POSt roaD

Post Road publishes twice yearly and accepts unsolicited poetry, fiction, and nonfiction submissions. Complete submission guidelines are available at www.postroadmag.com.

Subscriptions: Individuals, $18/year; Institutions, $34/year; outside the U.S. please add $6/year for postage.

Post Road is a nonprofit 501(c)(3) corporation published by Post Road Magazine, Inc. in partnership with the Boston College Department of English. All donations are tax-deductible.

Distributed by:

Ingram Periodicals, Inc., LaVergne, TN

Printed by:

BookMasters, Mansfield, OH

Post Road was founded in New York City in 1999 by Jaime Clarke and David Ryan with the following core editors: Rebecca Boyd, Susan Breen, Hillary Chute, Mark Conway, Pete Hausler, Kristina Lucenko (1999-2003), Anne McCarty and Michael Rosovsky.

Editors Emeritus include Sean Burke (1999-2001), Jaime Clarke (1999-2008), Mary Cotton, as Publisher and Managing Editor (2004-2008), Erin Falkevitz (2005-2006), Alden Jones (2002-2005), Fiona Maazel (2001-2002), Marcus McGraw (2003-2004), Catherine Parnell, as Managing Editor (2003), Samantha Pitchel (2006-2008), and Ricco Villanueva Siasoco, as Managing Editor (2009-2010).

Cover Art:
Gina Kamentsky, "Saga #2," 2013,
found metal, steel rod, ceramic and plastic figures, 9" x 16" x 5"

Copyright © 2015 Post Road   ISBN: 978-0-9849463-6-5

POSt roaD

Publisher
Post Road Magazine, Inc.
in partnership with the
Boston College Department
of English

Art Editor
Susan Breen

Criticism Editor
Hillary Chute

Fiction Editors
Rebecca Boyd
Mary Cotton
David Ryan

Guest Editor
Robert Chibka

Nonfiction Editors
Josephine Bergin
Pete Hausler

Poetry Editors
Mark Conway
Anne McCarty
Nicolette Nicola
Jeffrey Shotts
Lissa Warren

Recommendations Editors
Elizabeth Bologna
Annie Hartnett
Tim Huggins
Nelly Reifler

Theatre Editor
David Ryan

Layout and Design
Josephine Bergin

Web Designer
David Ryan

Managing Editor
Christopher Boucher

Assistant Managing Editors
Sarah Colwill-Brown
Christina Freitas

Copyeditor
Valerie Duff-Strautmann

Interns
Rachel Aldrich
Kaitlin Astrella
Christopher Kabacinski
Alexandra Machetanz
Caitlin Mason
Anna Olcott
Emily Simon
Katharine Stento

Readers
Joshua Barber
Lauren Bell
Jesse Brownstein
Daniel Cattolica
Kevin Cecala
Sara Danver
Katelyn Eelman
Brendan Flanagan
Catherine Gellene
Lindsey Hanlon
Laura Hayes
Allison Kolar
Sarah MacDonald
Mathew Mazzari
Marie McGrath
Linda Michel-Cassidy
Megyn Norbut
Joanne Nelson
Ben Olcott
Christian Petro
Leah Powell
Laura Smith
Bailey Spenser
Hannah Taylor
Cedar Warman
Caitlin Wilson
Eileen Zhang
Christine Zhao

Table of Contents

6   Contributor Notes

Fiction
13   Uprooted   *C.C. Robin*
23   Murmurings   *Jane Buchbinder*
53   Grandpap's Burials   *Casey Quinn*
83   Pity   *Lisa Gornick*
97   Allapattah   *Michael Hawley*
135   Mine Dont Never   *J S Khan*
225   Chiara   *Jonathan Wilson*

Nonfiction
59   Ma Picks A Priest   *Marianne Leone*
115   The Backyard   *Nicholas Ward*
149   Goodnight, Moon   *V. Hansmann*
159   The Pass   *John O'Connor*
215   Thin, Brilliant Lines   *Patrick Myers*

Criticism
40   Thinking/Cartooning   *Zak Breckenridge*

Poetry
29   The Secret Nancy   *Nancy Reddy*
129   Hogwash + Fullboat   *Christopher Robinson*
155   Our Town + Sinnerman   *Wesley Rothman*
169   Glenn Gould + Meeting Rain, Wutai Mountain
       Wang Jiaxin (trans. by Diana Shi & George O'Connell)

Art
65   Negative Space: Various Artists

Etcetera

    31 The Little Things *Will Dowd*

Recommendations

    20 *A Treatise on Shelling Beans* by Wieslaw Mysliwski, translated by Bill Johnston *Lynne Sharon Schwartz*
    56 *Just Kids* by Patti Smith *Brian Sousa*
    63 *All the Rage* by A.L. Kennedy *Ethel Rohan*
    81 Miranda July's *It Chooses You* *Shelly Oria*
    95 *I Love Dick* by Chris Kraus *Cari Luna*
  131 Three Lives *Megan Marshall*
  152 *The Learning Tree* by Gordon Parks *Katherine Karlin*
  172 An Altered Book by Cara Barer *Alexandra Chasin*
  213 The White Tide *Steven Church*
  223 *Die Leiden des jungen Werthers (The Sorrows of Young Werther)* by Johann Wolfgang von Goethe *David Samuel Levinson*
  235 *Becoming Abigail* by Chris Abani *Laura K. Warrell*

Guest Folio

  175 Swapped *Kate McMahon*
  179 The Sleeping Kingdom *Caitlin Keefe Moran*
  190 The Disappearing Wife *Simon Savelyev*
  200 Dandy *Ricco Villanueva Siasoco*

Contributor Notes

Zak Breckenridge is a recent graduate of the Master of Arts Program in the Humanities at the University of Chicago. His fiction and poetry has previously appeared in *The Glacial Erratic*. He will be on the road, collecting stories and ideas in the coming year.

Jane Buchbinder's stories have been published in *Ploughshares*, *Prairie Schooner*, *Boulevard*, *Black Warrior Review*, and *Green Mountains Review*. Her work has been cited as one of 100 distinguished stories in *The Best American Short Stories*. Earlier this year, her short story collection was a semi-finalist for the Iowa Short Fiction Award and the Mary McCarthy Prize in Short Fiction.

Susan Carr, a multifaceted artist, has an MFA from SMFA Boston and Tufts 2003. She is currently being represented by Giampietro Gallery, New Haven, CT.

Joaquin Carter is a Mexican-born New York based artist with a background in conceptual architecture. He is now exploring novel approaches in painting to create imaginary worlds defined by a progression of texture and structure.

Alexandra Chasin is Associate Professor of Writing at Lang College, The New School. Her books include *Kissed By* and *Brief. Anslinger Nation: A Documentary History of the Origins of Drug Prohibition, Starring Harry J. Anslinger* is forthcoming from the University of Chicago Press. Chasin directs *Writing On It All*, a public participatory writing program that runs every June on Governors Island in New York Harbor.

Steven Church is the author of *The Guinness Book of Me: a Memoir of Record*, *Theoretical Killings: Essays and Accidents*, *The Day After The Day After: My Atomic Angst*, and the forthcoming collection of essays, *Ultrasonic: Soundings*. His nonfiction has been published recently in *Passages North*, *River Teeth*, *Terrain.org*, *DIAGRAM*, *The Rumpus*, and many others. He's a founding editor of the literary magazine, *The Normal School*.

Astrid Cravens is a painter living in Brooklyn, New York. Her ESP collaborations can be found at eastsouthwestprojects.posthaven.com. Paintings at astridcravens.com.

Will Dowd is a poet and essayist from Braintree, Massachusetts. After attending Boston College as a Presidential Scholar, he earned an MS at MIT and an MFA at New York University, where he was a Jacob K. Javits Fellow. His work has recently appeared in *The Rialto*, *5 AM*, and *Barrow Street*. To see more of his broadsides or to order prints, please visit www.willdowdink.com.

Natalie Edgar is a second-generation Abstract Expressionist painter—a student of Ad Reinhardt and Mark Rothko at Brooklyn College, Meyer Shapiro at Columbia, and a friend of Willem and Elaine de Kooning. Later she married the sculptor Philip Pavia. She is the author of *Club Without Walls: Selections from the Journals of Philip Pavia*, and a former critic for *ARTnews* magazine with the legendary editor Thomas B. Hess. Also, she was assistant professor of Art History (1966-1994) at Queens College, and in 2010 she was a Pollock-Krasner Grant Recipient. Woodward Gallery, NYC, has been her representative since 1997.

Lori Ellison is a writer and artist living in Williamsburg, Brooklyn. Her work is in MoMA along with other private collections.

Lisa Gornick is the author of two novels: *Tinderbox* (Sarah Crichton Books/Farrar, Straus and Giroux and Picador) and *A Private Sorcery* (Algonquin). Her stories and essays have appeared widely, including in *AGNI*, *Prairie Schooner*, and *The Sun*, and have received many awards. She holds a BA from Princeton, a PhD in clinical psychology from Yale, and is a graduate of the writing program at NYU and the psychoanalytic training program at Columbia. A collection of linked stories, *Louisa Meets Bear*, is forthcoming, also with Sarah Crichton Books/Farrar, Straus and Giroux.

V. Hansmann was raised by wealthy people in suburban New Jersey; he grew up to be neurotic, alcoholic, homosexual, and old. His publishing credits to date consist of an anecdote in *The New York Times*, essays in the *The Common* online and *BLOOM*, and a poem in the British journal, *Structo*.

Michael Hawley's short stories have been published in *Alaska Quarterly Review*, *Boston Review*, *Cimarron Review*, *Columbia: A Journal of Literature and Art*, *The New Yorker*, *The Saint Ann's Review*, *Tupelo Quarterly* and other publications. His work has been nominated for Pushcart prizes and has received honorable mentions in *The Best American Short Stories* anthologies. He lives in New York City. (www.michaelhawleyfiction.com)

Karl Heine graduated from University of Bridgeport in 1982, with a BFA in Graphic Design/Illustration and minor in Photography. He is a life-long explorer in traditional and digital imaging.

Eminent among contemporary Chinese poets and essayists, **Wang Jiaxin**'s award-winning work has been translated into several European and Asian languages. The 2007 Luce Poet-in-Residence at Colgate University, and 2013 resident in the University of Iowa's International Writing Program, he has published eight poetry and eight literary essay collections. He is also a distinguished translator of Yeats, Tsvetaeva, René Char, and particularly Paul Celan. His *Darkening Mirror: New & Selected Poems*, edited/translated by Diana Shi and George O'Connell, is forthcoming this year from US publisher Tebot Bach. He is currently Professor of Literature and Director of the International Writing Center at Beijing's Renmin University.

Gina Kamentsky creates kinetic sculptures that exist in the somewhat chaotic and messy real world and animated films for the screen where gravity is a bit less of a concern. Her one of a kind automata and kinetic sculpture incorporates found objects, metal and mechanical components. Her sculpture work has been featured in *The Sunday New York Times*, *Metropolis Magazine*, and *LA. Style*, *The Boston Globe* and exhibited internationally.

Katherine Karlin's fiction has appeared in the Pushcart Prize anthology, *New Stories from the South*, *One Story*, *Alaska Quarterly Review*, *ZYZZYVA*, and many other venues. She teaches creative writing and film at Kansas State University.

J S Khan was born in the Seventh House, his moon in Gemini, and remains to this day ruled by a heartless Venus and scheming Mercury—being overall a volatile admixture of black bile and too much blood. Khan's deck bristles with wands, though swords and cups sadly divide his coins every time. Khan catches signals in the astra and transcribes them as parables. This parable (in particular) is dedicated to Amy Miara.

Marianne Leone is an actress, screenwriter, and essayist. She had a recurring role on HBO's *Sopranos* as Joanne Moltisanti, Christopher's mother. Her essays and op ed pieces on a variety of topics have appeared in the *Boston Globe*, *Bark Magazine* and WBUR's Cognoscenti blog. She is married to Chris Cooper, an academy-award winning actor. *Jesse, a Mother's Story of Grief, Grace and Everyday Bliss* (Simon & Schuster 2010), is a chronicle of the remarkable life and untimely death of her child. Jesse was an honor-roll student who loved to windsurf and write poetry. He also had severe quadriplegic cerebral palsy and used a computer to speak. He died suddenly at age seventeen.

David Samuel Levinson is the author of the novel, *Antonia Lively Breaks the Silence* (2013), and a story collection, *Most of us Are Here Against Our Will* (2005). You've probably never heard of either of them, but check them out because they're quite good, especially the novel. (At least, this is what his mom and dad tell him and since they're never wrong...) His latest short story can be found in Issue 26 of *Post Road*.

Cari Luna is the author of *The Revolution of Every Day*, published by Tin House Books. *The Oregonian* named Luna's debut novel a Top 10 Northwest Book of 2013. She is a graduate of the MFA fiction program at Brooklyn College, and her writing has appeared in *Salon*, *Jacobin*, *PANK*, *Avery Anthology*, *failbetter*, *Novembre Magazine*, and elsewhere. Cari lives in Portland, Oregon.

Megan Marshall is the author of *Margaret Fuller: A New American Life*, winner of the 2014 Pulitzer Prize in Biography, and *The Peabody Sisters: Three Women Who Ignited American Romanticism*, winner of the Francis Parkman Prize, the Mark Lynton History Prize, and a finalist for the Pulitzer Prize in 2006. She is at work on a short biography of Elizabeth Bishop, and will be researching a life of Elizabeth Hawthorne, Nathaniel's reclusive older sister, as a fellow of the Dorothy and Lewis B. Cullman Center for Scholars and Writers at The New York Public Library during 2014-15. She teaches nonfiction writing and the art of archival research in the MFA Program at Emerson College, where she is an Associate Professor in the Department of Writing, Literature and Publishing.

Kate McMahon lives with her husband and son in Brooklyn. When she is not practicing municipal law or tending to the needs of a small child, she spends much of her time meaning to write more fiction.

Caitlin Keefe Moran is an editor in New York City. Her work has appeared on *The Toast* and in the *Iowa Review*, *Pleiades*, and other outlets. She lives in Washington Heights.

Patrick Myers is a recent graduate from the Environmental Writing program at the University of Montana. His work draws upon, and is inspired by, the people he meets and the complex and unique ways in which they interact with their natural surroundings. He presented his work at the Wild Mercy Reading Series in Missoula, and "Thin, Brilliant Lines" is his first publication.

Recipient of numerous poetry awards, **George O'Connell** has taught in both the US and China, and at Peking University as Fulbright professor. With Diana Shi, he co-edited/co-translated the 2008 *Atlanta Review China Edition*, their work also appearing in Copper Canyon's *Push Open the Window: Contemporary Poetry from China*. Tebot Bach will soon publish their selection of poems by Wang Jiaxin, *Darkening Mirror*. Currently rendering Lan Lan's *From Here to Here*, he and Ms. Shi received a 2014 US National Endowment for the Arts Literature Fellowship in Translation. They direct *Pangolin House*, (pangolinhouse.com) an international journal of Chinese and English-language poetry.

John O'Connor is from Kalamazoo, Michigan. His writing has appeared in *Open City*, *Quarterly West*, *The Believer*, *Gastronomica*, and the anthologies *The Best Creative Nonfiction Vol. 1* and *They're At It Again: An Open City Reader*. He has also written for *The New York Times*, *GQ*, *Saveur*, *Men's Journal*, and *The Financial Times*, and for two years was a foreign correspondent for Japan's largest daily newspaper, *The Yomiuri Shimbun*. He currently teaches creative writing at Pratt Institute in Brooklyn, NY.

Shelly Oria's short story collection, *New York 1, Tel Aviv 0*, was published by FSG in November. Her fiction has appeared in *The Paris Review*, *McSweeney's*, *Quarterly West*, and *fivechapters* among other places, and won the Indiana Review Fiction Prize among other awards. Shelly curates the series *Sweet! Actors Reading Writers* in the East Village, teaches fiction and co-directs the Writers' Forum at Pratt Institute, and has a private practice as a life and creativity coach. You can find more information at www.shellyoria.com

Melanie Parke lives and paints in the tiny village of Chief, Michigan, population thirteen, with her husband, Richard Kooyman, who is also a painter.

Heidi Pollard is a painter and sculptor working in New Mexico. Further information and images of her work are available on the artist's website: http://heidipollard.com.

Casey Quinn is originally from Upstate New York. He has received scholarships from Bread Loaf Writer's Conference, The Community of Writers at Squaw Valley, and Hamilton College. This is his first published story.

Nancy Reddy's poems have recently appeared in *Tupelo Quarterly*, *32 Poems*, *Smartish Pace*, *Indiana Review*, and elsewhere. She holds an MFA from the University of Wisconsin-Madison, where she is currently a doctoral candidate in composition and rhetoric.

C.C. Robin lives in New York. This is her first published story.

Christopher Robinson's debut novel, *War of the Encyclopaedists*, co-authored with Gavin Kovite, will be published by Scribner in 2015. His work has appeared, or is forthcoming, in *The Missouri Review*, *Alaska Quarterly Review*, *Kenyon Review*, *Southern Review*, *Gettysburg Review*, and elsewhere. He is a recipient of fellowships from the MacDowell Colony, the Millay Colony, Bread Loaf, and the Djerassi Resident Artist program, to name a few. He has been a finalist for numerous prizes, including the Ruth Lilly Fellowship and the Yale Younger Poets Prize. He earned his MA in poetry from Boston University and his MFA from Hunter College. His secret underground lair is located somewhere in Seattle.

Ethel Rohan is the author of the story collections *Goodnight Nobody* and *Cut Through the Bone*, the latter longlisted for The Story Prize. She is also the author of the chapbook, *Hard to Say*, and a short ebook memoir, *Out of Dublin*. Her work has or will appear in *The New York Times*, *PEN America*, *World Literature Today*, *Tin House Online*, and *The Rumpus*, among many others. Raised in Ireland, Ethel Rohan lives in San Francisco. Visit her at ethelrohan.com.

Wesley Rothman's poems and criticism have appeared or are forthcoming in *32 Poems*, *Crab Orchard Review*, *Drunken Boat*, *Four Way Review*, *Prairie Schooner*, *Rattle*, *The Rumpus*, *Vinyl*, and *The White Review*, among other venues. He edits *Too Good Poetry* and teaches writing and cultural literatures at Emerson College, Suffolk University, and Grub Street Writers' Workshop. His work has received a Pushcart Prize nomination and a grant from the Vermont Studio Center.

Simon Savelyev is a writer and filmmaker in Los Angeles. He graduated from Boston College and UCLA film school, and now teaches at Studio 4. Most recently, he directed a segment of the forthcoming feature *Heyday of the Insensitive Bastards*, starring James Franco.

Julia Schwartz is a Los Angeles-based artist who has exhibited widely. Her paintings, influenced by years of psychoanalytic study, have been included in New American Paintings. As the Arts Editor for *Figure/Ground Communication*, she interviews other artists about their creative process. Her website is www.juliaschwartzart.com.

Lynne Sharon Schwartz's latest book is a collection of essays, *This Is Where We Came In*. Her novels include *Disturbances in the Field*, *Leaving Brooklyn*, and *The Writing on the Wall*. She has published several story collections, two books of poetry, *In Solitary* and *See You in the Dark*, and several translations from Italian. She is on the faculty of the Bennington Writing Seminars.

Diana Shi's translations of Chinese-language and American poetry have appeared in many publications east and west. She co-edited/co-translated the 2008 *Atlanta Review China Edition* with George O'Connell, their work also appearing in Copper Canyon's *Push Open the Window: Contemporary Poetry from China*. *Darkening Mirror: New & Selected Poems* by Wang Jiaxin, co-edited/co-translated by Ms. Shi, is forthcoming from Tebot Bach. Winner of the Chinese University of Hong Kong's Dawson Lee Memorial Prize, she is co-recipient of a 2014 US National Endowment for the Arts Literature Fellowship in Translation. Ms. Shi co-directs *Pangolin House* (pangolinhouse.com), an international journal of Chinese and English-language poetry.

Suzan Shutan combines manufactured and handmade materials in colorful minimalist installations that address issues of nature. She has exhibited extensively internationally and nationally, most recently at the Zacheta National Gallery of Contemporary Art and Kenise Barnes Gallery.
Artist website: www.suzanshutan.com.

Ricco Villanueva Siasoco has published in *Joyland*, *Fifth Wednesday*, *The North American Review*, and numerous anthologies including *Walang Hiya: Literature Taking Risks Toward Liberatory Practice* (Carayan Press) and *Take Out: Queer Writing from Asian Pacific America* (Asian American Writers Workshop). He was recently selected as a 2013 NYC Emerging Writers Fellow from The Center for Fiction. Ricco received an MFA from the Bennington Writing Seminars and taught writing at Boston College. He lives in New York City and is completing his first novel.

Cary Smith has been exhibiting his paintings in the US and Europe since the mid 1980s. He has had solo shows in New York at Feature Inc., Derek Eller Gallery, Koury Wingate Gallery and Julian Pretto. His work was included in the 1989 Whitney Biennial, in "The Geometric Tradition in American Art, 1930-1990," Whitney Museum, and most recently in "The Jewel Thief," Tang Teaching Museum, Saratoga, NY. Smith is scheduled to have a one-person show at the Aldrich Contemporary Art Museum in October 2014. He is represented by Feature Inc., NY, and lives in Farmington, CT.

Brian Sousa writes fiction and nonfiction, poetry and songs. His first book, *Almost Gone*, was published in 2013, and he is at work on a novel. Sousa also writes for the *Aspen Times*, and a number of magazines, including *Outside Magazine*. Find out more at www.briansousawriting.com.

Oriane Stender is based in Brooklyn. Collections include Fine Arts Museum of San Francisco, Federal Reserve Board, JP Morgan Chase, International College Center and Rose Art Museum/Brandeis University.

Ravenna Taylor works in pictorial abstraction employing oil paint, watercolor, or collaged torn materials in paper. Colors and geometrical forms are derived from nature, and from a fascination with systems, as can be found in measures, time pieces, game boards, and maps.

Lane Twitchell is a Brooklyn-based visual artist. His recent work uses processes of folded and cut material, which produce Mandala like forms. More of his artwork can be found at: www.lanetwitchell.com.

Don Voisine is a Maine-born, Brooklyn-based painter who shows regularly in the US and Europe. Collections include the Corcoran, National Academy, and Portland Museum of Art.

Nicholas Ward's writing has appeared in or is forthcoming from *Hypertext Magazine*, the *Eunoia Review*, *Hobart*, and the 2nd Story podcast, where he has been a company member since 2006. He lives in Chicago with Amadeus the cat.

Laura K. Warrell is a freelance writer living in Boston. She teaches at the Berklee College of Music and the University of Massachusetts Boston and is a graduate of the MFA program at Vermont College of Fine Arts. Her work has appeared in Salon.com, the *Boston Globe* and Racialicious.com, and she is a regular contributor to *Numero Cinq* magazine.

Jonathan Wilson's fiction, essays, and reviews have appeared in *The New Yorker*, *Esquire*, *Tablet*, *The Times Literary Supplement*, *The Paris Review Daily*, and *Best American Short Stories*, among other publications. He is the author of eight books including *A Palestine Affair* (Pantheon 2003), a *New York Times* Notable Book of the Year, and *Kick and Run*, a memoir. He is Fletcher Professor of Rhetoric and Debate, Professor of English and Director of the Center for the Humanities at Tufts University.

Charles Yoder has managed to make a long and productive career in the arts based on a life-long delusion that such a life was possible.

Mid-American Review is pleased to announce the

2015 Fineline Competition

for prose poems, short shorts, and anything in between.

2015 Final Judge:
Michael Czyzniejewski, author of *Chicago Stories* (Curbside Splendor, 2012) and *I Will Love You For the Rest of My Life* (Curbside Splendor, 2015)

Deadline: June 1, 2015
$1000 First Prize

500-word limit for each poem or short. $10 entry fee (payable online or by check/money order) for each set of three works. Contest is for previously unpublished work only—if the work has appeared in print or online, in any form or part, or under any title, or has been contracted for such, it is ineligible and will be disqualified. Entry fees are non-refundable. All participants will receive *Mid-American Review* v. XXXVI, no. 1, where the winner will be published. Submissions will not be returned. Manuscripts need not be left anonymous. Contest is open to all writers, except those associated with the judge or *Mid-American Review*, past or present. Judge's decision is final.

Uprooted
C.C. Robin

7:15 AM, Friday Morning

Maddie runs to the bus parked by the great white oak, her black boots sloshing through the mud. She climbs on board, boots squeaking on the rubber steps. Hot air blows down the back of her neck from the heat vent above. The stench of diesel fuel masks the sweet smell of her warm, cinnamon toast.

The bus snaps shut and jerks forward, catapulting her down the slick aisle. She lands in the empty seat behind Sam and Ali, who are always doubled up, no matter what, even if there is room. Swedish fish pelt her in the head. The 8th graders are shooting baskets again, using the straps of her backpack as the hoop.

Joey, *the* Leonard Middle School Deejay, is on board. He pulsates up the aisle, pumping his hands in the air to the beat, music blaring from his iPhone.

"Can you blow my whistle baby…" Joey whistles.

"Pipe down," George says, revving the engine, "pipe down."

Maddie deposits the backpack in her empty seat, air squeaking out of the vinyl seams. She plops her phone and breakfast on her lap.

"Hey," Maddie says, tapping the back of Ali and Sam's seat, chewing the toast.

"Hey," Ali responds. "Bring the sketch?"

Sam continues texting, not looking up.

"Sam?" Maddie says. "One sec, Ali."

Sam leans over to the right, whispering into Ali's ear and cackles.

Maddie settles back into her seat thinking, "*Who's the joke this morning?*"

Mom pings. *Eating your bkft?*

Yeah, yeah. Maddie takes another bite. She twists around with her knees on the seat.

"Peace," Joey says, raising his right index and middle fingers to his right eye.

"Peace." She takes another bite of her toast and sits back down.

"Yorkie, Yorkie, sketch?" asks Ali, pursing her lips to whistle the FloRida chorus.

Holding her breakfast, Maddie places her phone in her lap. "Looking," she says, as she unzips her bag.

The bus jostles down Bradford. Her phone slips to the floor.

"Catch itttt," Maddie says.

She hears a thump. "Nice save," she says stretching her arm beneath Sam's seat.

The wheels screech to the next stop on Old Murdoch Road.

"Heyyy," says Maddie. Her hand feels the wet boot locked down on her phone.

"My PHONE," she says, peering upside down—yanking the pink Hunter with her right hand and wedging her other hand under the boot. Sam's boot won't budge.

Maddie pushes up, reaching around Sam's seat.

"Phone, please," Maddie says raising her hand to Sam's face.

More pink Hunters squeak down the wet aisle.

"PHONE," Maddie says.

Sam slaps the phone in her hand. The cold metal stings her palm.

"Did I miss something?" Maddie rubs the wet phone on her jeans.

Sam leans over her seat and glares at Maddie. A Swedish fish pelts her in the face. She doesn't flinch.

"What?" asks Maddie chewing on her thumbnail. "What?"

Thunder rumbles as the bus makes a wide turn onto Palmer. Sam blinks and slams back into the coils of her seat.

Maddie texts Ali. *What's the deal with her?*
You told him.

Maddie pings back. *I told him what? Who is him?*

A crushed box of Swedish fish is pushed through the side of Maddie's window seat. She pulls it through without looking back.

Joey taps the back of Maddie's seat as a drum to the beat of the Beastie Boys: "You wake up late for school—man you don't wanna go. You ask mom, please and she still says no."

Mom pings. *Pick up at 2:35. Lower circle. Train @3:11.*

K. But don't want 2 go 2nite.

Mom pings. *No choice. Dinner with dad. Class in am. See u later.*

Maddie stares out the window at the pouring rain, passing her sister's elementary school. The janitor carries the Halloween banner inside, a dripping trail of orange paint trails on the blacktop.

Ali flips around, tapping on her window. "Hello. . .Yorkie. . .did you find it?"

"Right, right. . .looking." Maddie squeezes her head inside the loaded backpack. The warm air stings the back of her throat.

George pulls a leaver to stop at Haverford, right past the highway.

"I'll bring the tape and newspaper," says Ali, "Sam will bring—"

"She won't even talk to me," says Maddie.

"She'll get over it," Ali says, "and we will win *again* together."

Maddie rummages deeper in her backpack, "I'll bring the paint and brushes."

"She'll bring the paint tins," says Ali tapping Sam's shoulder.

Sam shows her phone to Ali, "Look at Katie in the blonde wig—she better have ordered one for me!"

Ali looks on, "And me. Perfect with the fluorescent pink leggings."

"In your seats, we're moving!" George honks, "Seats. Seats."

"It's here, I know it," says Maddie. She pulls out a zip lock bag hidden below her books and slides it behind her back.

"Here it is," she says pulling out her sketchbook.

"Let's see it!" Sam and Ali lean over their bench. Sam snatches the book from Maddie's hand.

"Hey, the caption—Bootique—get it?" Maddie reaches for her spiral bound sketchbook.

"Oooo. Pamela's boutique! Love the skull dress!" says Ali, chewing Laffy Taffy.

Sam snaps a picture of the witch wearing a black gown riding a broomstick and throws the sketchbook back to Maddie.

Maddie presses the clear plastic bag into the bottom of her backpack. She stacks the textbooks and sketchbook on top of her flattened black pants, Zeppelin T-shirt, fuzzy pajama shorts and EpiPen.

The bus hits a pothole and stops abruptly at Crossway. Kids skid down the aisle as the bus takes off. Gobstoppers roll down the aisle.

"That was a free sample," Ethan says. He opens his messenger bag revealing today's goods. Dollars and candy exchange hands as he walks back toward his seat next to Joey.

"This is certainly not sunny California. Nasty out," says Katie, also in Pink Hunters, landing in the seat opposite Sam.

"Can't handle a little frizzy hair, new girl?" Sam says tossing her Bazooka.

Mom pings. *Guess the guest on today's show...*

A clue pls?

Maddie leans over the seat, pulling the foam from the ripped pleather. "So we'll meet up in front of the window at 3."

Sam whispers to Ali. Maddie hovers over their seat.

"Can't. Have to meet at 9," says Ali.

"I'm at my Dad's tonight in the city," says Maddie. "I have art class in the morning—remember?"

"Oh yeah. Your art class is exactly what I am thinking about. Well, we have the sketch now," Sam holds up her phone, "So splitting the contest winnings two ways is much better than three."

"Let me see, let me see," says Katie.

"This picture *is* the $500 winner," says Sam. She holds up Maddie's picture.

"Well maybe it's for sale," says Katie. "But I do have the bigger window." She holds up her entry card.

"Whatever LA. The paintings all have to be the same size—no matter how big the windows are," Sam snaps back in her seat.

"You have to fight for your right to partyyyyy," Joey hollers from his seat.

"Party," the bus hollers back in unison.
"Maddie, you've got to be there, without you it will look like my little sister did it," Ali whispers.
"Ok. Ok," says Maddie.
Text to Mom. *Can't go to Dad's 2nite*
Ping from Mom. *Y.*
Can't. Window painting contest is in a.m. -not p.m.
Ping from Mom. *Art class?? Dad?*
Maddie chews on her nails.
I know mom. But…
Ping from Mom. *I guess that's it then-will deal with it. Txt dad pls.*
Thx mom. Thx! Thx!! Who is guest on show?
Ping from Mom. *Current celeb-boy.*
Maddie stands up and hangs over seat. "Hey…my mom says—"
"The dance store opens at ten. They'll have the leggings," says Ali.
"I'm an extra small, so is Ali," says Sam, "What are you—a medium?"
"A small," says Katie. "I guessed your head size right—an extra large?"
"If the wig is too big, I am sure it will fit you," says Sam.
"I'll bring the lipstick, hot pink," says Ali.
Maddie slides down back to her seat, out of sight.
Maddie texts Dad. *Hey about tonight—*
Ping from Dad. *Ok. No prob. C u tomorrow. All ok.*
Right Dad. Sushi after art class?
Ping from Dad. *Yes…with Carey too.*
Maybe I'll just go to Syd's then.
Ping from Dad. *Bring Syd. 7pm. Sushi Garri.*
Whatever. Cu tomorrow.
  The bus approaches the stop at the five corners. The Metro Diner, Brian's Ice Cream Shop, Balducci's Market.
  Maddie stands up again and taps Ali's window. "Hey, I can be there at 9. Will leave for city at noon."
  "GREAT!! Without you," Ali says, "we would NEVER have a chance."
  Riders pile on, 8th graders use their hands as megaphones. "Move on shorties, make it to 8th grade and you'll get your own seat."
  Joey's tunes are muffled against the bus chatter. "I know caught up in the middle," FloRida sings, "I cry just a little when I think of letting go…"
  The light turns green. The bus passes Tudor and colonial mansions peak through hedges on Heathcoate Road.
  Maddie shrugs down in her seat. Joey tosses a red gooey ball overhead. She flicks it off of her phone. Another lands on her phone.
  She turns around, "Hey…that's some serious ammunition."
  Ethan warms the Swedish fish in the palms of his hands, making perfect pea-size pellets. As he masters the pellets, Joey rolls them into their original candy casings.

Maddie presses her forehead against the cold glass of the window. Tattered paper skeletons and cobwebs litter the lawns.

Ping from Mom. *Did u figure out the guest? Hint—his friends drink blood.*

Is he a wolf?

"Last stop ahead, last chance for a sugar high—two for one Skittles, Bazooka, Hershey's," Ethan walks the aisle, hustling the remnants from the bottom of his bag.

"In your seats, we're moving!" George speeds past the last stop.

"Stop the bus. There is someone at the stop!" says a kid.

"He's back," announces an 8th grader in the exit row pressing his face against the window, "He's back!" Phones, water bottles, candy and wrappers roll forward as the bus halts on a decline. Kids open their windows and peer out. "He's back."

Maddie wipes the condensation from her window. A wiry boy breezes down the hill. His Babolat Racquet bag replaces the backpack. She chews on her nails and sinks into her seat.

"What's *he* doing back?" Sam pushes her nose to the back window.

"Who is THAT?" asks Katie.

"Well, he's the one and only," says Sam.

Ethan squeezes into Sam and Ali's seat.

"Yep. It's him," Ethan says looking out the window. "I guess the hedge fund king is back from London."

"He's hot," says Katie.

"Don't even try," says Sam.

"Looks like I have a very good customer coming aboard," says Ethan walking up the aisle.

Mom pings. *Any guess?*

Sam reaches over Ali to open the window. "Ohhh, look at his hair. I like it long. It's shiny and wet."

Katie snaps her phone posting to Instagram. The caption—he's mine!

George blares his horn. Maddie's cheeks are hot. Her hair curls from the dampness behind her neck.

Maddie texts Mom. *Twilight. Taylor Lautner.*

Mom pings. *Autograph for u:)*

"Candy, candy. It's now or never later," says Ethan.

"I'll take four boxes." Maddie grabs a few rumpled dollars from her jacket pocket.

"Whoa. Don't chew them all in one place."

"Let's do the wobble baby. Wobble baby, wobble baby," Joey grinds in the aisle.

George honks again. "Settle down, settle down."

"Do the wobble baby, wobble baby," the bus riders wobble in their seats, shaking the bus.

Maddie perches forward. A body swings up the stairs. He bangs his wet knuckles with George's. It is Mike. Mike Kaplan.

He shakes his wet hair over the first row of 6th graders, peeling his hand out for candy.

"Wobble baby, wobble baby," iPhones blare.

The bus roars. Mike wobbles down the aisle in his duck boots.

"Double up, double up," Mike says, high fiving the 7th graders.

The music stops.

"Didn't anyone save my seat?" Mike says.

"Oh…there it is, THERE it is," he shakes his wet head, spraying Maddie.

"Double up, MADELINE." Red ammunition balls fly thru the air.

"Ahhh," Mike puts his arms in front of his face as more red balls shoot out from behind Maddie. He waddles backward, losing his balance.

"It's MADISON," she says.

More balls shoot out.

"Whatever, Maddie New Yorkie, MOVE," says Mike, "MOVE."

The bus stops at the red light on Secor. A single red ball hits Maddie from behind. Joey says, "Move." Maddie's body is weighted lead.

"Daydreaming belongs in your sketchbook," Mike says. He scoops her up and throws her on top of Sam and Ali. Her backpack lands on her stomach.

Katie snaps a photo. "An Instagram hit!" says Katie.

"Get her off of me," Sam screams at Mike.

Mike scoops up Maddie again—cradling her up one row.

"Wow, you ok? Want some candy?" the 6th grader asks—now sitting next to Maddie.

Maddie stares at the maroon pleather in front of her, chewing her nails.

"That picture! Already getting followers," says Sam, "Look at my hair!"

"Well, it's my posting," says Katie. "It looks like I'm getting the followers."

"And a lot of them," says Ali looking down at her phone.

The bus turns into the school entrance on Orienta Road.

Joey pings. *Listen.*

Ping from Mom. *Taking bus home or want me to pick u up?*

Maddie's cheeks are hot. She is silent, holding her breath, fiddling to find her notebook.

"Five hundred twenty-five thousand six hundred minutes," Seasons of Love chorus plays from *Rent.*

The bus screeches to a stop behind another yellow bus.

Maddie shuffles into the aisle. Mike is behind her. He yanks the straps of her backpack tightly. "Have a good day Yorkie," he says, rubbing the joint of his index finger against Maddie's scalp.

"In daylights, in sunsets, in midnights, in cups of coffee…"

Maddie steps off the bus and stands there in the icy rain. It's 7:35 AM. More pink Hunters greet Sam, Ali, and Katie. They run ahead into the doors of Leonard Middle School. Maddie hears the first bell ring. ≈

A TREATISE ON SHELLING BEANS by Wieslaw Mysliwski, translated by Bill Johnston

Lynne Sharon Schwartz

The speaker who seizes our attention at once with a mild yet tenacious grip is the caretaker of a cluster of vacation cabins in a rural part of Poland. He manages his small domain with the precision and rigor of an exacting deity. In his spare time he engraves nameplates for the graves in the nearby woods. One night a visitor arrives who wants to buy beans. The two commence shelling beans together, while our gregarious narrator tells the story of his life, and of Poland under communist rule, after the transforming experience of the war.

This is the simple framework of Wieslaw Mysliwski's brilliant and heartbreaking novel, *A Treatise on Shelling Beans*, published in Poland in 2006. Mysliwski is a major literary figure in Poland, winner of many national awards. In addition to this novel, an earlier one, *Stone Upon Stone*, is also available in English, both thanks to the prolific and widely honored translator, Bill Johnston. I read *Shelling Beans* the way I remember reading books in childhood, impatient for the school day to be over so I could return to the story, and especially the narrator, who speaks like an intimate friend.

Within this framework Mysliwski sets a series of digressions, rather like interlocking circles, from the banal details of ordinary life to ongoing philosophical quests, often in the space of a single paragraph. The homely act of shelling beans, for instance, which was a ritual in the narrator's family and indeed his entire village, becomes freighted with metaphorical association.

The site of the resort cabins was once the village where our narrator spent his childhood. He was the sole survivor of a brutal Nazi assault that obliterated the village and all its people: an orphaned boy hidden in the potato cellar until he's discovered and nursed back to health by a group of partisans. After a series of grim picaresque adventures, he finds himself in a military-style orphanage, where he is trained as an electrician and, more important, learns to play the saxophone, his great passion. He plays in bands abroad for many years, then returns to his native village, although, as he puts it, you can never recover your original place: "Places die once they've been left...A person's only place is inside themselves...Everything that's on the outside is only illusion, circumstance, chance, misunderstanding. A person is their own place, especially the last place."

The world of the novel, a mélange of chatty anecdote and metaphysical speculation, is in constant flux. Reality and dream sometimes change places. Nothing is stable—not time, not place, and not even character. The narrator often encounters people he seems to have met before; characters echo one another, resonances stretching across years. Even the enigmatic visitor resembles an old acquaintance, the narrator cannot quite place. Memory, we are told,

> is no more than a function of our imagination. Imagination is the place we feel connected to, where one can be certain that that's where we actually live. Then when we come to die, we also die in it. Along with all those who have ever died before, and who help us die in turn.

The only firm element is the mesmerizing voice of the narrator, full of anecdote and wit and rumination: "The world," he says, "is what is told."

Like the great twentieth-century European writers who evoke an entire society through the perceptions of a single character and sensibility—Proust in France, Bohumil Hrabal in Czechoslovakia, Saramago in Portugal, Robert Musil in Austria—Mysliwski has not been infected by the American virus of minimalism that counsels: less is more. Quite the contrary: more is more. His esthetic is one of liberal inclusion, and his novel is stunningly rich in detail, encyclopedic. We're regaled with droll passages not only about the ubiquitous beans, but about hats; train travel; electricity, saxophone reeds; candlesticks; his mother's Christmas dinners; shaving, and dogs—the narrator has two, one of whom he rescued from the nearby forest and nursed back to health as he himself was rescued and nursed.

The nature of life under postwar communism is portrayed with offhand remarks: "These days the soul is a commodity like anything else. You can buy it and sell it and the prices aren't high." The system is illustrated by the complaints of a longtime shopkeeper now forced to operate under absurd bureaucratic restrictions. It's also mirrored in the deprivations, petty cruelties, and strict regimen of the orphans' school where the narrator spends his adolescence. Even the war is replicated in a wild rebellion staged by the boys: tired of the constant power outages leaving them in the dark, they break windows and generally destroy everything in sight. Worst of all, they destroy the musical instruments they've been taught to play by their affectionate and alcoholic music teacher. In their blind fury they even attempt to hang this one teacher they love. When the rampage ends and the investigation begins, the innocent music teacher is arrested. "Long live music, boys," he shouts as he is carried off.

The destruction of the instruments is the most telling and tragic outbreak of violence. For music is the narrator's *raison d'etre*. His saxophone teacher at the warehouse where he has his first job, tells him, "You have to play with your whole self, including your pain, your tears, your laughter, your hope, your dreams, everything that's inside you, with your whole life. Because all that is music. The saxophone isn't the music, you are." By now the narrator's rheumatism prevents him from playing—his fingers are too stiff. Without his music his identity drains away. "Beyond playing it was like I didn't exist. Who knows, maybe I actually didn't, and it was only playing music that kind of summoned me out of nonexistence and forced me to be."

The exploration of identity that infuses the entire novel leads to the question of who is the visitor. He assumes various shapes, gradually congealing, as it were, into his true self. At first we take him at face value—a passing stranger who wants to buy beans. At various points he seems a ghost from the narrator's past. Or an incarnation of one of his younger selves. As more details emerge—his age is indeterminate, untouched by time, he has no gray hairs, he doesn't come out in photographs—the narrator grows suspicious. But he is not disconcerted when he—and we—realize that here is the inevitable visitor who turns up at the end of a long life. For beneath the speaker's casual tone is a profound vein of grief and skepticism dating from the early loss of family and home. All is imagination, illusion, and chance. "Death is just a transition from one illusion into another." He is ready, after one last round of checking on the cabins. "The world is what is told," he concludes, and he has told his story. And we are transformed by hearing it.

Murmurings

Jane Buchbinder

For the years leading up to the siege, the little white house on Walcott Street contained a wild thicket of giggling, a red, wee-wah delight, and hope. It also contained grace. And a rounded, rocking ease. The new owners—at least our peripheral sense of them—seemed an affable addition to the landscape. The short, bumpy one seeded our yard; the tall, weedy-looking one pruned the bushes. While she planted the flower garden, he snipped parsley and plucked sugar snap peas. They came outside in the early evenings just to smell the earthen, fertile air. Just to spy on gestation. It wasn't uncommon to see them pressing their faces together in that strange human way—a slow, sienna, humming motion—over their herb garden. Because we had heard them so many times before, it was easy to imagine the rolling and moaning rituals they would engage in after they went inside.

We had been casually observing the couple, though not in the crude manner of humans. Grasses have their own way of looking and listening. With great precision, we perceive emotion through vocal tone and intensity rather than words. We "see" form and color through the density of visible light waves. This is how there had been thousands of witnesses to the couple's fizzy, golden dinners with friends. The bounce of their laughter. Their indigo wooing and snuggling at night.

Meanwhile, we enjoyed our mindless cohabitation with the crisp New England April, the shining showers of May, June's chlorophylatinous surges, and the sweat lodge of a long, purging summer. Our bodies reveled in their unfurlings. We never complained about droughts, though we were depleted and frequently trounced upon. We didn't challenge or question our fate. The truth is that before ingesting their liquid we hadn't thought about our survival—much less anyone else's.

But that came to an end early last spring. That's when we started to feel the couple's heat. The chartreuse weight of their wanting. They were craving to grow something of their very own. Their nighttime passion turned into sad, violet contortions; their mornings into a rushed, yellow, mechanical pumping. Each smashing session was followed by an odd stillness that lasted only through a lunar cycle. Smash and rest. Smash and rest. This went on for months. Until, that is, they opened the spigot behind their faces and released a slow, steady stream of water—their eyes, noses, and mouths turned, by some trick of human magic, to leaky hoses.

From their windows, we witnessed how a steady mist of sadness can turn piles of books and magazines into tiny waterfalls. Trusty appliances rust into squeaky lamenters. Cheerful figurines become weepers. A rainbow tried to make the best of the situation by arching between the living room and kitchen. But the tall one just grimaced at the ceiling, while the bumpy one coughed into a dirty handkerchief. Then a thick fog rolled in. By the end of winter, the sorrow spores had expanded to droplets. Drizzle replaced by downfall. The humans seemed to slide into sedation, so sunken and dampened, so ochre-smudged and dissolving. They were oblivious to the fact that they had changed from a perambulating demolition to a destructive force. But a house is different. It has perspective. And sharp boundaries. It can only hold so much.

Eventually rivulets of sadness pushed their way through the old stone foundation. Thin sheets of groaning squeezed through door and window frames. The yard was doused, even if it was frozen. And so it happened that, with the spring thaw, we—the lawn surrounding the sobbing house on Walcott Street—drank in the human's fluids. It was our feeding season, so we slurped them in, in great gulps. Then, like them, we started to drown.

We were awakened by the stench of our putrefaction.

As if we had been slumbering. As if the little lives we had lived up until now flittered any which way, directed by the nutrients that fed us.

It was just nine months ago when the little white house on Walcott Street began its awful raining. We didn't question why we had been chosen to receive the alarm; we weren't yet capable of such thoughts. On instinct, we rallied to the call.

All of us—thousands of inert, gurgling seedlings—shimmied like tadpoles, beneath the surface of our small yard. We popped from our soggy shells to form a dense, husky mound, and then vomited until the poison freed us. Awakened and cleansed, as if someone had breathed life into us for the first time. So greenly prickled, so sharply alert. But those strange sensations are not what moved us.

Their suffering had nearly killed us. It was no longer possible to root beside them like a benign appendage. That's why we convened on their marshy yard. We gesticulated at one another with wild flickering colors until we determined a plan. This is what started our murmuring.

We set to work immediately. Even though we had no idea how to multiply or move. Over and over we flung ourselves into a mad, useless snarl. A repeating humiliation. Why had we gained awareness without ability? And what exactly was ability? Conceiving, itself, seemed impossible. Yet the home, and all it held, roused us to action.

We murmured for months without understanding one another. Our sounds, a vibration within our roots. It was agonizing at the beginning— all sharps and points—as fear and longing filled our bodies. And then something more powerful overtook us.

*

By early spring, the house was surrounded by a shallow, widening moat. Its seepage attracted a swarm of mosquitoes. Mad spawners. Within days, the air was animated. It gyrated and hummed within its own ecosystem. Our yard would have been uncomfortable for visiting humans, had there been any. But the couple had ceased their social customs. They were flattening, softening, muffling to a dull, smothered pink. Their mouths puckered. Beige and dryness invaded them. When they left the house in the morning and returned at evening they didn't even notice the buzzing or biting. Their ears and eyes seemed glazed, as if they were turning inside out.

This worked out well for the mosquitoes, whose feasting was a rapid competition. During the seconds that they were privy to flesh, the man's and woman's hands, necks, and faces were freckled with dense, raspberry clustered bites. The mosquitoes were swelling as the humans were shrinking.

Around the same time, we discovered that our dearest friends, the worms, had not been as lucky as we. A flotilla of their bodies spun by us in slow spirals, inspiring us to work faster, harder. We stretched to touch their bodies one final time as they drained toward the slope of the driveway.

We weren't the only ones to say good-bye to the worms. Their ambidextrous bodies attracted a bevy of birds to the plot. How we despised their waxy cawing! The swollen, viscous scent of bird genitals invaded the air, creating a hot, amber dome above us. But it also led to a fertilizing rain of the most sensuous droppings. Our private thrill! By late spring, their shower, along with the long-awaited sun, helped us to spawn in grandiose proportions: the first of our milestones accomplished.

There was no time, however, to pat each other on the back. Even as we were thriving, the house and its inhabitants were withering. Drying. Pucing.

With a force of multitudes, we set upon phase two: migration.

We were working on advanced ambulatory techniques, one summer day, when the bumpy one surprised us with a visit. Her purposeful gait had been replaced by something too slight. Her hue too pale, almost, for color. She had turned into a cold, floating mass. Sunlight glinted off of the pruning sheers dangling from her grasp. The shrill sound of her clipping turned us to witnesses of a massacre. One by one she decapitated our companions: the sleepy-headed roses, the frenetic lilies, the vainglorious dahlias. Even the buds—she had no mercy—then the bud-less stems! If we had had mouths we would have awakened her with our screams. If we had had hands we would have grabbed the clippers before she snipped the magnolia limbs and rhododendron leaves into jagged claws. We watched the force of life bleed from our friends. We were in a rage, clicking and flashing as the woman floated back toward her house, but she didn't notice us. She just walked away, a lime desperation vibrating inside her footprints.

We took off the rest of the day. We cried, wishing we had never been roused from our grassen slumber. Never cared or hoped to make a difference. We didn't understand our new understanding. Why, we wondered, had we been chosen? Then we wondered who or what could ever answer our wondering. Exhausted by too many things, our bodies fell limp.

The next day, we agreed to abandon our thoughts—our aptitude was discouraging—and focus upon the simple sensations of work. We forced ourselves to new levels of vigor. Our murmurings grew to grunts and moans. Over time, we became stronger, more flexible, while the white house continued to shrivel: shingles gap-toothed, rafters warped, corner studs buckling.

By June, the couple's sobbing had ceased. They came and went in their burlap shroud. Their speech depreciated from grunts and moans to murmurings, and then vaporized into the air. They no longer touched each other. Their exhausted sobbing turned a brittle acid yellow.

Meanwhile, we, the grasses, had learned to labor together. We worked furiously for months while the humans were sleeping, a powerful indigo ringing up from our blades. By some inexplicable trick of will and adaptation, we learned to transport ourselves.

The hardest part was turning the corner from the yard to the foundation of the house itself. The physics were confounding. The most eager among us uprooted but could neither secure their roots nor find their way back home. Some among us were dedicated to the dying, so others could focus on the journey itself. By the end of September, a couple of young shoots caught hold of the space between shingles and coached our kindred on the passage. We hissed, in awe, trying to conserve our energy for the work ahead of us. Triumphant little tufts began to sprout around the foundation. Soon enough, grassy rows bent their backs to help a next row knit itself between the clapboards. We were taking over the house. We never felt so alive.

It is late December, now, and we have fully consummated our union with the little house on Walcott Street. We have arrived. Every moment of doubt, every ounce of confusion and despair, the tonnage of exhaustion we have ignored until now: trivial. The residue of striving oozes from our roots as tears stream from our tips. The soft cloak of our bodies, at last, wraps around the drying house. We share our breath with its skin. We are home.

Thousands of beaming blades on the yard huddle around us, nodding furiously at our accomplishment. We hum a celebratory tune, then burst into a gross, convulsive laughter. Most of us are tone deaf. Who knew?

After delirium slides off our bodies, stillness falls upon us. As if the air is a blanket weighing us down. We vegetate for a couple of days, nearly forgetting about the humans. When the house's sadness starts to chill our roots, we know it is trying to pull us under its spell. Too tired, still, to rouse ourselves, we whimper feebly, understanding that we are just another shadow in the couple's blinded lives.

An idea to form an idea and then an action plan floats among our brethren, sisters, cousins, aunts, uncles, and the generations of parents and grandparents still with us, but it can not seem to find a form or language. And then the new we—a furry and flocculent home—slump against the pallid landscape and fall asleep.

Days pass and the winter sends the last shining slivers of life underground for safety. Our bodies, stiff and tense from stagnation, awaken then stretch into the frosty air. We watch the man and woman shuffle in and out of their verdant den, utterly unaware that we have moved in.

Again, we drink their poison and spit it out. We cough and wretch, but we aren't afraid of the malignancy. We have already suffered the vaccination. The frozen ground also refuses the contagion; it rolls off the driveway and into the sewer's vast annihilating dilution.

And then, late one night, as the first snowfall drifts down from the sky, the blanched couple tiptoe outside, tenderly brushing the cracked tips of their fingers against us. They circle us, a crusted curiosity on their faces. Then they step back to drink us in with their sad eyes—a surprising role reversal—their rounded shoulders and heavy arms drooping toward to the ground. A fallen awe unclenches their jaws; their breathing reveals a sour, umber wind.

A sigh seeps from us. We suck in the frigid air, trying to absorb the heat of their sadness. We are silent but weeping, now, as their dry eyes moisten and their boney, oddly fiery frames make their way onto the barren yard.

The humans help each other to their knees. Then they strip, revealing their beastly, pendulous bodies. They slouch against one another up for a long time. A bonfire of bones. We still ourselves at 90° against the force of gravity. We will not miss a sound or an emanation.

Their rubbing begins only after the frozen air forces the bulbs of their joints to shiver. It starts slowly; they are tentative, like humans who are unfamiliar to one another. But as they recall the iridescent feel of one another's skin, their kneading hastens then turns to a fury. They smash their mouths together, as we had seen them do so many months ago. Then they start to cry: a stream we must taste so we can know, from the inside, if they are going to survive. We are sobbing—we can't help it—as they send great gulping sounds into one another.

Have we helped, or did it hurt them to answer our call? Groaning sounds rattle our roots as the humans grunt and squeak. The small one grabs the tall one's face, her voice scratching the word "Roy" into his eyes; he looks into her, choking on the sound "Bev." The entire light spectrum is flashing through our bodies as they lower themselves to the frozen ground. They pull at each other's hair and skin. They bite each other's mouths. They beat their flesh against one another like giant frenzied birds. When their howls flare into the sky, we can't stop ourselves from joining in. ❧

The Secret Nancy
Nancy Reddy

The Dark and Handsome Stranger Mystery
He's been trailing her all over town. She hears
him just behind her on the sidewalk
walking home. She feels him watching her
as she scrapes the dishes clean. She can hear
the ghosts behind her writing. Nancy reads
the local papers, checks with all her sources.
No one's missing. No poisoned swooning
debutantes, no jewel thieves at the Mayor's
inaugural soirée. Nancy presses
her face to the glass. He's standing in her yard.

The Clue at the Abandoned Drive-In
She doesn't know his name. The ghosts won't speak
but urge her back again toward town, toward
a volunteer job at the local library,
toward spying even on a new and suspect
neighbor, Miss McDonald. Nancy knows
what good girls do, how they wear gloves to drive
and wash the dishes, wear slips and stockings
under summer dresses. She won't. She's off the plot.
Her stranger never smiles, never speaks. She feels
his eyes on her as she undresses.

The Sign of the Burnt-Out Streetlamp
 Ned always was a timid thing, daring
only once to graze her thigh when Father
glanced away. But this man has hands. He finds her
as she's sleuthing and under lamplight fingers
her silk slip's ribboned hem. She's ready
for bed. He's below her window, waiting,
her flashlight now the beacon blinking *yes*,

blinking *come*. And when he mounts her trellis
and enters her window, when he lifts her nightdress—
she won't say no and won't be sorry.

The Little Things
Will Dowd

One afternoon last winter, while I was lingering in the gift shop where my mother works, I became convinced that a new literary genre was being born in America.
    The inspirational quote.
    They've been around for a while.
    They grace the front of your aunt's get-well card, the back bumper of the car that cuts you off, the side of the disposable coffee cup you turn in your hands so as not to burn yourself.
    But now they've ascended to the wooden wall sign.
    There's not a home in my suburban town without one.
    They have replaced the novel and the painting in one fell swoop.
    They have their roots in the headstone epitaph, the wartime propaganda poster, the philosophical billboard and street graffiti.
    Happiness is learning to dance in the rain.
    Enjoy the little things in life for someday you will realize they were the big things.
    Don't give up hope—when the sun goes down, the stars come out.
    The words—stock, stale, stenciled—encourage two contradictory impulses: motivation and passivity.
    They try to light a fire under you without striking a match.
    It's existentialism without the dread.
    Memento mori without the death.
    Carpe diem without all that aggressive seizing.
    It made me wonder: What would I—a skeptic and snob—hang on my wall?
    At the same time, I was becoming interested in biography as a minimalist art.
    As haiku.
    According to Richard Holmes, my favorite practitioner of the craft, a biographer must possess "the ability to give a snapshot impression of a whole life caught from one fleeting but revealing angle."
    Is it possible to find a shape within a life that reveals the life?
    Is a life a fractal?
    I don't remember consciously deciding to blend my two preoccupations—the form of the inspirational sign and the content of the micro-biography—but I suspect the link was made for me.
    Many signs appropriate the quotes of long-dead geniuses who currently rest in peace in the public domain.

Even the most weightless words acquire gravity when attributed to Albert Einstein.

There's no sense of the actual lives lived by these luminaries, of the suffering they endured or inflicted, of the absurdities they committed or survived.

Just a kind of brand recognition.

I think that offends me the most.

To find these stories, I scoured letters and journals in library basements.

I wanted to discover fresh shapes in previously ransacked lives.

At the same time, I was wary of imposing these shapes.

In the writing, I was inspired by the clarity and rhythm of Jacques Prévert's poetry.

In the graphic design, I tried to disrupt the reading experience.

To slow it down.

To force the reader not to scan or skim but to truly look.

When I first showed these broadsides to a friend, she was concerned. "Once they're on the wall, that's it. They won't change. Won't they be boring after a while?"

This is now a valid anxiety for any two-dimensional artwork that is not a touchscreen.

My aim—or rather my hope—is that these broadsides provoke in the reader a desire to reread what she has just read.

News that stays news.

That's one of my favorite definitions of poetry.

The other comes from Jacques Prévert.

Poetry, it's the prettiest nickname we give to life. ❧

WHEN NIKOLA TESLA
(INVENTOR, PIGEON ENTHUSIAST)
WAS THREE-YEARS-OLD
HE PRODUCED
A SHOWER OF SPARKS
FROM HIS HAND
STROKING MAČAK
(HIS CAT)
IS NATURE A CAT?
THE BOY WONDERED
AND IF SO
WHO STROKES ITS BACK?
GOD?
STOP PLAYING WITH THE CAT
HIS MOTHER SAID
YOU MIGHT
START A FIRE

EVERY TIME
VAN GOGH
WENT FOR A WALK
IN ARLES
THE LOCAL TEENS
THREW CABBAGES
(YES, CABBAGES)
AT HIS HEAD
IT WAS NOT
HIS GRIMY SMOCK
HIS CHEAP STRAW HAT
HIS STENCH
OF COFFEE COGNAC
AND TURPENTINE
HIS LACK OF TEETH
IT WAS THE WAY
HE WOULD
SOMETIMES
DROP TO HIS KNEES
AND STARE
INTO THE HEART
OF A WILDFLOWER
WITH SUDDEN
MONSTROUS
AWE

SHE WAS CHRISTENED
MARÍA DE LA CONCEPCIÓN
BUT EVERYONE CALLED HER
CONCHITA
BLOND THIN SPRITELY
CONCHITA
SHE WAS SEVEN
WHEN SHE CAUGHT DIPTHERIA
THE DOCTOR SENT
FOR A SERUM MADE IN PARIS
WHILE THEY WAITED
HER PARENTS
DISTRACTED HER
WITH LITTLE PRESENTS
HER BROTHER
A THIRTEEN-YEAR-OLD
PAINTING PRODIGY
MADE A DEAL WITH GOD
SPARE CONCHITA
AND HE WOULD NEVER TOUCH
ANOTHER PAINT BRUSH
ANOTHER PENCIL
ANOTHER PIECE OF CHALK
NOT EVEN A TWIG
OF CHARCOAL
SNATCHED FROM THE EMBERS
OF A FIRE
THE SERUM ARRIVED
TWENTY-FOUR HOURS
TOO LATE
CONCHITA WAS BURIED
IN A LOCAL CEMETERY
UNDER A NUMBERED CROSS
HER PARENTS
COULD NOT AFFORD
A HEADSTONE
TO BEAR THE FAMILY NAME
PICASSO

LEONARDO DA VINCI
WORKED HIS WHOLE LIFE
FOR RICH MEN
DESIGNING GIANT
CROSSBOWS
FLEUR-DE-LIS
FORTRESSES
MECHANICAL LIONS
THAT COULD VOMIT
FLOWERS
HE ALSO WORKED
FOR HIMSELF
FILLING NOTEBOOKS
WITH BEAUTIFUL
ERRONEOUS IDEAS
THE SURFACE OF THE MOON
HE WROTE IN ONE
IS COVERED
BY A VAST
LUMINOUS SEA
TODAY THE NOTEBOOK
IS KEPT
IN A DARK
AIR-LOCKED VAULT
IN THE MEDINA HOME
OF BILL GATES

ALEXANDER SCRIABIN
(RUSSIAN COMPOSER,
INCORRIGIBLE MYSTIC)
WAS WORKING
NIGHT AND DAY
ON HIS MAGNUM OPUS
THE MYSTERIUM
A SYMPHONY
HE BELIEVED
WOULD BE SO
TRANSCENDENTALLY
BEAUTIFUL
IT WOULD END
THE WORLD
WHEN HE CUT
HIMSELF SHAVING
THE CUT
BECAME A FURUNCLE
WHICH BECAME A CARBUNCLE
WHICH BECAME INFECTED
BUT THIS IS
A CATASTROPHE!
WERE HIS LAST WORDS
HE NEVER FINISHED
THE MYSTERIUM
THE APOCALYPSE
IS ALWAYS
A PRIVATE CONCERT

ISAAC NEWTON
WHO HAD NO MONEY
HAD TO WAIT ON
HIS FELLOW STUDENTS
AT CAMBRIDGE
HE CLEANED THEIR BOOTS
COMBED THEIR HAIR
MADE THEIR BEDS
ATE THEIR LEFTOVERS
AND EMPTIED
THEIR CHAMBER POTS
WHEN THE SCHOOL
CLOSED
IN THE SUMMER OF 1665
DUE TO AN OUTBREAK
OF PLAGUE
THAT REFUSED
TO DISTINGUISH
BETWEEN RICH STUDENTS
AND POOR STUDENTS
NEWTON RETURNED
TO HIS FAMILY'S
PIG FARM
AND INVENTED
CALCULUS

EVERYBODY KNOWS
PERCY SHELLEY
IS THE ROMANTIC POET
WHO DROWNED
BUT JOHN KEATS
DROWNED TOO
IF YOU THINK ABOUT IT
LYING IN BED
IN THE MIDDLE OF ROME
HIS LUNGS FILLED UP
WITH FLUID
THAT'S TUBERCULOSIS
FOR YOU
HE CAUGHT IT NURSING
HIS DYING BROTHER
I AM IN THAT TEMPER
THAT IF I WERE UNDER WATER
I WOULD SCARCELY KICK
TO COME TO THE TOP
HE WROTE IN A LETTER
AT THE TIME
WHEN THE BODY
OF PERCY SHELLEY
THE ROMANTIC POET
WHO DROWNED
WASHED UP
ON THE BEACH AT VIAREGGIO
IT COULD ONLY
BE IDENTIFIED
BY THE BOOK
FOUND IN HIS BREAST POCKET
A VOLUME OF POEMS
BY JOHN KEATS

Thinking/Cartooning

Zak Breckenridge

"...it designed for the different generations under one roof the character of their journey through time."

— Martin Heidegger, "Building Dwelling Thinking"

Comics such as Art Speigelman's *Maus*, Alison Bechdel's *Fun Home*, and Marjane Satrapi's *Persepolis* draw international interest and acclaim. Comics test the limits of what can be done with the combination of text and image on the page—which can perhaps most notably be seen in the work of Chris Ware and Lynda Barry. We also, incidentally, live in a time of crisis for Heidegger studies. With the collection and publication of some of Heidegger's "black notebooks" by Peter Trawny and his new book *Heidegger and the Myth of the Jewish World Conspiracy*, Heidegger scholars have been forced to seriously reconsider whether and to what extent Heidegger's philosophy could be contaminated by Nazism. Joshua Rothman describes a panel discussion on Heidegger and Nazism, of which Trawny was the centerpiece, as "dim, airless, and funereal," and the discussion itself as "halting and desultory." These notebooks raise the question of whether or not a person capable of holding such poisonous opinions about Jews is capable of producing any valuable thought at all. Heidegger scholars and non-scholars for whom Heidegger is an important figure, such as Trawny and Rothman, are anxious not only about what this means for the academic consideration of Heidegger, but also the damage that this does to their philosophical outlook. It seems that the received ways of understanding Heidegger are no longer sufficient and that we need new ways of considering him as a thinker.

So although the timbre of the question is radically different between the two areas of study, the study of comics and the study of Heidegger are both hungry for revision. I want to single out Chris Ware's most recent graphic novel *Building Stories*, which is made up of fourteen distinct pamphlets contained in what looks like a game board box and is doubtless one of the most formally innovative graphic novels ever, and a few of Heidegger's insights about space, art, memory, and teaching in order to think about the output of these two figures alongside one another. Rather than just using Heidegger as a lens through which to read Ware's work, I want to see what can be illuminated about both Heidegger and Ware by considering them side by side. Ultimately, I want to propose that in the case of these two men a distinction between "philosophy" and "art," or even "cartoons," is insufficient. Heidegger is, in addition to being a philosopher, an artist, who has to inhabit the aesthetic and poetic in order to convey his thinking to a reader. Conversely, Ware has somewhat famously stated that "drawing is a way of thinking," a quote that became the subtitle of the first edited collection considering his work.[1] This suggests that the aesthetic production of comics, at least in the case of Chris Ware, is, in addition to being an art object, a way of thinking both ontologically and phenomenologically. Hopefully this can open the way for deeper consideration of comics as a medium and Heidegger as not just a philosopher, but also as a teacher and an artist.

Building

Heidegger's essay "Building Dwelling Thinking," originally presented as a lecture in 1951, provides a philosophical account of space in opposition to a Cartesian view in which space is described in terms of "the purely mathematical construction of manifolds with an arbitrary number of dimensions." The problem with such a view is that in it "'the space,' 'space,' contains no spaces and no places. We never find in it any locales."[2] Heidegger, through his characteristic excavation of Greek and Germanic etymology, arrives at an account of space as the primary character of man's existence in the world. He claims that the German word for building, *bauen*, originally means "dwelling," and claims that it survives in the first- and second-person singular conjugations for the German verb "to be," *bin* and *bist*: "*ich bin, du bist* mean I dwell, you dwell. The way in which you are and I am, the manner in which we humans *are* on earth, is *buan*, dwelling. To be a human being means to be on earth as a mortal. It means to dwell."[3] Space is not merely an abstract extension that surrounds us in certain geometrically describable ways, but instead sets the terms of how we experience our existence in the world.[4]

In *Building Stories*, Chris Ware is also concerned with people's spatial existence in the world. The title *Building Stories* is a pun: it is about stories that take place in, through, and around buildings, and it also asks the reader, by providing booklets but no order in which to read them, to build their own version of the story. My concern here is with the former meaning of the pun (the latter is discussed below). Many of the

---

[1] Ball, David M. and Martha B. Kuhlman. "Introduction: Chris Ware and the 'Cult of Difficulty.'" *The Comics of Chris Ware: Drawing is a Way of Thinking*. Jackson: Mississippi University Press. 2010. p. xix.

[2] Heidegger, Martin. "Building Dwelling Thinking." *Martin Heidegger: Basic Writings*. Ed. David Farrell Krell. New York: Harper. Harper Perennial: Modern Thought. p. 357.

[3] "Building Dwelling Thinking." pp. 349-57.

[4] Heidegger's view of the subject, which he terms Dasein (literally "there-being") is also distinctly spatialized. Thus Heidegger not only disagrees with a view of space which is abstract and removed from subjective experience, but also disagrees with a view of the subject which is abstracted from the world that surrounds it. cf. Being and Time ch. 19-24.

stories contained within *Building Stories* are centralized around a three-story tenement building in Humbolt Park, and shows how the contingent fact of the spatial relationship between the tenants shapes their lives. For instance, in the second page of a four-page fold-out board, Ware depicts a couple living on the second story that fights over money. The man, alone, looks down at the woman who lives above them as she walks out of the building, wonders about how she lost her leg, and fantasizes about having sex with her. Later, his girlfriend goes to the flower shop where the woman living above them works, who, upon realizing that they live in the same building, gives her a free bouquet. The final two panels, circles in the bottom right corner, depict the second-floor couple cuddling on the couch while the woman upstairs sleeps by herself. It is the space of the building that determines the outcome of the narration.

However, this page, and the other three in this series, deal with space in an even more interesting way. Not only does the narrative center around the building and the spatial life of the characters, but the actual narrative is laid out spatially. Instead of employing narration or even speech bubbles (these pages have a few speech bubbles with symbols or ideograms in them, but no text as such), Ware conveys the unfolding action and the emotional timbre of these sequences by relating objects and people on the page. On the first page, for instance, we are introduced to a handwritten classified ad, in the drawer of a side-table in the third-floor apartment, which is printed in the newspaper in the box outside the restaurant where the woman goes for the date that she has scheduled as a result of the classified ad. This is all conveyed through the spatial arrangement of images on the page; narrative and emotion come solely through this practically architectural arrangement. Ware both represents a life that is lived essentially in space, through our dwelling, and thematizes it in his use of the medium.

If both Heidegger and Ware are working to examine the spatially determined character of existence, space is really an intermediate step on the way to interrogating the everyday. For both Ware and Heidegger, truth speaks through the everyday, which means that understanding comes from the consideration of the everyday. Ontological thinking, for Heidegger, must proceed from the analysis of Dasein in its everydayness: "the manner of access and interpretation…should show that being as it is *first and for the most part*—in its average everydayness. Not arbitrary and accidental structures but essential ones are to be demonstrated in this everydayness."[5] It is by understanding the everyday that the essential structures of human being can be discovered. The pages of *Building Stories* are filled with depictions of sleepless nights, meticulously sliced

---

[5] Heidegger, Martin. "Being and Time: Introduction." Basic Writings. p. 59.

Post Road Criticism | 43

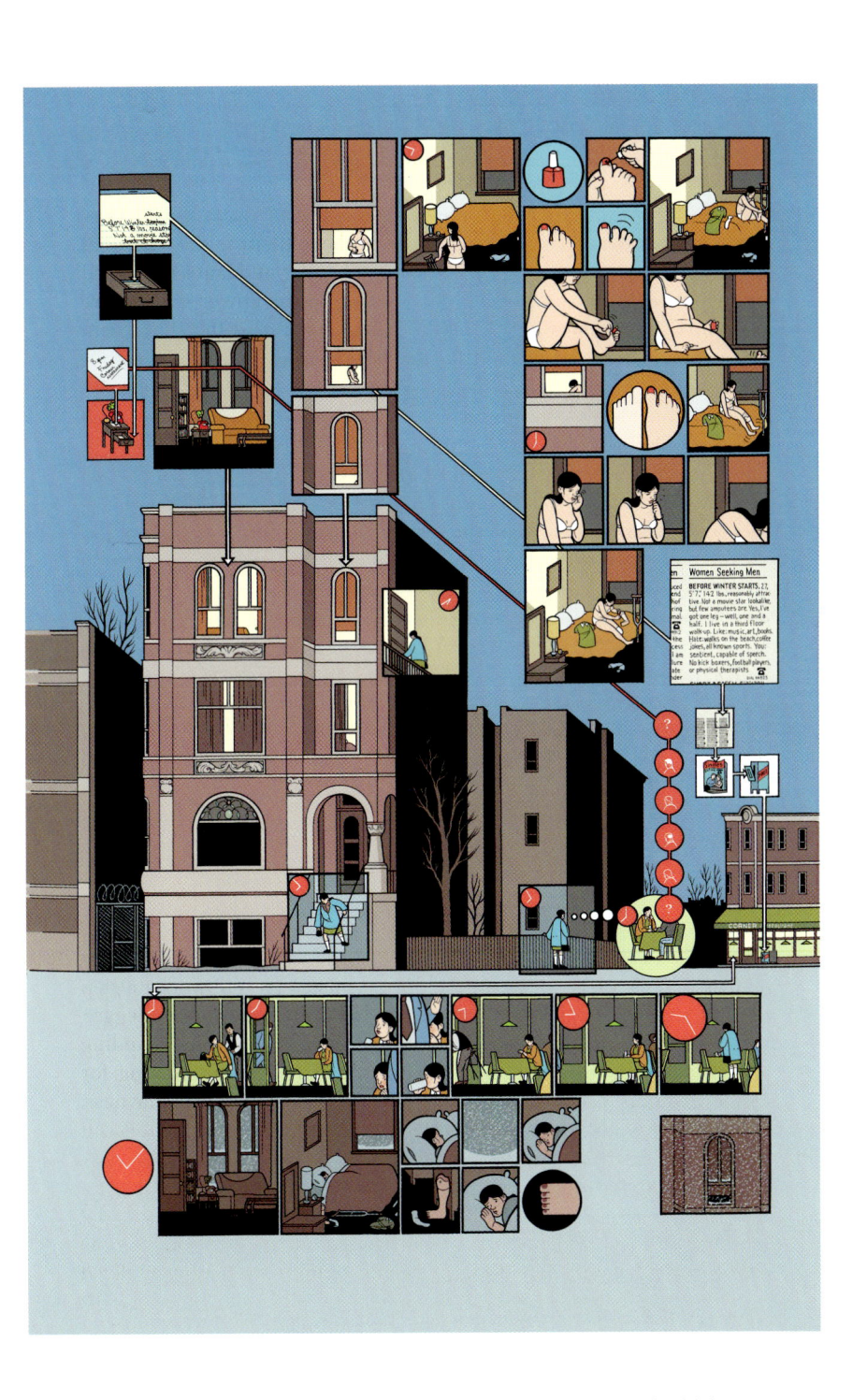

apples, grocery shopping, balancing checkbooks, and etc.: it tries to exemplify the everyday through the form of comics. If attention to the everyday is the path toward ontological thinking, then Ware is right alongside Heidegger on that path.

Finally, Heidegger situates himself clearly within a philosophical conversation by responding explicitly to the shortcomings of past attempts at thinking space, ontology, technology, etc. Similarly, the conversation in which Ware situates himself aesthetically has to do with comics: the limits of the form, the possibility of faithful representation in comics art, and the growth of "literary" comics as a contemporary movement. However, Heidegger frequently takes recourse to poetic and aesthetic tools in order to do the thinking that he finds necessary. In "Building Dwelling Thinking" he places at the center of his argument a downright poetic description of a bridge: "The bridge gathers the earth as landscape around the stream. Thus it guides and attends the stream through the meadows. Resting upright on the stream's bed, the bridge-piers bear the swing of the arches that leave the stream's waters to run their course."[6] In "What Calls for Thinking?" he centralizes a few lines from a Hölderlin poem in order to think about signification, memory, and thinking itself. In order to make his philosophical intervention, Heidegger relies on an aesthetic method. Only by changing, and frequently, aestheticizing his mode of thinking is Heidegger able to do the necessary thinking. Placing this alongside Chris Ware's statement that "drawing is a way of thinking," both Ware and Heidegger begin to appear as philosopher-artists.

Creation

What does it mean, though, to call Heidegger and Ware thinkers? What is thinking here? This question, that of the structure of thinking, occupies quite a bit of space in Heidegger's corpus. For him, "Every questioning is a seeking. Every seeking takes its direction beforehand from what is sought."[7] Thinking thus has, to a certain extent, the character of discovery. Heidegger expands on this in a later essay, writing: "What must be thought about turns away from man. It withdraws from him... Whatever withdraws refuses arrival. But—withdrawing is not nothing. Withdrawal is an event." We, as those seeking to think, are then presented with something, an object of thought, which does not immediately reveal its essence to us. In turn, "what withdraws from us draws us along by its very withdrawal."[8] We are thus called to thinking by something that is as yet unthought; the object of thinking withdraws, inviting us to seek it. In

---

[6] *"Building Dwelling Thinking."* Basic Writings. *p. 354.*

[7] *"Being and Time: Introduction."* Basic Writings. *p. 45*

[8] Heidegger, Martin. *"What Calls for Thinking?"* Martin Heidegger: Basic Writings. Ed. David Farrell Krell. New York: Harper. Harper Perennial: Modern Thought. *p. 374.*

this view, then, there is a certain passivity to Heidegger's thinking subject: it is pulled toward a concealed truth by that truth's very concealment.

However, thinking is not merely passive discovery; it also has an element of *poieses*, of creation. Heidegger arrives at this creative element in thought, and identifies thinking as an element of poetry, by way of memory:

> Drama and music, dance and poetry are of the womb of Mnemosyne, Memory. It is plain that the word means something else than merely the psychologically demonstrable ability to retain a mental representation of something that is past. Memory thinks back to something thought...Memory is the gathering of thought upon what everywhere demands to be thought first of all...Memory, Mother of the Muses—the thinking back to what is to be thought—is the source and ground of poesy...Surely as long as we take the view that logic gives us insight into what thinking is, we shall never be able to think how much poesy rests upon thinking back, recollection. Poetry wells up only from devoted thought thinking back, recollecting.[9]

This is a dense but centrally important passage. First, for Heidegger, creation rises out of memory. Second, remembering is not simply retaining: the subject is not a vessel filled with memories. Rather, remembering is an active thinking-back, and memory watches over that which remains unthought. Thus creation finds its root in the form of thinking which is remembering. However, considering thinking as a creative act does not contradict what I have been calling the passive dimension of thinking. In order to explain the process of learning, Heidegger takes recourse to the example of a cabinetmaker's apprentice: "If he is to become a true cabinetmaker, he makes himself answer and respond above all to the different kinds of wood and to the shapes slumbering within wood—to wood as it enters into man's dwelling with all the hidden riches of its essence."[10] Through this example, we can see that both cabinetmaking and thinking are simultaneously acts of creation and discovery. This is because creation is always a proper response to an essence; it must first of all respond to that which calls it. The shapes slumber in the wood as truth slumbers in the world, but it is only creation which can bring them forth.

Considering thinking, memory and creation in this way has significant implications for thinking about Ware's work. Ware himself has said that *Building Stories* is "from start to finish about memory."[11]

---

[9] *Ibid. 376.*

[10] *Ibid. 379.*

[11] Sattler, Peter J. "Past Imperfect: 'Building Stories' and the Art of Memory." The Comics of Chris Ware: Drawing is a Way of Thinking. Jackson: Mississippi University Press. 2010. 206-22. p. 207.

As he describes the style of drawing that he employs in his cartoons, "I want the black lines of the strip to have the same clarity as typography, because I think that a typographical approach more accurately reflects the way we remember and abbreviate reality as ideas rather than as images."[12] Ware not only works to evoke memory in the way that he draws objects and characters; he also, through the particular interplay that he creates through image and text, as Peter Sattler argues, works to evoke the experience of remembering in the reader. By stringing almost unrelated images together with a continuous memory-narrative, Ware not only represents memory but tries to recreate it as an experience in his work.[13] So if drawing is a way of thinking, memory is an essential dimension through which this thinking operates.

Let's consider more fully the particular form that this thinking takes. Ware says of his process: "I guess it would be admitting too much to say that I make it up as I go along, but that pretty much comes down to what I do. Things happen on the page that I simply would not be able to plan if I was plotting it out very carefully or scripting it beforehand."[14] Considering this alongside the fact that Ware has referred to cartooning as "memory drawing,"[15] we might think of Ware as being much like Heidegger's cabinetmaker. Rather than setting out to make something before he encounters the page, Ware sits down to discover the shapes, patterns, and stories that slumber in the page.[16] Through this process, he creates in terms of memory; he creates a process of thinking-back as he discovers the essence of the cartoon that calls him to draw.

However, thinking is never completed. Even if we are called to think, summoned by the object of our thinking, thinking does not naturally draw to a close. Heidegger writes at the end of "Building Dwelling Thinking" that "enough will have been gained if dwelling and building have become *worthy of questioning* and thus have remained *worthy of thought.*"[17] Thinking as a creative act is thus not merely an activity which can be engaged in and completed, but a practice. The basic definition

---

12 *Quoted in Chute,* Outside the Box. *p. 223.*

13 *Sattler's essay is a wonderful, attentive, and creative piece of criticism to which I cannot do justice here. Further consideration of Sattler's insights would be essential, however, for continuing the comparison between Ware and Heidegger.*

14 *Ibid. 229-30.*

15 *Sattler. "Past Imperfect." p. 206.*

16 *For an entirely different but very illuminating consideration of comics as a kind of carving or sculpture, see Scott Bukatman's essay, "Sculpture, Stasis, the Comics, and Hellboy," in the forthcoming Spring 2014 issue of* Critical Inquiry.

17 *Basic Writings. p. 362.*

that Heidegger gives of Dasein at the beginning of *Being and Time* is that "in its Being this being is concerned *about* its very Being."[18] The defining character of our subjectivity is thus its questionability. I have already touched briefly on Heidegger's interest in the category of *withdrawal*, but I want to give this matter a bit more attention. "What withdraws from us draws us on along by its very withdrawal," he writes. "Once we are drawn into the withdrawal, we are. . .caught in the draft of what draws, attracts us by its withdrawal. . .As we are drawing toward what withdraws we ourselves point to it."[19] The object of thinking, which withdraws, opens us up to an opacity; we seek truth against the world's essential presentation of its withdrawal.[20]

Ware not only parallels Heidegger's account of thinking in his method of creation, but also thematizes this problem of withdrawal in *Building Stories*. In other words, Ware presents us with characters for whom their own Being is a problem, and shows this both graphically and textually. Particularly in the case of the unnamed main character, a young woman with one prosthetic leg who lives on the third floor of the tenement building, Ware gives us access to her dead time, the ways in which she second-guesses and criticizes herself. Lying on her bed, waiting for a plumber to arrive to fix her toilet, she recollects: "It was as if all my failed ambitions were closing in on me as the hours ticked by . . .I had to face it: I'd never be an artist, I'd never be a writer. . .I'd never be **anything**" [bold in original text]. Confronted, in her bored, empty time, with the fact of her mere being, she is forced to consider herself as a problem. Again and again, Ware shows us characters who are unsure, characters who are called to participate in a perpetually incomplete process of thinking.

On the graphic level, Ware works through the problem of characters' withdrawal and opacity to one another and to the reader. Sattler points out that in *Building Stories* Ware makes "this record of remembering one that is simultaneously inside and outside, subjective and objective."[21] Through his use of memory images, which blend objective reality and subjective distortion into a seamless whole, Ware builds a certain opacity into the drawings. This opacity is most evident in the many panels that show characters' faces turned away from the reader and/or from one another. A striking example of this is the first panel of a thin, white

---

[18] Basic Writings. *p. 53*.

[19] *"What Calls for Thinking?"* Basic Writings. *p. 374*.

[20] *For a more complete discussion of man's openness to a closedness in Heidegger's thought, see Giorgio Agamben.* The Open. *Trans. Kevin Attell. Stanford: Stanford University Press. 2004. Particularly chapters 12-14.2010. 206-22. p. 207.*

[21] *Sattler 212.*

"MOMMA, I DON'T KNOW HOW I FEEL RIGHT NOW.
I MEAN, I DON'T KNOW HOW TO SAY IT.
I'M JUST NOT HAPPY OR SAD,
I'M IN BETWEEN."

fold-out series of images that string together poignant memories of the main character's daughter. We see the girl's sandy blonde hair, the pink roll of a shoulder, and a hairband; her face is turned enough that we can see the edge of her lips, the tip of her nose, and the thin line of a single eyelash. The caption reads, "Momma, I don't know how I feel right now. I mean, I don't know how to say it. I'm just not happy or sad, I'm in between." The girl, as she turns away from her mother and the reader, admits that she is opaque to herself. She withdraws, and incites a seeking which is a thinking toward her as a being. As if to enforce Heidegger's comments about memory watching over what insists on being thought, this moment is lodged in the main character's memory. It is an object of thought worthy of being remembered because it points to, without fully understanding, the girl's withdrawal from herself, the girl's withdrawal from her mother, and implicitly, her mother's withdrawal from herself. This moment stays as a memory because it points to the interpretive problem that is human existence.

Thus Ware is through and through a thinker in the Heideggerian sense. His creative process pays attention to its medium and develops organically out of that medium; it is a kind of thinking-creation. Further, *Building Stories* represents characters for whom their own Being is a problem, and thematizes the call to thought in large part through his depiction of averted faces. Through the comparison with Ware, we also see that thinking is, even for Heidegger, a creative act. As we see the two of them puzzling over parallel problems in such radically different media, genre boundaries blur. Heidegger becomes a poet-thinker, Ware a graphic philosopher.

Teaching

The focus on thinking in the work of Ware and Heidegger does not stop with the piece's completion. Rather, they invite their readers to think with and through their work. The centerpiece of Sattler's argument about memory in *Building Stories* is that "Ware attempts to capture and encode nothing less than the very phenomenology of memory...Ware cares less about representing the memory of an experience than about reproducing memory *as* an experience...'Building Stories' attempts to reconstitute memory, coaxing its readers not only to remember feelings, but to *feel* remembering."[22] This suggests that *Building Stories* is not just an aesthetic object that can be experienced and set aside; it works to create an experience in which the reader must participate. This brings us back to the second meaning of the novel's title: out of the fourteen memory-stories contained in the box, the reader has to actively *build* the story in his or her own way. In this sense, *Building Stories* is a piece of narrative which is always created anew upon every individual reading. If, then, *Building Stories* is essentially an aesthetic piece of thinking, it invites (calls) the reader to think and create along with it.

Both Ware and Heidegger are recognized within their respective fields for their difficulty. If we think of this difficulty as resulting, at least in part, from Ware's meticulous project of "encoding emotion" in his work, forcing the reader to participate in the work's unfolding, then perhaps Heidegger's difficulty can be thought of in a similar vein. Heidegger rejects the straightforward descriptive modes of modern philosophy in order to better grasp what is, for him, philosophically fundamental and which remained ungraspable with the previous philosophical vocabulary. Heidegger spends the very first pages of *Being and Time* dismantling the philosophical commonplace that Being must remain unthought:

> On the foundation of the Greek point of departure for the interpretation of Being a dogmatic attitude has taken shape which not only declares the question of the meaning of Being to be superfluous but sanctions its neglect. It is said that "Being" is the most universal and emptiest concept. As such it resists every attempt at definition.[23]

In order to respond to this gap in philosophical thinking, Heidegger must create a new language to apprehend this supposedly unthinkable interpretive problem. Consider such an apparently nonsensical thought as "Dasein is a being that does not simply occur among other beings. Rather it is ontically distinguished by the fact that in its Being this

---

22 Sattler. *"Past Imperfect." p. 207.*

23 *"Being and Time: Introduction."* Basic Writings. *p. 42.*

being is concerned *about* its very Being."[24] This thought, though, is not completely obscure: rather, it merely requires attentive consideration by the reader. At the same time that Heidegger works to interpret Being, he asks his reader to interpret alongside and through his writing.

Heidegger's creation of this new philosophical language is not by any means haphazard. He is attentive to etymologies and works to find hidden essences buried within language: "It is language that tells us about the essence of a thing, provided that we respect language's own essence...Man acts as though *he* were the shaper and master of language, while in fact *language* remains the master of man."[25] In much the same way Heidegger sees man as dwelling essentially in the world, he also sees man as dwelling within, rather than merely employing, language. Much as the cabinet slumbers within the wood, meanings slumber within language. If we extend this paradigm to reading Heidegger himself, his style of writing invites us to attend to the essence of his thought contained within his language. Thus we must think with, and therefore create within ourselves, Heidegger's thought.

In this sense, much like Ware's comics, Heidegger's thought is not simply a set of propositions which can be read, understood, and internalized. Rather, he works to induce the perpetually unfinished creative work of thinking in his readers. "What Calls for Thinking?" which is reconstructed from a series of lectures entitled *What is Called Thinking*, contains a brief reflection on teaching which is indicative of how Heidegger views the relationship between his thought and those receiving it:

> Teaching is more difficult than learning because what teaching calls for is this: to let learn. Indeed, the proper teacher lets nothing else be learned than—learning...The teacher is ahead of his apprentices in this alone, that he has still far more to learn than they—he has to learn to let them learn... If the relation between the teacher and the learners is genuine, therefore, there is never a place in it for the authority of the know-it-all or the authoritative sway of the official...We must keep our eyes fixed firmly on the true relation between teacher and taught—if indeed learning is to arise in the course of these lectures.[26]

If this is the outline of a Heideggerian pedagogy, then his primary concern is not depositing information in the minds of his students but rather inciting thought in them. This is curious for a lecture course, but

---

[24] *Ibid. 53.*

[25] *"Building Dwelling Thinking."* Basic Writings. *p. 348.*

[26] *"What Calls for Thinking?"* Basic Writings. *p. 380.*

it means that the call to thought is actually contained in his thought itself. It provides a language through which his students can think. With both Ware and Heidegger, then, in addition to being a creative act, thinking is a collective, participatory act. The meticulous, arduous, and deep thought performed by both Ware and Heidegger is not intended to be a complete and bounded product, but instead calls us as readers to think with it and through it.

This is, of course, only the beginning of what can be said about the comparison between Chris Ware and Martin Heidegger. Much could be said about Branford Bee in relation to Heidegger's reflections on animals and boredom in his 1929-30 lectures. More could be said about their various conceptions of space, building, and dwelling. Volumes could probably be written on the history and usage of "draw," "withdrawal," and "draft" as Heidegger uses them alongside Ware's comment that "drawing is a way of thinking." The list could go on. This piece is meant to open up the possibility of considering comics philosophically and philosophy aesthetically. Perhaps comics are a philosophically privileged medium, or perhaps their philosophical potential is only now being tapped.

I wonder if thinking of Heidegger aesthetically might open up productive ways of considering Heidegger's thought that neither dismiss him out of disgust for his politics nor ignore this troubling aspect of his character. What makes Heidegger's Nazism so troubling, according to Joshua Rothman, is that "philosophy has a math-like quality: it's not just a vocabulary, but a system. A failure in one part of the system can suggest a failure everywhere." If Heidegger is capable of thinking such short-sighted and poisonous thoughts, of what value can the rest of his thinking be? I wonder if, perhaps, this view underestimates the strength of Heidegger's challenge to philosophy. If his thought is primarily creative and participatory, rather than systematic and mathematical, then breaking out of the framework that Heidegger himself created, no matter how meticulously, does not contradict his values as a thinker. I will not pretend to have solved the problem of Heidegger's Nazism, but perhaps he was a deep enough thinker that, with his help, we could today overcome some of his shortcomings.

What I hoped to show here is that drawing Heidegger's philosophy into conversation with comics not only provides ways of reading these comics, but also can furnish us with new ways of considering philosophy. On the other hand, with the serious critical and theoretical reception that comics are now receiving, the possibility that they are capable of doing substantive philosophical work is worth considering. If thinking is a creative and participatory act, then we, as readers of Ware and Heidegger, are heeding the call. ❧

AGNI

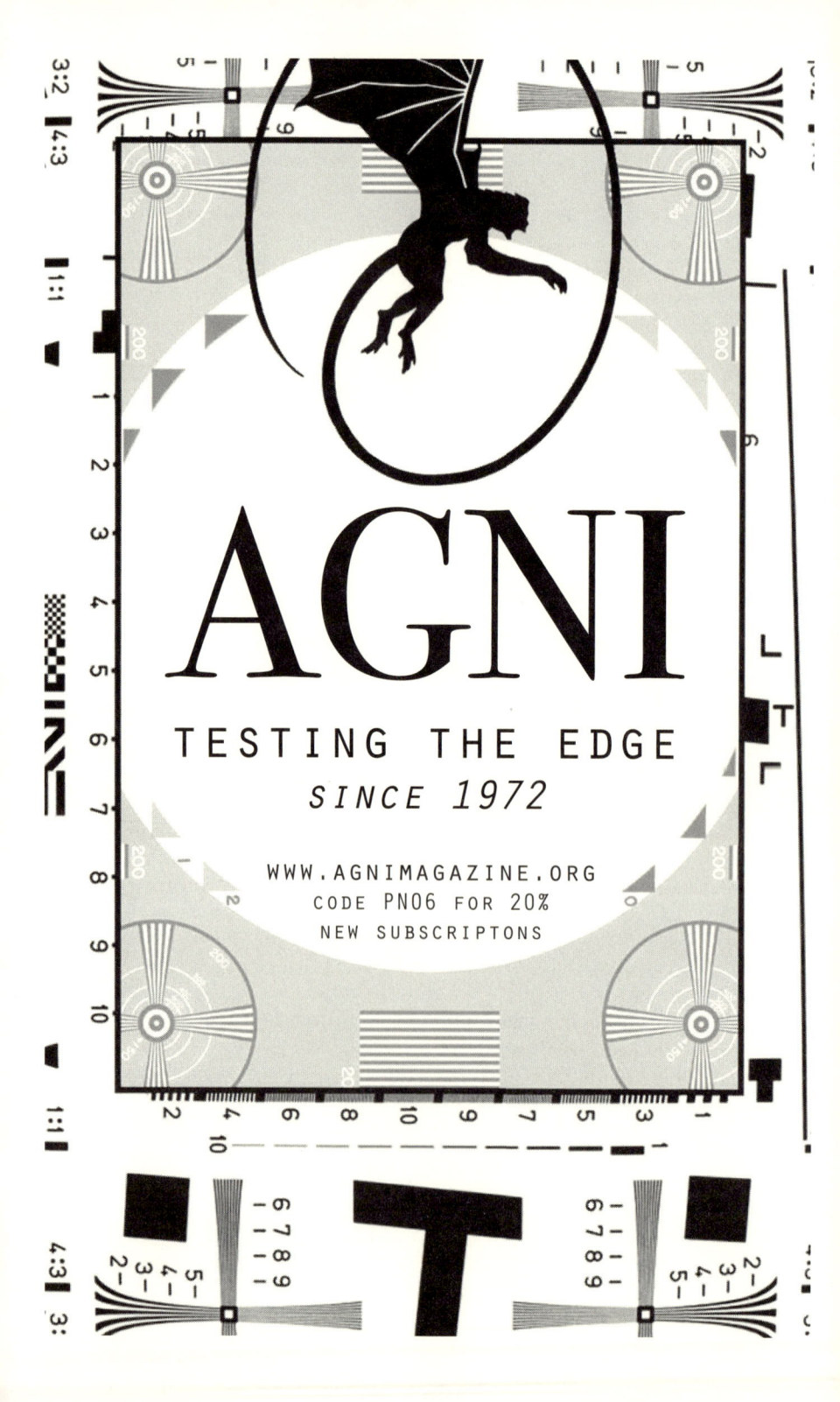

TESTING THE EDGE
SINCE 1972

WWW.AGNIMAGAZINE.ORG
CODE PN06 FOR 20%
NEW SUBSCRIPTONS

Grandpap's Burials
Casey Quinn

At noon, Grandpap takes aim and shoots the crow in our garden.

"Get it, boy, sniff it," he says, shooing me with one hand. I burst out the back door into the heat, sprinting towards the trellis on which the grapevines grow.

The crow is four feet, four inches and boy-shaped. Two mustard-colored seashells form a teepee over his mouth. A black mask is sharpied around his two blue eyes. Glued feathers crisscross up and down his forearms like tic tac and toe. Timmy Jensen was in my third grade class—before he became a crow and formed a one-boy flock, flapping up and down our suburban street, marring tulips and rummaging gardens the way he imagined a crow would. He was troubled long before Grandpap shot him down.

"Don't he know crows don't eat no grapes?" Grandpap asks. His face is patched with pink splotches. I don't think he has shot a boy before, but I can't be sure.

I nudge the body. The crow whimpers.

Buckshot punched holes in the back of his black jeans, and shiny red-flecked metal juts out from his haunch like bits of asteroid. His wings are sun-faded trash bags. In the daylight, the plastic Hefties are more vermillion than black. When I point out the wing discoloration and that the Timmy is still alive, Grandpap shakes his head.

"Cruddy crow," Grandpap says, and spits close to Timmy's face. Grandpap kicks Timmy in the stomach. Timmy groans but remains dead.

"Nope. See, he's dead. Dead crow is dead crow," Grandpap says. This makes me uneasy. I do not think Pap's defense will hold up. At least not here. Grandpap is from the south; things are different down there.

Mikey Henderson, age seven, and my brother, age five, bound towards us with shovels.

The boys bring three. I take the extra and Grandpap hobbles back towards our Cape-Cod. Once he's out of earshot, I turn to Timmy Jenson. "Stop faking it dummy, we know you're alive," I say.

Timmy makes dead crow noises. He lifts a wing slightly then lets it fall.

"Come on, get up," I say. I prod his crow face with my foot. He squawks and bats me away, then resumes death. Mikey and my brother look at the body. Then me. They shrug and sink their shovels into the ground. Grandpap returns, dragging a lawn chair.

Grandpap drinks sweet tea until the hole is big enough. Then he rises, walks over and rolls Timmy Jenson with his heel. Timmy lands with a groan. The four of us gather around the grave and look down. The hole is only three feet deep, the same depth of our Golden's grave. After one night, raccoons discovered Milo and dragged pieces of him to the four corners of our yard. I wish the same for the big faker, Timmy Jensen.

"What now, Pap?" my brother asks.

Grandpap looks at us three. His hair is gone. His teeth are yellow, mostly gone. He taps his chapped lip with his one unscarred finger. "Ice cream?"

I hold my tongue. It is not okay to shoot our neighbors and then leave them in an open grave, but in this heat, a little Rocky Road won't hurt.

"Where's your grandpa from again?" Mikey asks after we pile into the bed of Grandpap's truck.

"Pap's from 'Bama," my brother says in his recently acquired twang.

"Where's that?"

"Ma says that's where we ain't supposed to go."

I peg my brother with a pebble.

The horn shrieks. Swerving into the other lane, Grandpap shakes his scrawny fist at a Honda, then guns past.

"Why'd he shoot Timmy Jenson?" Mikey asks.

"He didn't mean to," I say.

"You sure?" Mikey asks.

I punch Mikey in the shoulder.

Of course Grandpap meant to. At 11:50, he found me crying after Timmy chased me, shrieking "Gonna eat your eyes. Gonna get 'em." Grandpap had me load the buckshot and open the window. We looked down the barrel together, but he pulled the trigger. I'd swear it in a court of law, just not about the crying part.

Mikey looks over but says nothing. He's not as dumb as my brother. He knows we've done bad.

"What flavor you getting?" my brother asks, "I'm getting Razz-burry with sprinkles."

"Chocolate and vanilla," Mikey says.

My brother turns to me.

"Rocky Road," I say.

Grey clouds suture the last strip of clear skies above. We pull the tarp over us when the rain starts.

"You like Timmy Jenson?" Mikey asks.

"Nah," I say. But, in fact, Tim was my best friend before his parents' divorce and crow transformation.

"I'm glad we killed him," my brother giggles.

Mikey and I avoid one another's eyes.

It's hot under the blue tarp. I peek out but don't recognize the flash of buildings. Rain pocks the blue fabric then dribbles down the sides onto my feet. I flick the fabric wherever drops collect and think of Timmy Jenson down in his grave. Had he lifted himself from the hole we dug, run home, and told on us, or were his eyes still closed? Was Timmy that eager to die? After the showers break, we remain under the tarp. Our plastic sky is perfect blue, no clouds.

  The truck slows, then halts. We wait a few minutes before peeping out. Steam rises off the hot asphalt. We slip out from under the tarp and off the truck bed. There are only cornfields and the newly paved road that splits them for miles and miles. The cab door is open, and we tell ourselves Grandpap went for a wizz. A blackbird is perched on a cornstalk. It watches us as it reaps unripe kernels. We wait and wait, but soon even my brother realizes something is wrong. ò

JUST KIDS by Patti Smith

Brian Sousa

Suggested, optional soundtrack: Patti Smith, *Horses.*
"I had no proof that I had the stuff to be an artist, though I hungered to be one."
– Patti Smith, *Just Kids*

Some believe certain books arrive in our lives for reasons we don't understand, like mysterious strangers knocking on our doors. With Patti Smith's soul-bending memoir *Just Kids*, this seemed to be the case: an old friend gifted me the book a few nights before I packed my car and once again obeyed Horace Greeley's famous advice: "Go West, young man."

Let me be more specific: I'd left my teaching job of seven years, given up my tiny-yet-coveted apartment in the Back Bay of Boston, and decided to move to Aspen, Colorado with my girlfriend. I had no plan of any kind, other than to write and play music, explore the vast mountains on foot and snowboard, and attempt to break a routine that was grinding my muse down to a fine dust. I rapidly folded, then ripped my old life apart, hoping the highways would provide new dotted lines to follow.

Fast-forward a few months, to when I opened the black cover adorned with a simple photo of Smith and artist Robert Mapplethorpe. If you don't know the backstory, Patti Smith began as an aspiring poet in New York City in the late 1960s, but it wasn't long before she was performing her poems with a guitarist, and enduring poverty to dedicate her life to art in its many forms. Smith ultimately followed a crooked path to become one of the most influential performers and songwriters, not only within the New York City punk rock movement, but in the world. Robert Mapplethorpe, her best friend and partner in life and art, was a photographer who shattered conventionalism with his boldly sexual, controversial work. The book is both memoir of Smith's life—she is still touring and writing music—and beautiful tribute to her relationship with Mapplethorpe, who died of AIDS in 1989.

The strength of the writing relies both on Smith's lyrical, philosophical prose, but also the subject at hand: a fumbling, disconnected period of mutual creative discovery, followed by the stuttering-then-scorching rise of both artists. Smith and Mapplethorpe meet as teenagers, and together they attempt to gain traction in the sprawling NYC art scene. They fail yet exult in their creations, they succeed and are wracked with doubt. The two are constantly working—painting, writing, promoting— and though they both realize their visions, it is in ways and forms that neither expected.

The story is not remarkable for the way it ends—we know Smith will create the now-classic album *Horses*, and we know Mapplethorpe will be eulogized by his own brilliant portfolio, among other things—but for its description of how willing each artist is to fail completely.

This was a reality I could relate to this past fall. I thought I was leaving the rigors of academia for a life filled with freedom and the clack of my keyboard. I envisioned rapid success; after all, I just needed time to create. But real-world concerns crept in, even in snowy, sunny Aspen, and finding inspiration for my novel proved difficult. Normally, when I can't write prose, songs and poems fill my notebook, but for a while, I couldn't create at all. Smith's words about her own periods of creative paralysis resonated: "I taped sheets of paper to the wall, but I didn't draw. I slid my guitar under the bed. At night, alone, I just sat and waited."

But pragmatic questions continued to assail me, yanking me from my work. Was I just avoiding the social and economic realities of adulthood? While many of my friends were enjoying promotions or starting families, I was working odd jobs, unable to even afford a sandwich from the coffee shop where I wrote. Smith, too, endured periods like this. She writes of herself and Mapplethorpe only being able to afford one visit to the art gallery among the both of them: "He waited for me, and as we headed towards the subway he said, 'One day we'll go in together and the work will be ours.'"

My dilemma was existential, too. I wanted to believe I was driven by forces out of my control, some artistic impulse that set me apart from the masses. But maybe this was just an easy fantasy? Why was I writing; what was the point? As I examined my role as an artist, Smith, eerily in tune with my own ego, did the same:

> In my low periods, I wondered what was the point of creating art. For whom? …Are we talking to ourselves? And what was the ultimate goal? To have one's work caged in art's great zoos—the Modern, the Met, the Louvre? I craved honesty, yet found dishonesty in myself…It seemed indulgent to add to the glut unless one offered illumination.

But as she self-analyzed, Smith also produced a stunning amount of work. As I finished her book, I realized this. And I stopped doubting myself, and pushed harder. My emboldened journal entries at the time reflect this:

> Patti Smith told you things you should've figured out a long time ago: you are an artist. So allow yourself to create, lose, learn, screw up, and continue. Write every day, and stop worrying so much about the practicality of it.

So I continued to create, once again filling pages with words, once again pulling my guitar from underneath my bed. It didn't matter if no one was listening when I sang songs in crowded bars. It didn't matter that

I didn't have an agent or publisher for my novel yet. I would get there. And even if I didn't, I would be doing this work anyway. I always had. I always would.

Once I realized this, the future regained its addicting shine. As Smith writes, "No one expected me. Everything awaited me." ❧

Ma Picks a Priest

Marianne Leone

"I rest my case."

My sister, Lindy, thrust a statue of Saint Anthony in my face, ticktocking him like a metronome. Saint Anthony was wearing a rakish pink scrunchie stuffed with red and yellow artificial flowers around his waist. We were arguing about holy cards and which saint Ma would want on hers. I had pushed Saint Rocco in honor of Ma's part-time job booking illegal numbers for the local wise guys. I thought I remembered her telling me that Saint Rocco was the patron saint of gambling. He was often depicted as a ragged man with bleeding leg sores being licked by a faithful dog. (I later found out that he was invoked to ward off infectious diseases.) I supported my vote for Saint Rocco with the fact that Ma had a statue of him right by her bed. My sister pointed out that Saint Anthony was there, too. So was Saint Jude, a flame shooting out of his head like he had just been electrocuted, and Saint Francis, decked out like a mad pigeon lady in Central Park with birds clinging all over his monk's robes, even covering his privates. But Saint Anthony had the scrunchie with the flowers. And Ma had put it there herself.

"Look at him. He's *decorated*," my sister said. We both cracked up. Then we cried. Again.

We had been on an emotional roller coaster for two days now, ever since Ma died suddenly at the age of eighty-four. The doctors said it was a cerebral hemorrhage. She woke up with a headache and was dead by two the same afternoon. Ma would've liked the idea of leaving in such a hurry, like one of our childhood Christmas trees that was stripped and tossed every year the day after Christmas, at her urgent behest.

Now my brother Michael, Lindy, and I were orchestrating the wake and funeral, checking off chores with the same haste as we used to devour desserts, Ma waiting impatiently to clear the dinner table. Apart from the quibble about her favorite saint, we knew exactly what to do. From birth to marriage to death, there was a clear trajectory if you lived in the Lake, an Italian-American part of Newton, Massachusetts, where the circle of life had a really tiny radius. You were baptized at Our Lady Help of Christians Church, you got your wedding dress at La Sposa, you were laid out across the street at Magni's Funeral Home, and your funeral Mass sendoff returned you to Our Lady Help of Christians Church.

Andrew Magni led us through the downstairs coffin display. We bypassed the over-the-top one with the carved version of the Last Supper on the cover, paused briefly by the hot pink number so my sister and I could instant eyebrow message each other, and settled finally on a shiny metal canister with a coppery glint. Back in his office, Andrew informed us that none of the regular priests at Our Lady's were available and we would have a substitute to say Ma's funeral Mass from the next parish over, St. Bernard's. The name of the parish rang a tiny, distant bell muffled by my memory of Ma's last non-encounter with priests a few months before she died.

We were at Newton-Wellesley hospital. Ma had complained of a headache and partial loss of vision in one eye and the doctors wanted to make sure she hadn't had a small stroke. I stayed with her so that her spotty English language skills wouldn't make her seem unhinged to the medical staff; they were testing her mental competence with questions about what day it was, what month, and what year. She answered correctly. They asked her who was the current president that year, 2004.

"Eh. I can' remember his name, but I know he's a *basta!*"

I looked at the hospital personnel.

"You can't possibly question her sanity now."

Nevertheless, the doctors decided to keep Ma overnight. They sent in a very young, squeaky-voiced hospital clerk, who rattled off a list of questions in a fatally bored voice.

"Religious Affiliation?"

Ma looked at me and shrugged.

"What's 'e want?"

"He wants to know if you want to see a priest."

Ma's voice was strong, resolute.

"No. No priest."

I turned to Squeaky.

"You got that? No priests."

Squeaky didn't realize that to my mother it was as if he'd asked: "And would you like to have a visit from the Angel of Death?"

Later, I settled Ma in her intensive care room—there were no beds available in the regular part of the hospital. She relaxed, lulled by the electronic wallpaper of the television mounted in the corner. Restless, I wandered into the hall. I stopped at the neighboring cubicle, listening as a priest droned the "Our Father" to a frightened, demented old woman who was emitting cries of alarm like a baby bird dislodged from the nest. I edged closer. "Home. Home," the old woman cried. She lay huddled on her bed in a wilted heap, barely distinguishable from the bedclothes. The priest sat four feet away and recited his prayer as if he were alone in the room, as if he were direct-dialing his old buddy God for a dinner date, as if the old woman were already dead.

Ma was right about priests, I thought.

About a month after the hospital event, I was on a flight from Los Angeles heading home to Boston. We were in first class, courtesy of the studio that was promoting my husband, Chris' film. I sat beside an entitled middle-aged guy who wasn't about to give up his window seat so I could sit with Chris. That was okay. Chris and I could survive five hours one row apart. And we were in first class. Who was I to complain when there were warm cookies available and I had actual legroom? Just six rows back in the economy gulag there were cramped throngs with serious future chiropractor bills looming and no warm cookies. I didn't hold it against the window-hugging guy, and over lunch we made polite small talk. I asked him why he had been to LA. He said he was at a religious convention.

"Oh, really? What do you do?" I asked brightly, with only a tinge of heart-sink at the word "religious." I knew that my own contentious nature and the twelve years I put in as a parochial school POW would inexorably draw me into talking about religion. I was a lemming in sight of the cliff.

"I'm a priest," he said, with a kind of mock sheepishness, like he was revealing unwillingly his superpowers.

I leapt off the cliff.

"I hope you don't think you're more spiritual than I am because you have a penis and can change water into wine."

That came out so abruptly I almost looked around to see who said it.

The priest raised his arm for the stewardess like he was bestowing a blessing.

"I'll have a scotch, please."

Over the next five hours we discussed my theory of the imminent demise of the Catholic church. Well, I scattershot bullet points at the priest, and he dodged them. It was strange. I remembered the worshipful way the nuns would ask the priests if they would give us a blessing back in high school when they visited our classrooms. The nuns would duck their heads girlishly and we students fell obediently to our knees in a thudding horde. They had a glamour then, the priests. They handled God every day. A tiny, retro part of myself wanted the God spillover from the guy sitting next to me in the window seat. But I also wanted him to explain to me why any woman would want to join a club that from birth designated her as a second-class citizen. He talked about the programs he was involved in for troubled youth. I talked about the Magdalene laundries in Ireland, the Catholic-run slave-labor institutions for unwed mothers that only closed in the nineties. I asked if his youth programs were like that. He kept ordering scotches. Even though he was the one drinking scotch, my memory of the rest of the discussion is hazy, though I know it touched upon my years of torment in parochial school, the priest pedophile scandals, and my gratitude to renaissance cardinals for commissioning 3-D pornography from artists like Bernini so that we could today view Italian sculptures of women in "spiritual" ecstasy, like Santa Ludovica and Teresa of Avila.

What I couldn't remember now, at Magni's Funeral Home was the name of the parish to which my sacerdotal seatmate had said he belonged. But I didn't dwell on the priest. I thought instead of Ma, her fierceness stilled forever, on display in her burnished copper casket. I remembered asking her on New Year's Day what her resolution was for 2004, and her growly answer: "to be dead this year." And then her practiced hold for my laugh, her timing as polished as any late-night comedian's. Her pitch-black humor, which had taken seed in the arid mountain soil of her impoverished girlhood, was as gnarled and twisted as the Montepulciano grape arbors of that region, and as dry and delicious as the dark wine they produced. I don't remember ever hearing a belly laugh from Ma. She favored the snort of derision, the head toss, the "ha!" that was more like a spoken confirmation that she got the joke. As measured as her own laughter was, she was sly about amusing her audience. She knew she was funny but she always played it straight. She acted the innocent, watching us laugh, eyelids at half-mast, appraising the reactions. Ma would never make me laugh again, I thought.

On the day of Ma's funeral I entered the church as the substitute priest was setting up shop for the requiem Mass he was about to say.

It was my scotch-drinking seatmate from the plane.

I snorted with laughter, shaking my head, my laugh a replica of my mother's. I was wrong about Ma making me laugh again. ☙

ALL THE RAGE by A.L. Kennedy
Ethel Rohan

The greatest brilliance in one of my favorite short stories, J.D. Salinger's "A Perfect Day For Bananafish" (originally published in the *New Yorker* in 1948), is how it depicts the difficulty of communication between its characters—characters whose conversations, desires, and demons are rendered on the page with enormously effective indirectness. As I read the twelve stories in A.L. Kennedy's new collection, *All The Rage*, I reveled in how Kennedy also tells things slant—an insistent obliqueness that works to, yes, render the difficulties of communication amongst her characters, but also, like Salinger, to invite the reader more fully into her stories by making us work to understand, identify, and connect.

I've been a fan of A.L. Kennedy's work for several years now, ever since I first read her short story collection, *Indelible Acts*. The central themes across Kennedy's impressive body of work are love and relationships—love blooming and breaking and broken, and lovers trying to put themselves back together or willing to risk harming themselves all over again. Thankfully, the theme of love in its many states is also ever present in Kennedy's fifteenth book, *All The Rage*, as is Kennedy's growing refusal in her work to tell anything straight on. There's this ironic feat the fiction writer must pull off: make the real out of the fabricated. Kennedy approaches making the real out of the fabricated by rendering how cryptic people and life can be, gloriously refusing to be obvious and direct. Thus Kennedy gets at the truth in her fiction by mirroring the truth of people and of life: both are often hard to figure out, explain, and negotiate.

All The Rage is peopled with a wide range of characters—young and old, monogamous and adulterous, sober and addicted, in and out of love, the lost and the found, the open and the closed—characters with experiences, emotions, logic, and motivations that resonate, and that also sometimes seem impenetrable. Kennedy's fiction demands readers interact and infer to arrive at the point of understanding—or not. As I read, I could almost hear Kennedy urging me to *Pay attention, Keep up, See harder, Know we can't always know.* Above its stellar prose and skillful crafting, what I found most captivating and compelling about A.L. Kennedy's *All The Rage* is its honesty about what we know of people and our world and also what we can never know of people and our world, at least not fully, and such limits are true even of fiction writers, the creators of people and worlds.

I leave you with an excerpt from one of the stories I found perhaps the most obscure and compelling amongst the obscure and the compelling in *All The Rage*, titled "Baby Blue":

There wasn't a fountain.
There never has been.
I don't know why I added it.
I want to describe my genuine circumstances on the occasion in question, but I can't.
I don't remember a bus stop, a journey of that kind. I usually drive. There would have been parking and, before that, the customary instances of discovery, bits of waiting—I'm sure there must have been—only I had no idea they might be of importance and paid them no heed.
But I was neither in an alien country, nor suffering unusual conditions.
That rubbish isn't true.
I did get lost. True.
I was raw-eyed. True.
I had passed a shallow night holding on against a memory of altitude and claustrophobia. Doesn't everyone? True.

Go read *All The Rage*. Go give yourself the gift of gorgeous. Go allow your mandatory involvement with these stories. Go risk your heart. ❧

Negative Space: Various Artists

Natalie Edgar, *South Ferry*, 2011, Oil on canvas, 42" x 58",
Courtesy the artist and Woodward Gallery, NYC

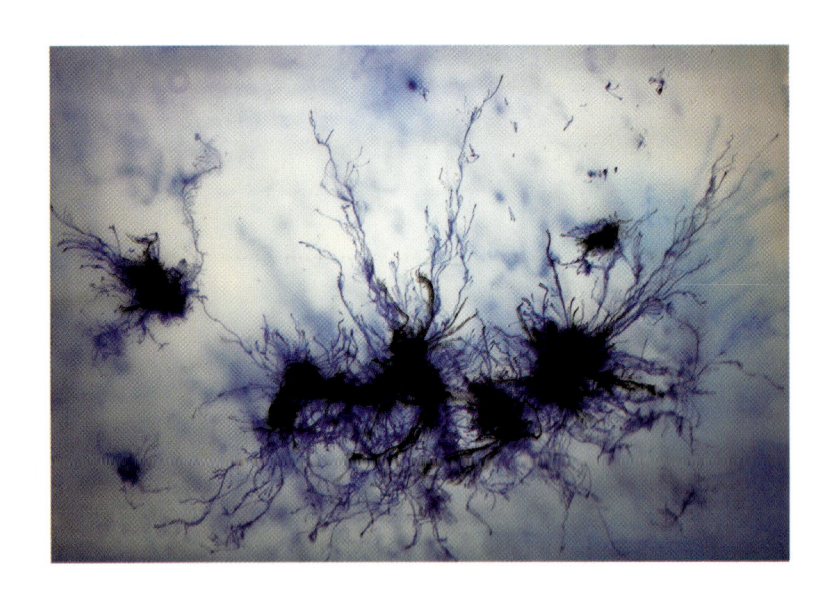

Joaquin Carter, *The Confrontation*, 2009, Ink and watercolor on Mylar, 20" x 30"

Karl Heine, *Green Panes—Broken Sky*, 2013, Digital photography, 16" x 28"

Lori Ellison, *Creases*, 2013, Ballpoint pen on college ruled paper, 11" x 8.5", Courtesy the artist and McKenzie Fine Art, New York

Heidi Pollard, *Swat*, 2010, Cellulose, gypsum, polymer, wire and oil paint, 55" x 32"

Astrid Cravens, *Hurricane ESP*, Visual component of audio-visual collaboration with writer/musician Rick Moody, 2012, Inks and casein on paper, 14" x 10"

Julia Schwartz, *1.9.31.24*, 2013, Oil on canvas, 12" x 12"

Don Voisine, *Dub Stride*, 2013, Oil and acrylic on wood panel, 32" x 32",
Courtesy the artist and McKenzie Fine Art, New York

Cary Smith, *Pointed Splat #2* (pink/yellow, with color blocks), 2013, Oil on linen, 50" x 50"

Ravenna Taylor, *Rhyme Scheme V,* 2011, Paper, photos, gouache and collage, 9" x 11.25"

Lane Twitchell, *Self Centered Asunder*, 2013,
Enamel on cut Melinix mounted to acrylic, ink and pencil on panel, 36" x 36"

Charles Yoder, *Tree Rings*, 2012, One color linocut on 30g An-Jing paper, 16" x 27", Edition of 14

Oriane Stender, *Endless Column* (detail), 2013,
Ink, beeswax on book pages, 7" x 26" (6 pages)

Melanie Parke, *Morning Table*, 2013, Oil on canvas, 30"x 40"

Susan Carr, *Burnt Mattress, Birthday Photo*, 2002, Photograph, 4" x 6"

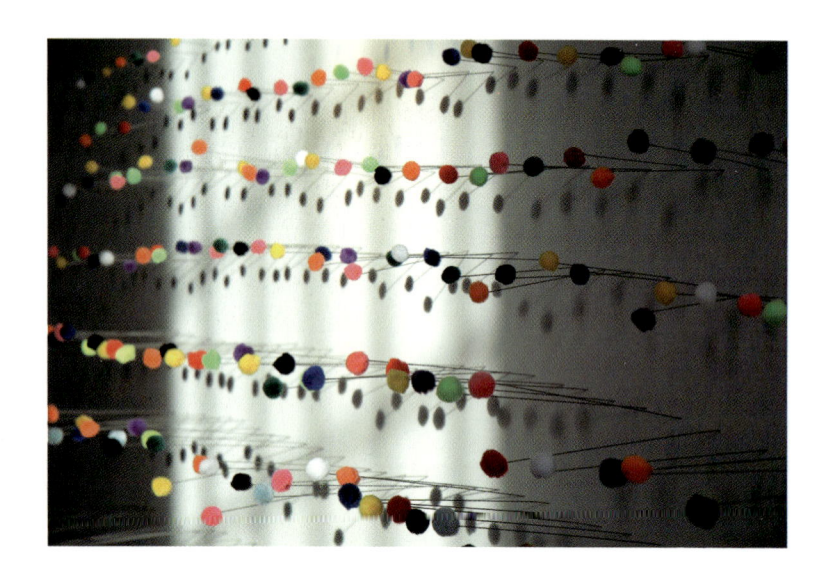

Suzan Shutan, *Flock* (detail),
Exhibited 2013 (Biennale Internationale d'Art Non Objectif, Pont-de-Claix, France)
and 2010 (Artspace, New Haven, CT), Wire and pom poms, size variable

Miranda July's IT CHOOSES YOU
Shelly Oria

Some books are not so much books as they are tiny angels sent to help humans figure something out—something we seem to keep fucking up. For instance: the creative process. I know for a fact that the creative process is something many humans keep fucking up because I am a human who keeps fucking up her creative process, and also because I am a human who helps other humans with this problem. I do this for a living: I work as a creativity and life coach. I also do this for friends, of course, and sometimes for strangers at parties, because when you mention the words *creativity unblocking* to anyone, what usually happens next is that the person in front of you turns into a blinking question mark. What does that mean, he or she asks, how does it work?

The conversation that follows is long. Sometimes it goes on for years. For a while, back in 2011, Miranda July's *It Chooses You* saved me a lot of time. I would carry a copy of the book with me and take it out of my bag in relevant moments. Instead of the usual creativity talk, I would just say, "Read this book; it will solve all your problems." Then I would take it back from them because it was my book and they could get their own.

You may be wondering if when I said, "it will solve all your problems," I was speaking hyperbolically. The answer is yes, I was. As a writer, I appreciate the drama of hyperboles. Isn't it funny how we always want something, someone, to solve all our problems? And isn't it funny how nothing and no one ever does? And how even though we know this, we keep forgetting? So I always figure: if I can make someone feel for a fleeting moment that she's arrived, that I am that someone offering that something that can fix it all—why not do that? It's a kind gesture, dishonest and quick though it is. If you meet me at a party, I hope you'll do the same for me.

But while it may not solve *all* of your problems, *It Chooses You* is a pretty powerful creativity pill. It is a book that describes a creative journey—namely, Miranda July's struggle with her film *The Future*—and shows how that journey is, or can become, its own work of art. In the beginning of the book, July is hitting wall upon wall in her attempt to finish that screenplay. In her procrastination, she becomes obsessed with the *PennySaver*, or, to be exact, with the lives of the people behind the ads. She calls them, and if they agree, she shows up at their houses with her assistant and photographer and interviews them. If you've ever read or watched Miranda July's work you understand that she does this with heart and humanity and humor. The outcome is beautiful in the way that only the most tender efforts can be.

For me, *It Chooses You* is a book-long reminder. It reminds me that everyone, including a brilliant artist whose work inspires me, has days when they feel lower than dust, and months when a project is wholly out of reach. It reminds me that I can always turn to my work and ask it: "Who are you? What are you trying to be?" And it reminds me that if I do, I will be opening a new window; this miniscreen within my screen can become its own work of art, if I am brave enough to let it. And maybe most of all, *It Chooses You* reminds me to be curious. It reminds me that being curious is being alive, and that every "creative block" is in essence a crisis of empathy, a failure to ask questions or care about the answers.

I stopped carrying the book with me at some point. It's not a small book, not a light one. My bag is often filled with heavy items of various kinds—a laptop, a big water bottle, a journal. After a while, conversation seemed easier than the extra weight.

A few minutes ago, my friend Caitlin texted me some thoughts about love. Caitlin now lives and loves in Portland, Oregon, after many years here in Brooklyn. I am writing this piece, I told her. It's about that Miranda July book *It Chooses You* and about creativity and curiosity and aliveness; what word should I end on? Wonder, my friend Caitlin, who's one of the best writers I know, said. End on wonder. ෴

Pity
Lisa Gornick

In 1967, the summer after I turned eleven, my family moved to a ranch house on a cul de sac in a town not far from Baltimore. The house was laid out in a T with boxy bedrooms and low bumpy ceilings like a reptile's skin and a dining square off the rectangular living room that reminded me of math sheets demanding computations of the area of ungainly shapes. My father, recruited to head the Physics Department at the nearby branch of the university, had bought the house without my mother or the rest of us having ever seen it, and I hated it on first sight for lacking the nooks and crannies, the polished banisters, window seats, crawl spaces, attics, gardens, and gazebos of the houses I knew from the children's books I loved. Technically a suburb, the town was in truth sub-rural with scant connection to the city, which in those days was in the depths of its decline with a largely abandoned downtown, what little of which remained functional would be decimated during the race riots the following spring.

Of course, it had never occurred to my father to inquire about the local schools or the character of the community. My younger brother and I got our first introduction when the girl who lived on the other side of the cul de sac told us she wasn't allowed to play with us since her mother, who'd correctly surmised from our surname, Steinberg, and my father's olive complexion, that we were Jews, had informed her she was at risk of having her blood let in one of our barbaric rituals. We were, I would soon learn, the only Jewish family in the town where the religious diversity ranged from Catholic kids who attended one of the many parochial schools and evening fellowship classes, to Catholic kids who went to parochial school and to Friday night mass so they wouldn't have to get up early on Saturday morning, to Catholic kids who went to the public schools where they either rested lightly before landing in quasi-industrial jobs or settled permanently into personas—sloppy drunk, football hero, lusted-after cheerleader—they would keep for the rest of their lives.

The town was rife with anti-Semitism, slurs about kikes and money-grubbing Jews, but none of it felt personal since none of the kids who said these things had actually ever known anyone who was Jewish, and other than the keen neighbor across the street, it seemed never to have crossed anyone's mind that our family might be Jewish any more than that we might be space aliens. It became a never-ending ordeal for my brother and me to one by one tell our friends we were Jewish, something I dreaded doing, not out of fear of losing my friends—my brother and I were both popular—but because of the embarrassment of having to say to someone who hadn't even known she was insulting me that she had been, and then the awkwardness of having to digest the apologies.

In my last month of tenth grade, my father bought a camper van and took off cross country with a thirty-two-year-old female post doc from his lab. My parents were vague about the meaning of this arrangement, but when my goodie-two-shoes mother started smoking cigarettes on the patio at night and my father did not return to the house by September, my brother and I surmised that a permanent change was under way.

Our mother took a job at a local nursing home. Neither she nor my brother, who was busy with football practice, got home until seven each night, so it fell to me to start dinner. Whereas my brother was invested in being part of the school, I was biding my time until I could move away and begin what I thought of as my real life. In ninth grade, I had been a peripheral part of the popular group with a boyfriend who was on the varsity baseball team; our dates focused on fights about his pressuring me for sex, which I would not have been adverse to if he weren't so dull. In tenth grade, I spent a few months hanging out with the pot smoking kids, not really smoking that much pot myself since I didn't like the way it made me feel—tired and stupid—but for a while finding the novelty of the marijuana rituals and the loquaciousness of the other kids when they were stoned kind of interesting. The new dinner responsibilities gave me a good excuse to do what I really wanted, which was to spend my afternoons lying on our living room couch and reading until it was time for me to put on the franks and beans or chicken and rice.

Most of the teachers were lifers who'd been teaching the same tired curriculum for decades, but every once in a while there was a new teacher who tried to "engage" the kids. That year, the new teacher was Mr. Mitner. Mr. Mitner was cute in a pale Irish way with nice features and a neat head that seemed a little small for his long frame. He'd majored in English at Fordham, where he'd commuted from his mother's home in the Bronx. His first year at my high school, he coached the Boys JV Basketball Team and taught Honors Eleventh Grade English: *The Scarlet Letter*, *The Great Gatsby*, *Catcher in the Rye*, *The Merchant of Venice*, and some Flannery O'Connor stories. For the first time in all my school years, I actually listened because he actually had things to say about the books that weren't totally obvious. I wasn't much of a talker in class—it wasn't interesting to hear myself talk; I already knew what I thought—but Mr. Mitner would call on me sometimes, inquiring in an arch way, "So, Ms. Steinberg, how would you describe the moral universe of Daisy?" or "What do you think Salinger means by the image at the end of the book?"

The week Mr. Mitner assigned *The Merchant of Venice*, he asked me to come see him at lunch. "Please have a seat, Ms. Steinberg," he said when I slouched into his classroom. He smiled at me and pushed his bangs off his forehead. With his jacket hanging on the back of his desk chair and his shirt sleeves part way up his arms, I could see the fine black hairs on his arm. He sat on the edge of his desk and swung his legs back and forth. I didn't find him particularly attractive but I could see why a lot of the girls in my class and even some of the popular cheerleader girls had crushes on him—one in particular who'd bragged that she'd driven him home after two of the basketball games, insinuating that something had happened, which no one believed.

"I want to talk with you about our next book, the Shakespeare play." He paused until I looked up from my lap. "One of the themes in the play is anti-Semitism. I was worried our class discussion might make you uncomfortable."

I laughed, more out of nervousness than finding what Mr. Mitner said funny—nervousness since I wasn't used to teachers talking with me about anything beyond a reprimand for reading during class or an occasional *good job* as they handed back a test. "Mr. Mitner," I said, "I've been in this town since I was eleven. I've heard kids say every prejudiced thing you can imagine about Jews, in front of me only because they never thought anyone in this school could possibly not be Catholic."

Mr. Mitner looked at me. "Well, I'm pleased to hear that. I grew up in the Bronx where every other sentence contained a racial epithet. Mean, vulgar insults. The adage, what doesn't kill you makes you stronger, is true."

I thought about whether I should respond, and then ended up half mumbling, "What doesn't kill you makes you harder."

Mr. Mitner squinted at me in a way that made me squirm. It was as though he were seeing me for the first time. Then he smiled. "Well, Ms. Steinberg, perhaps you'll write a paper on that: what doesn't kill you makes you harder."

Honors Eleventh Grade English fumbled through *The Merchant of Venice* and I wrote my final paper on the question of whether Shakespeare was an anti-Semite or was depicting anti-Semitism. Mitner gave me an A+. Over the summer, a rumor circulated that Mr. Mitner had been seen at a movie with Julie Ralston, a girl who had just graduated and was working in her uncle's auto parts store. By the end of the summer, my brother referred to her as Mr. Mitner's girlfriend.

"Yuck," I said.

My brother looked at me curiously. Now that he'd started to shave every day and was going to be on the varsity basketball team, he refused to act like my little brother, challenging me at every turn with his superior understanding of how everything worked.

"Why yuck? She's graduated, she's eighteen, an adult. And Mitner was never her teacher."

I couldn't defend why I felt it was yuck—maybe because Mitner had been my teacher, maybe because he'd made me squirm that day in his classroom.

At the beginning of my senior year, I decided I wanted to go to college in New York. My father, who by then had settled into a crummy house in downtown Baltimore in a neighborhood that had been heavily looted during the riots that followed Martin Luther King's assassination, had to come in to talk to the guidance counselor because she'd never heard of Barnard. The guidance counselor thought that since I was a smart girl, I should go to Sweet Briar in Virginia where the smart girl from last year's class was now.

"Sweet Briar is an excellent school, Professor Steinberg," she told my father. Although it was November and in the thirties outside, there were sweat circles looping down from her armpits. "And they take good care of the girls. No boys are allowed in the dormitories..." she said with a meaningful glance at me.

"My daughter wants to go to Barnard," my father announced in a voice that signaled end of subject and perhaps reminded the guidance counselor of the physics class she'd failed in college because she shut up about Sweet Briar and looked up the address to request the Barnard application.

Mr. Mitner wrote one of my letters of recommendation and it must have been good because I got in. Over the summer, I worked as a waitress in a diner and had my first boyfriend who wasn't a kid: Hank, a 26-year-old black short-order cook who played drums for an R&B band and had gone in 1969 to a youth Communist conference in Europe with Angela Davis. He'd had a baby with a girl in Oakland, California, which was where he'd grown up, and he lived in the black part of town, where I'd really never been before, with his grandmother, who he'd come east to take care of for a while. Hank laughed when I told him I was a virgin, but he was gentle and sweet as he led me through the basics and made sure I got something out of it "because baby, it ain't no fun for me if it ain't fun for you."

In late August, my father and brother drove me to New York and, after we unloaded my stuff and I met my roommate who'd grown up on West End Avenue and we went with her to have coffee and pie at the Chock Full O' Nuts, my father and brother drove off and I literally cheered, right there on the corner of 116th Street and Broadway about what felt like the beginning of my real life.

When I came back for Thanksgiving, my first time home that semester, my brother told me that Mr. Mitner was now the Boys Varsity Basketball coach. The season had begun and after games, Mr. Mitner sometimes had the team over to his house for a party, where he would let the boys bring beer if they had a designated driver. According to my brother, the thing with Julie Ralston was over and Mr. Mitner was openly dating one of the Spanish teachers, Señora Marta Gomez.

A Columbia sophomore, Rolly Thines, who I'd gone out with a couple of times and then stupidly slept with, after which I'd had to admit that the only thing we had in common was that he was also from Maryland, though in his case from one of the tony prep school neighborhoods of Baltimore that I'd not known existed before coming to Barnard, offered me a ride back to New York the Saturday morning after Thanksgiving, which I took and then regretted since he spent the whole trip trying to convince me to go down on him while he was driving, which I thought was both repulsive and dangerous. We arrived in New York mid-afternoon, no longer speaking. My dorm was open, but no one else on my floor was back. I unpacked my things and wondered how to spend the rest of the day. I could have called my roommate who was at her parents' apartment, but I felt like I'd be intruding, a hanger-on to whatever parties she would be going to with her friends also home from college. I lay down on my dorm bed and fell asleep.

I woke to the phone ringing. To my surprise, it was Mr. Mitner. "How did you get my number?" I blurted.

"Your brother gave it to me a while back. I'm here in the city, visiting my mother. You didn't go home for the holiday?"

"I did. I came back early because I had a ride."

"So, what are you up to now?"

"Not much. No one is here. I guess I'll get some reading done for my classes next week."

"Why don't I take you to dinner? You can tell me about your classes."

I put on a skirt and some boots and took the subway to 79th Street to meet Mr. Mitner at an Italian place he'd suggested. Mr. Mitner was seated when I arrived. He had on a crew neck sweater and his hair was a little shorter than the last time I'd last seen him.

"Good to see you, Mr. Mitner," I said.

He stood and gave me a peck on the cheek while I awkwardly wiggled out of my jacket and settled the book bag I was carrying because I didn't own a purse. "Now that you've graduated and are in college, you can call me Jim," he said.

"Jim."

"Everyone calls me that except my mother who calls me Jimmy still."

While Mr. Mitner, Jim, talked with the waiter about which bottle of wine to order, it occurred to me that no matter what I called him, he would still be Mr. Mitner to me. He poured me a glass, and for a moment I thought that I should tell him that I was not yet eighteen, but that seemed silly since like everyone else in my dorm who was still seventeen, I had a fake ID and we all drank at the bars near school, just not with our former high school teachers.

Mr. Mitner told me about growing up in the Bronx, in an enclave of Irish-Catholic families, and going to a parochial high school where he'd been on the basketball team, and then to Fordham, and how in all of those years, he'd hardly ever been to Manhattan save at the holidays when his mother would always take him on the Sunday before Christmas to see the tree at Rockefeller Center and the 10 AM Rockettes show and, until he was way too old, Santa at the Lord & Taylor's department store.

"I once dated a Barnard girl," he said with a little laugh. "Sophie Jacobsen. A little nymphomaniac."

I had heard my brother's friends talk about what they imagined to be Mr. Mitner's hot sex life, first with Julie Ralston, who'd never been considered a catch before she dated Mr. Mitner but whose stock had risen in all of their eyes afterwards, and then with Señora Gomez, who had a way of arriving just as they left the parties at Mr. Mitner's house, occasioning a lot of tittering and on one occasion, Corky, the team clown, climbing a trellis to look in Mr. Mitner's window, resulting in a fall from which he'd been lucky to have only sprained a wrist.

It was a clear night, and Mr. Mitner suggested that he walk me back to my dorm. We walked up Broadway, talking about George Orwell's essay "Shooting an Elephant," which I'd read for my British literature class and that Mr. Mitner told me was his favorite essay ever—the way shooting the elephant was an act of cowardice, how doing something wrong out of fear of humiliation was even lower, in his mind, than simply doing something wrong, and how he'd come to realize that this was also true about being intimidated into doing something right, that this was also a sort of cowardice.

Mr. Mitner looked at me meaningfully, as though he was sure I must be catching the drift of what he was saying, but I felt lost in the same way I had with the poems by Thomas Hardy in the same class—that there was a dark labyrinthine meaning that eluded me.

"The curse of a Catholic boyhood," he said in what I knew was intended to be a mocking voice but struck me as a little creepy and made me wonder if his calling the girl he'd known at Barnard a nymphomaniac had been a thought he'd had about me, as though he knew about the incident in the car earlier in the day with Rolly Thines trying to get me to go down on him and it had been transposed in Mr. Mitner's mind into something I'd initiated.

When we got to my dorm, Mr. Mitner insisted on escorting me up to my room since the dorm was basically deserted, after which I felt like I had to invite him to come in.

I turned on the overhead light and my desk lamp and offered him a glass of water, which I went to get from the bathroom down the hall. He looked at the books on my shelves and then sat in my desk chair drinking the water. Having no other alternative, I sat on the edge of my bed.

Mr. Mitner came to sit next to me. He seemed a little disheveled, with his shirt tails out, but I thought it was the wine and the late hour. He took my hand in what at first I hoped was a fatherly gesture, but then he shoved it into his pants which he must have unzipped when I'd left the room. He squeezed my hand around his substantial erection, then pushed me back on the bed and put his wet mouth over mine in a way that made me gag.

He felt heavy, heavier than Hank or Rolly Thines had ever felt, and between the weight of him against my diaphragm and his saliva in my mouth, I felt like I was suffocating and gagging all at once.

"Mr. Mitner," I gasped after I managed to free my mouth. "You can't do this."

Mr. Mitner sat up. He put his hands over his face and bent over so his head was almost touching his knees. "Oh, my God," I could hear him moaning. Then he slid off the bed, onto his knees, and started to pray, his back towards me, "Lord, forgive me, Lord, forgive me," over and over again.

"Mr. Mitner," I said, "Please, it's alright."

Still on his knees, Mr. Mitner whispered, "I almost violated you."

"You stopped."

We remained in silence for a while, my hand feeling dirty from having touched his penis. Then, Mr. Mitner got off the floor, and sat back on the bed, this time a few inches away from me so no part of his body was against mine. "Can I tell you a secret?" he said. "Something I've never told anyone?"

I wanted to say no, but I didn't feel able to say no to Mr. Mitner who had given me an A+ on my *Merchant of Venice* paper and written my college recommendation letter which was part of how I'd ended up in this dorm room in the first place.

"I'm a virgin. Twenty-six years old and still a disgusting virgin."

My eyes must have opened wide because Mr. Mitner then said, "I know. It's shocking. It shocks even me."

I looked at the floor, averting my gaze so he wouldn't see that behind my shock, it also struck me as perverse, as though he'd confessed to being a foot fetishist or having had sex with animals.

I kept my eyes on the floor while Mr. Mitner continued. "At first, it was because of my upbringing. I truly believed that I had to wait until marriage. And then, as I got older, twenty, twenty-one, and started understanding that this was just one of those things people say but you're not supposed to really do, it was out of embarrassment."

Mr. Mitner cupped his hands over his knees. "I was too embarrassed to tell the girls I went out with, all of whom had already lost their virginity, that I had no experience. Last spring, with Marta, Señora Gomez, was the worst: all the lies about needing to get up early and wanting to wait until we could go away together because I was terrified that if I tried to have sex with her, she'd be able to tell that it was my first time and she'd be horrified."

The look on Mr. Mitner's face was unbearably pathetic. I felt humiliated just seeing it. Even though my neck was hurting from the effort of pushing Mr. Mitner off of me and I knew what he'd done was wrong, I felt sorry for him.

I lowered the shade and turned off the overhead light and then I took off all of my clothes and climbed over Mr. Mitner so I could get under the sheets.

Mr. Mitner looked at me wide-eyed. It occurred to me that he had probably never seen a naked grown woman—I supposed that was what I was. He bent down and unlaced his shoes.

Mr. Mitner left on his red and green boxer shorts. I held open my sheets. He was a little flabbier than I had expected and he had hardly any hair on chest. He suckled at my breasts for what seemed like too long a time and moaned but not in the way I'd heard from Hank or from Rolly Thines. I reached down to confirm what I suspected: the erection was gone.

I made some efforts to resuscitate Mr. Mitner's erection, something I'd never had to do with Hank or Rolly, but my own expertise was minimal. Afterwards, I blamed myself for giving up too quickly, but from the way Mr. Mitner's skin had felt clammy and his breathing shallow and his penis soft like a baby's foot, I was 99% sure there was nothing I could have done to help Mr. Mitner,

Mr. Mitner left before I woke up. I took a long hot shower and changed the sheets on my bed and then went back to sleep. When I woke up, it was two in the afternoon, and there were only a few seconds before I remembered Mr. Mitner and a gloom fell over me again.

Mr. Mitner called three or four times before I came home for winter break, but each time I would wildly motion to my roommate, *NO NO*, and she would sweetly tell him that I was in the library or at a friend's performance. Once she even said I was at class even though it was ten at night. I hoped he would take the hint, but his letters continued, each restating how he couldn't wait for me to come home for Christmas break. There was a restaurant he was not going to try until I was home to go with him and some books he had bought for me and something "special" he had for our first night together again. His last letter, before the break, concluded with: "I know, my little beauty, that it will be different next time."

I slept with Rolly Thines the weekend before winter break and then again the night before he drove me home. In the car, we smoked a joint and he told me the story about how he'd lost his virginity at fourteen with his Jamaican nanny's daughter and how afterwards the nanny had said to him, "Now you the man," which I thought was hysterically funny and couldn't stop laughing about until Mr. Mitner's flaccid penis resting against my thigh came to mind and I had to open the window to keep from throwing up.

It was four when we got to my mother's house, too early for my mother to be home from work. There was a car in the driveway, which as we approached I recognized with a sinking feeling as Mr. Mitner's car.

I climbed out of Rolly's car and Rolly handed me my duffel bag and squeezed my butt as Mr. Mitner got out of his own car.

I didn't actually say "What are you doing here?" but it must have been obvious that this was what I was thinking because Mr. Mitner said, "Your mother invited me to dinner."

I tried to come up with a reply, but my thoughts were still muddled from the joint, muddled in a way that now felt distinctly unpleasant.

"She said you'd be getting in around four, so I thought I'd come over early to have a visit first with you."

"This is Rolly. Rolly Thines. He gave me a ride."

Mr. Mitner peered at Rolly as though he'd caught him plagiarizing a paper. Then he held out a hand to shake. They made some small talk about the holidays and the basketball game that would be on television that night and then Mr. Mitner took my duffel and Rolly whispered in my ear, "I'll call you, babe," and got back into his car.

I unlocked the house and excused myself to use the bathroom. By the time I returned, Mr. Mitner had settled into the living room, in what I still thought of as my father's chair.

I sat on the couch, my legs tightly crossed. Mr. Mitner stood. He glared down at me, then lowered himself beside me.

"So, are you fucking him?"

"What?"

"Are you fucking that stuck-up little piece of shit?" He put his hands on my forearm and twisted hard, giving me what as kids we'd called an Indian rope burn.

"Mr. Mitner, stop! You're hurting me."

He released my arm, but I could still feel his leg against mine. "That's why you didn't return any of my calls, right?"

I looked at my shoes and then at my watch and prayed that my mother would come home early.

Miraculously, the front door opened. It was my brother with two friends, all of them in basketball shorts and shoes. Three sweaty angels.

The rest of the vacation was horrible: pretending to my mother and brother that I was just being irresponsible in not returning Mr. Mitner's calls. When I finally called him back, it was on my mother's insistence; she actually stood next to me at the phone, refusing to leave until I dialed, lecturing me about how it was rude not to return a teacher's call—once your teacher, always your teacher and deserving of that respect. It got to the point where I thought, well, maybe I just had to let him try again to have sex with me so he could get over it.

Mr. Mitner nearly wept when I called him from the payphone at the Seven-Eleven to say that I was coming over. By the time I arrived, he had pulled the drapes shut in his living room and bedroom and lit so many candles I feared he might set the place on fire.

"Undress me," I instructed.

Mr. Mitner got onto his knees and pulled off my boots. He unbuttoned my denim shirt and tried to unfasten my bra but got stuck on the hooks. I reached around and unhooked it. He petted my breasts in a way that made me feel anxious.

I tried to help him. I got out of the rest of my clothes myself and panted into his ear and acted like as much of a hussy as I could muster from my limited experience with Hank and Rolly Thines. I did everything I'd ever read about in *Cosmopolitan* magazine, but it was useless. He'd get hard but lose it before he could actually enter me.

Mr. Mitner called me twice more before I went back to school. On the second occasion, I asked him not to call me again.

"I can't help you," I said. "I tried. I honestly did."

Mr. Mitner moaned into the phone.

"Maybe it's me. Maybe I'm not your type." I liked this line of reasoning since it seemed that it let him save face. "When you meet a girl you really love, it will work. Trust me," I said.

Mr. Mitner moaned again, and I realized with horror what he was doing.

"If you call me again, I'll call the police." I slammed the phone.

I married Rolly Thines's second cousin, John, who I met at Rolly's sister's wedding the summer before my senior year. I had gone as Rolly's date, though more as a matter of convenience for him since I was home that summer and bringing one of the girls he was sleeping with in New York where he had taken a job trading bonds would have meant too much of a commitment for him. With me, he just had to show up the day of the wedding at my mother's house and could return me that night, which he didn't even have to since John, who was more sober than Rolly after the wedding, offered to drive me home.

John was a second year pediatric cardiology fellow at Hopkins, and for the first year we were together, I kept pinching myself that someone as funny and smart and kind as he was could like me so much. We married the month after I graduated, inheriting from his aunt a house with the nooks and crannies I'd always wanted—a pantry and a sun room and a linen closet tucked under the attic eaves—in a shabbily genteel neighborhood not far from the university. Perhaps because I was so grateful at the cards fate had dealt me, we had more kids and much earlier than I had ever imagined, three girls and a boy by the time I was thirty-one. I never planned to be a stay-at-home mom, but with four kids and a husband who worked long hours with very sick children, work that was more important than anything I would ever do with my English B.A., it seemed both ethical and logical that I should devote myself to providing a home for John and our children along with whatever small volunteer work I could manage.

My oldest three children were of similar temperament to John and me, bookish and introspective, but our youngest child, our daughter Amelia, was cut from a different cloth: a scrappy tomboy who outran the boys in kindergarten, and with a mind just as fast and intrepid. An excellent shooter, she was a starter on her high school basketball team by ninth grade, a feat that delighted my brother, who lived by then in Boston but would travel down two or three times a year to watch Mealy, as he called Amelia, play.

In her junior year, Amelia's team made it to the regional championships. John had a dangerously ill child in the hospital, so it fell on me to drive Amelia and three of her friends to the Wilmington sports complex where the games were played. The girls piled out of the car and disappeared into the steamy locker room to change into their uniforms. In the stands, they settled into the stew of their team, huddling together and twirling one another's hair, as they watched the game before their own.

I took a seat at the top of the bleachers, luxuriating in this interlude between the drive and my daughter's game when I could drink the milky coffee I'd brought in a thermos and lose myself in *Anna Karenina*, which I had not read since high school when I'd hidden it on my lap under my desk. I slipped back a century, into the hunt: Levin and his hound Laska and Stepan Arkadyich and the silly Veslovsky on their expedition for snipe—for Levin, a horrible first day, and then his vindication the next day, trekking twenty miles solo before daybreak to return with a full booty of birds.

When a hand touched my shoulder, I started. "Is that you?"

I don't think I would have recognized the voice alone, but something about the touch, almost like a claw, made me bite my lip even before I saw the face, larger looking now with a heaviness along the jaw and hoods over the eyes.

"Mr. Mitner?"

He laughed. "I've changed that much? Well, you look great. Hardly any different."

I glanced down at my daughter, still with her friends on the bleachers.

"What brings you here?" he asked.

"My daughter's team is playing."

Mitner looked at the court where girls in the same baggy shorts and athletic tops that I'd been watching for years now seemed too scantily clad, their coltish limbs exposed as they raced between the baskets, their high ponytails swinging behind them. I could see that Mitner thought my daughter was playing in the game going on below us, an error I did not feel inclined to correct.

"And you?" I asked. "What brings you here?"

"I'm the coach for the Barrondale Girls Varsity. They just played. Actually, I'm the principal for the school, but I coach this one team."

I knew I should say something nice about his being the principal, about his career having taken this turn, but a copper taste had invaded my mouth and I felt as though I literally could not speak. I glanced at my watch, making the clucking sounds and gestures people make when there is something they need to do. I gathered up *Anna Karenina* and my coffee and coat. "Well, nice to see you," I said.

Mitner was staring at me in a way that made me certain that my face must be betraying the misery he was causing me. He smiled, but it felt more like he was baring his teeth, and I recoiled, fearing in that moment that he might reach out and twist my arm.

It took me several weeks to get Mitner out of my mind, to not feel as though by his mere presence he had soiled me, to not fear that I would come home to find him parked in my driveway. For a few days, I was obsessed with the thought that I needed to warn Amelia about him, lest he try to track her down, but the rational part of me knew that made no sense, that even if Mitner had figured out that she was not one of the girls playing on the court below us, she had her father's last name, which he would have no reason to know, and there were eight teams playing that day, each with at least a dozen girls.

Still, I began working out a speech to deliver to Amelia about why if she ever heard from someone named Mitner she was never to respond, but before I could finish, I laughed out loud. Even at sixteen, there was no chance that Amelia would be taken in by Mitner.

I didn't think about Mitner again until more than a decade later when my brother sent me Mitner's obituary from the *Times*. By then, Mitner had become the superintendent of a Massachusetts school district. The obituary mentioned his years as a basketball coach and his work with an international organization that funds schools for girls in Africa, to which donations in his name could be made.

There was no mention of a spouse or any offspring. Was it possible that Mitner had gone to his grave a virgin? And then for a moment, I felt my eyes well. Pity for myself, for the girl I had been, but also for Mitner—that the sucking and grunting and crying and arm twisting had accomplished nothing, that I had been unable to help him, and that it was all now such a long time ago. ❧

I LOVE DICK by Chris Kraus
Cari Luna

Yes, I know. The title. It's delicious in a way, isn't it? But, yeah, I hesitated to read the book in public. I found myself hiding its cover in my lap as I read it on the playground while my kids played, or on the bus. I placed it facedown, its spine turned toward the wall, whenever I set it down. That edge of self-consciousness I felt when reading the book, the awareness of the sharp double entendre of the title, was a part of the experience of reading *I Love Dick*. Had I read it without its cover, or if I'd read an eBook version, I wouldn't have had that discomfort and hyperawareness of myself as a woman reading a book with I LOVE DICK on the cover. And that discomfort? It echoed and underlined Kraus's discomfort and self-awareness in the text.

For the record, the eponymous Dick is a person, Kraus's love interest. *I Love Dick* is part epistolary, part diary, and deeply confessional. It begins when Kraus and her husband, Sylvère, have dinner with his colleague, Dick, and end up spending the night at Dick's home. Kraus believes Dick has been flirting with her over the course of the evening, and in the morning determines that she and Dick have experienced a "Conceptual Fuck." She becomes infatuated with him, and then falls in love with him, though after that one night, he is entirely absent. She falls in love with him, or with the idea of him, on her own. She shares this with Sylvère, and the two begin writing letters to Dick over a short, frenzied period. These letters, which become a sort of art project between the married couple, comprise the bulk of the text.

*I Love Dick i*s memoir (maybe), it's polemic, it's epistolary fiction (maybe), it's couples therapy acted out through laptop and fax machine. It's a woman breaking her marriage down in the pursuit of a man, her sexuality, her identity. But no. . .even as I try to pin it down, objections arise. It's not really Kraus breaking her marriage down. The marriage was already stalled out, at least sexually, before the story began. "Because they are no longer having sex," Kraus writes, "the two maintain their intimacy via deconstruction: i.e., they tell each other everything." In fact, it is Kraus's obsession with Dick that rekindles their sexual relationship, at least temporarily. But the obsession is not about her husband.

What I love most about this book: Kraus realizes, as does the reader, that her obsession with Dick has nothing to do with him. It isn't about him, either. He was the cipher, the object of desire necessary to set the whole exploration of self in motion. She purports to love Dick, but he is nothing more than catalyst. This book, be it novel or memoir or some hazy middle ground, is about a woman named Chris Kraus, and her journey by way of (what feels like, and so what functions as) brutally honest self-exposure. Kraus writes: "WHO GETS TO SPEAK AND WHY...IS THE ONLY QUESTION." In *I Love Dick*, Kraus speaks boldly, baldly, and often out of turn. She lays herself absolutely bare. She made me uncomfortable sometimes, until I wanted to cringe, to look away. But I didn't. And in the end I was left having witnessed and explored one woman's lived experience in a way that was profoundly new. ❧

Allapattah

Michael Hawley

Palms, palmettos, lancewood, camellias. For twenty minutes, Mavis Hawthorn named the plants she knew, happy to answer the stream of questions from the blond-haired seven-year-old in the back seat. Sylvie seemed to have a special fascination with flora—until she switched focus to birds.

"What's that bird?"

"Grandma's driving, honey," said Gordon in the passenger's seat. Their granddaughter was born when they were both over seventy, and he hoped they were "up" for her five-day visit.

"It's a stork," said Mavis, bending close to the wheel. "A wood stork."

They had picked her up at the Sarasota airport, where they had rendezvoused with Scott and Irene before the newlyweds caught their connection to the Keys. There was little time, beyond a rushed cup of coffee, for the Hawthorns to get a sense of their son's new wife. Naturally, Sylvie was the center of attention.

"What's *that* bird?"

"I'm not sure," said Mavis. "Ask Grandpa."

Gordon labored to turn in the seat. His face was soft and deeply lined. His voice, too. "We get mostly snowbirds this time of year. Know what those are, honey?"

"What are what?" she answered nonsensically.

Gordon frowned. "Snowbirds. People who spend just the winters down here. From the north. Like you."

"Snowbirds," said Sylvie, wrinkling her nose. "Snowbiiiiiiiirds."

Mavis glanced in the rearview mirror. Sylvie's language capacities seemed stunted for her age, yet her kooky-cloying intonations suggested a wily intelligence.

They hadn't seen her since their move to Florida. That they were a thousand miles from Lansing didn't help, or that Gordon was terrified of air travel, or that Scott never came to see them.

"If you like birds," said Mavis, patting her corkscrew perm with one hand, "I'll drive you out to the rookery."

"What's that?"

"You'll see. I take lots of pictures there. Me and my neighbor, Ellen."

"No, that thing, that bird!"

Gordon turned up the radio. Dime-sized liver spots showed through the gossamer remnants of his hair. Sylvie poked at one with her finger.

"Stop that, now," he chuckled.

Sylvie sat back. She watched the flight of a snowy egret gliding over the tree line. They didn't have birds like that in Michigan. Or bushes so rubbery-looking.

"Another day in paradise," said Gordon. "What we say every day. Isn't it, hon?"

Mavis nodded, stroking his knee. Though he wore khaki shorts all year round, Gordon didn't leave the house enough to garner much of a tan. "*Just as well,*" he liked to say. "*No one ever got skin cancer from watching television.*"

A car from the adjacent lane cut sharply in front of them.

"Not even a signal!" Mavis thumped her fist on the steering wheel.

"Rhode Island plates," said Gordon. "Figures. Still, you gotta thank God for the snowbirds. Without them, the state would never have built these highways or keep them up so nice." His lower spine was starting to hurt as it always did around noon.

They passed a condo development under construction. The only thing finished was the monumental, gilt-lettered sign—Luxor Suites—and concrete pylons flanking the entrance. On the banks, evergreen shrubs stood ready for planting.

Mavis glanced back at Sylvie. Huddled close to the door, she was licking at the window, her tongue moving in broad, flat swaths up the glass.

"Sylvia Hawthorn!"

The waitress at Meals-a-Deal had feathered hair and a girlish face, except for the creases at the edge of her mouth and teeth too white to be real. Leaning over Sylvie's shoulder, she tapped her pen at several items on the menu.

"Bacon gravy and biscuits, see? Or a BLT. Or a hamburger and bacon. Just a side of bacon? You're sure that's all you want?"

Sylvie nodded.

"You ought," said Mavis, "to have this Vegetable Medley thing along with. Right, Grandpa?"

Sylvie looked at Gordon and smiled, her lips curled tight to her gums. This girl, he thought, would be quite the looker, with her fair hair just starting to mellow, her daddy's cheekbones and Mavis's dimpled chin. And the eyes. The light just poured from her eyes when they looked at him—until the smallest thing yanked them away.

"Bacon," said Sylvie, glaring at the waitress. "Make it crispy, crunchy, crispy. Pleeeeeeeeeease."

Gordon took a Vicodin from his shirt pocket and downed it with a sip of iced tea.

As they awaited their food, Sylvie's grasshopper curiosity lit on the wooden statue of an Indian chief poised outside the restrooms. It was roughly hewn and off-proportion, with a small alligator sitting at his feet.

"Look at that!" she shouted, dramatically gripping her side of the tablecloth. "That snake thing's looking at me!" Her voice had taken on a bone-cutting shrillness.

"It's an alligator," said Mavis. "Now stop with the tablecloth. You'll pull the glasses off."

Sunset threw a coral wash over the roofs of Casa Verde. Sylvie caught her breath at the security station when the crossbar raised to admit them.

"What's that thing, that pond?"

"Lake Pearl," said Gordon. "One of five man-made lakes here at Casa. You can see gators on the banks sometimes."

"Where? I don't see them."

"Not now. In the morning. They sun like cats. Grandma has pictures."

"What's that tree?"

"It's a grapefruit," said Gordon. "You don't see the fruit on the branches?"

Sylvie expelled a sigh of impatience. "All the houses look alike. Short, short, short."

"Mobile homes are all one storey," said Gordon, the painkiller putting a fuzz on his words. "They don't make them tall and they don't come with basements. That's the beauty of them. No musty basements. No stairs. Paradise."

"Manufactured homes," Mavis corrected, pulling into the carport. "Looks like Ellen and Zeke are back. We'll have to ask them over."

Casa Verde's eastern periphery was defined by a stiff wire fence. In the distance, a flatwood forest of pine and hickory stood against the darkening sky. Controlled burns, Gordon explained, kept the intervening brush at low rise. He waited with Sylvie on the rear patio while Mavis made pineapple smoothies inside.

"In the morning, you can see wild pigs at the fence if you get up early enough. Your room faces back."

Sylvie stared at a spot in the woods, her brows knit tight, as if even then she could see one. Gordon knew not to pay much attention. The girl's mind was full of strange turnings. It would likely be a tiring week for Mavis, he thought, though of course they were glad they could host her. Until now, Scott hadn't asked them for a single favor. He rarely made contact at all.

"Let's go inside, honey." Despite the Vicodin, standing for any length of time sent darts of pain up his back.

Sylvie walked out into the yard and halted at the birdbath. She pointed toward the forest.

"You don't see anything, Sylvie," he said, limping after her. "It's too dark."

He laid a hand on top of her head. Her fine straight hair felt like silk.

"One thing you *won't* see is a panther, if that's what you're looking for. The Greenies are lying. Anything to erode folks' property rights and beat back civilization. Sometimes you can see Indians, though. Seminoles. They go out in parties, trapping gators and pigs. They have a special license to do that. Along with all the other privileges."

He thought of the gambling revenues, hand over fist, in Port Charlotte.

"Seminoooooles."

"Let's get off the grass, honey. Mavis would never forgive me—Shit."

Sylvie was looking down at her legs, where at least a dozen tiny red ants dotted her left shin. Gordon thought he heard her snicker. Then her lips drew back in a clench-jawed grimace. Standing still like that, with her hands to her sides, she launched a series of piercing shrieks that brought the neighbors running.

Sylvie lay on the foldout guest bed, gazing at the window and the darkness beyond. From the living room, the unfamiliar voices of a man and woman mingled with those of her grandmother, though the words amounted to little more than decoration in the air, less distinct to Sylvie than the harping of crickets and tree frogs that called through the window screen.

Gordon had given her an antihistamine tablet and—over his wife's distracted objections—half a Vicodin.

Mavis, for her part, had treated the stings with vinegar and soda, then daubed them with Calamine, Sylvie screaming all the way through. She hadn't struggled or scratched at the welts, but applied every crumb of her will to hollering, like that was what she did to relax.

Exasperated, Mavis had left a traumatized Gordon with Sylvie in the guest room and gone to commiserate with the neighbors.

"These things happen," said Ellen Fishman. "It wasn't your fault."

Ellen was slim and fit—remarkably so—with hair that was a shade of light red meant to disguise its thinness.

"I'll have to watch her every minute," said Mavis. "I don't think Gordon's. . .equipped."

Ellen looked at her husband and smiled inscrutably. Zeke set his empty glass on the table. "Refreshing, Mavis."

The Fishmans seemed wary of expressing opinions when it came to anything. Mavis attributed this to the fact that they were relative newcomers to Casa Verde and the only resident Jews. Which might also explain their congenial silence when it came to politics. Gordon had pegged them as left of liberal.

Aside from Ellen's interest in photography, it was her calming presence that Mavis especially liked. She had perennially friendly, light blue eyes that seemed to make no judgments except when framing a shot. Ellen's photos had been published in several magazines, something Mavis had given up on after more than fifty submissions.

"Well," said Mavis through a bursting sigh, "things can only get better. Right?"

The first glint of dawn brought the red-bellied woodpecker to the guest room window—*tap, tap, tap*—the tip of its beak on the mirror glass. The Hawthorns had forgotten to warn their granddaughter about nature's little alarm clock. *Tap. Tap-tap.*

When Mavis looked in, Sylvie was standing in her jammies by the window, peeking out through the blinds.

"Little pest, isn't he?" Mavis sat at the edge of the bed. "Just pecking away at his own reflection. I'm sorry if he woke you, sweetheart."

Sylvie turned from the window. She brought her hand to her grandma's forehead and, with the tip of her middle finger, copied the action of the woodpecker.

Tap. Tap-tap-tap. Mavis forced herself to sit still. She thought it uncanny that the girl could guess the bird's pattern without even looking that direction.

"Let's check your ankle, Sylvie."

A light red blotch covered the area but, aside from three little pustules, there was no further swelling.

"You've got to watch out for the anthills. In fact, don't go outside by yourself. Okay?"

"Okay, May."

"Call me Grandma. Let's get dressed and we'll have some breakfast. Then we'll go for a walk. Maybe we'll see momma gator."

"Where's that guy, that Grandpa?"

"Sleeping. He'll be up by the time we get back. Then we'll all go to church. It's Sunday."

Sylvie turned back to the window. The bird had moved to the other side of the window, where it continued its noisy pursuit. It would keep up this racket for an hour or so.

"Look," said Mavis as she opened the blinds.

A haggard-looking jack rabbit gimped slowly past the birdbath.

"What's that?"

"Don't tell me you've never seen a bunny."

It stopped at the fence and sank down, panting. Mavis could see the bumpy ridge of its backbone and regretted having pointed it out.

Sylvie drew closer to the window, her nose touching the glass. She giggled.

"Never seen a bunny? Sure I seen a bunny. Duh!"

The rabbit had twisted onto its side and, except for one twitching foot, lay still. Mavis took the girl's hand and led her away from the window.

They ate breakfast on the veranda.

"A lanai, we call it down here," said Mavis, referring to this part of the house.

Sylvie liked the sound of "lanai" so much that she kept repeating it between bites of cereal. The Fishmans rode by on their double bicycle and waved at them.

"Zeke and Ellen," said Mavis, before the inevitable questions started. "They were here last night. They're Jewish. Ellen runs a taffy shop in Punta Gorda. Taffy's candy."

"What's Jewish?"

Mavis straightened the drape of the sweater hanging on the back of her chair. "Jews are…complicated."

Sylvie smiled, her pale green eyes beaming. "Why, May?"

"For one thing, they're a different religion. Though the Fishmans aren't really religious." Explaining this was pointless, thought Mavis. "And call me Grandma, not May. That's not my name, anyway."

Sylvie reached across the table as if to resume the pecking routine, though the bird was out of sight and hearing. Instead, she plucked something off Mavis's glasses—an insect. The child held it gently between her thumb and forefinger. She looked at it closely, her eyes nearly crossed. It had a green metallic carapace and transparent, V-shaped wings. She blew on it, a dim whistle streaming from her lips. She closed it in the fingers of her other hand and crunched it in her fist.

Wading fowl by the dozens paced the banks and shallows around Lake Emerald. Egrets, herons, ibises. A large gray bird with a two-foot neck stepped out from behind a white bougainvillea and sprinted across the street.

"That's a sandhill crane," said Mavis, her voice hushed. She wished she had brought a camera instead of Gordon's binoculars.

"It's got a red hat," said Sylvie.

"So it does. Both the male and female have them."

The crane stopped in the grass. It preened under one of its wings, then swung its head up to stare across the lake. Mavis raised the bulky binoculars and put the lanky bird into focus.

"It must have a nest in the woods somewhere. Out past the canal."

"Grapefruit!" said Sylvie.

She was pointing to a lime tree, but Mavis just nodded.

"Are we going to church, May?"

"We're going to see the gator first. Isn't that what you want?"

"Babies," the girl scowled. "That Grandpa guy said so."
"Well, you can't see one without the other, Sylvie."
The crane kept its place on the bank as they walked.
"Try to be quiet," Mavis whispered. "Let's see how close we can get."
The girl tracked beside her, silent as a cat. The crane stood less than eight yards off. At four feet high, it was fully mature. Of course, Mavis thought, if she had brought her camera, the bird would not have stood still for so long.

A golf cart hummed up the street behind them—Julius Capetto on his way to the clubhouse. He stopped the cart, obeying Mavis's outstretched hand.

Eight yards narrowed to seven, then six. Mavis glanced down at her granddaughter, whose interests for once seemed akin to her own. Sylvie clasped her hands behind her back and took careful, quiet steps through the grass.

The crane thrust its neck an inch forward. Its legs flexed and it pushed off the ground. Mavis watched it fly over the lake and the clubhouse.

"Dirty birdie!" Sylvie hollered. "Damn!"
"Hey! Don't swear or we're turning around right now."
Sylvie flapped her arms and ran back toward the lime tree.
"That was quite the heron," said Julius, advancing in the golf cart.
"It was a crane," said Mavis.
Julius picked a white plastic bag from the cart seat.
"Take some oranges," he said, handing the bag to Mavis. "The frost this year made them extra sweet." He wiggled the bill of his cap. "Is that your granddaughter?"
"Yep. Scott's daughter. Silvia Hawthorn. She'll be eight this fall."
"Pretty girl." He called out to her: "I wouldn't pick those limes yet, sugar. They're hard as rocks."
Sylvie flapped her arms and circled the tree.
"Enjoy," said Julius. "I'll stop by later and check in on Gordon." He continued around the bend of the street.
"Damn that snowbird!"
"Stop it, Sylvie! Come on, if you want to see the alligator."
Mavis turned and started walking. For weeks she had entertained the fantasy of playing grandmother: hunting for sharks' teeth on the beach, making smoothies, riding the Ferris wheel in Venice. Sadly, though, when it came down to it, she already wanted the week to be over. She wondered how Sylvie's father stood it. Presumably, Irene knew what she was in for.

Mavis heard the girl behind her, scuffing through the grass.
"Aren't the azaleas pretty, sweetheart? Come, let's walk on the pavement."

In five minutes, they had reached Lake Pearl. On the far end stood the security station.

"Do you know where you are now?"

"Paradise," said Sylvie without hesitation.

"There she is on the shore. Momma gator."

Drawing closer, they could see the ten-foot reptile half-submerged in the water, its heavy tail draped up the bank.

"She's a big one," said Mavis. "You can't see it now, but there's a hole dug into the rise behind her."

"Where? I don't see that! Where?"

"Just past the tip of her tail. Her babies are in there. Hatched a few weeks ago."

They ventured within twenty yards of it. The mud-colored beast turned its head their direction. Its jaws cracked. Every movement was slow and deliberate, as if requiring great forethought to execute.

"We shouldn't go any closer," said Mavis. "Gators can move very fast when they want to. See those legs? You especially don't want to mess with a mother."

"Grandpa said babies. He *said*!"

"They're in that hole, Sylvie. Where momma can keep an eye on them. Their little cave cradle. Do you want to try the binoculars?"

"Hey, no way."

Mavis put down the bag of oranges and looked through the barrels of the instrument. Grass screened most of the hole. She took a few steps closer. She thought she could see the head of one baby—a black little snout, a tawny yellow eye.

"How do they get here, May?"

"The gators? They swim. There's a canal between us and the nature preserve."

Something splashed in the lake.

"What's that?"

Mavis turned the binoculars until they took in a large black bird surfacing in the water.

"They're called anhingas," she said. "They're diving birds. In a few minutes, he'll be sitting on the bank, his wings spread out, drying off."

Mavis shifted her magnified gaze toward the head of the alligator. It had backed up onto the bank so that only its forelegs were left in the water. Its head was raised, its jaws tightly closed. It looked like a statue, regal and serene, until something hit the side of its head, near the eye, and plunked down into the grass. Mavis found it in her sights—a lime. She lowered the glasses and turned.

Sylvie's face held an expression that Mavis had never seen on a child—a bizarre fusion of terror and delight that bared her teeth and blazed from her eyes. The girl raised her hand and pointed.

On her first step away from the charging reptile, Mavis lost her footing. She fell face-down and hard in the grass. Gasping for air, she tried to get up. Her limbs wouldn't budge. Who would believe—without actually seeing its hunkered sprint, its chopping limbs, its spine as pliant as a snake's—that anything so leaden in appearance could really move that fast?

The jaws closed over Mavis's foot and a lurch of the head brought her quickly down the bank. The alligator tugged her out into the water, then, climbing over her, flogged its armored tail repeatedly in the mud.

Sylvie sat on a wooden bench on the other side of Lake Pearl. Ten minutes had passed since the fracas on the opposite bank had given her the chance to peek into the nest and see what gator babies looked like. They weren't all that small. They were black and prickly, with sharp little claws and shiny yellow eyes. The one she had taken had squirmed feistily in her fingers; she had had to hold on tight until she was able to slip it into the plastic bag from which she had dumped out the oranges.

Staring out at the lake, Sylvie watched as the sky grew over the water and vanished in silver ripples only to reappear. The light seemed to come from all over the sky, different from the kind she was used to. It flashed from the water and from the metal and glass of passing cars.

"Lanai," she said.

The white crossbar at the security station raised and lowered. From where she sat, it looked as small as a toothpick.

A heron flapped down to the grass in front of her and stepped to the water on its black stilt legs. It pecked at something lying in the mud before wading in to hunt for tadpoles and minnows. Sylvie gripped tighter to the bag. It was moving again, the baby gator inside of it trying to escape.

A car had stopped on the far shore, where the mother gator could be seen on the bank. Two people stood nearby, watching it. A mud-colored thing, like a large twisted rock, lay by the water's edge. Mavis Hawthorn.

Sylvie tuned her ear to the sigh of the breeze, to whispers in the grass, to the sound of her nails scraping the bench. She watched as other cars gathered, and a white van with screaming red lights, while the security crossbar raised and lowered, and the water's surface filled with clouds and waves of wrinkled silver.

Gordon sat motionless in his recliner, his hands clutched to the pair of binoculars found on the bank at Lake Pearl. A cooking show played on the muted TV, the chef concocting a marinade for gigantic swordfish steaks. The bird-call clock above the kitchen sink sounded—the two o'clock oriole chirrup.

In the guest room, Ellen Fishman tried to keep Sylvie occupied with games of tic-tac-toe. The previous evening, after the girl's screeching marathon, Ellen had returned with Zeke to their house through a silence that seemed almost impossible. She had practically felt the rents in her brain caused by those feral, heart-shivering calls. In bed, she had laid awake for hours, waiting as if for those cries to resume, then imagined or dreamed that they were answered from some burrow or treetop in the forest preserve.

"Hey, your turn!" Sylvie stared at the thinness of Ellen's red-dyed hair and laughed. "Under your hairdo, you're bald!"

Ellen peered over her readers at Sylvie—"Isn't everyone?"—then scrawled a requisite *O* on the grid.

At the front of the house, Julius Capetto bumped around in the kitchen, mixing Gordon a gin and tonic. Julius was father-in-law to Deputy Miles, who sat on the sofa with Zeke Fishman.

Above the sofa hung one of Mavis's bird photographs that had won second prize at the Naples art fair. A spoonbill descending into its nest had been captured in the soft light of dusk.

"I just want to see her," said Gordon, his voice in cracking falsetto. "I want to go to the hospital."

Zeke shared a look of concern with the deputy, then spoke to his grieving neighbor.

"She's not there, buddy. The ambulance took her to the morgue."

"I'm so sorry, sir," said Deputy Miles. Despite his youth, the condolence had weight, his manner both grave and gentle. "She'd been gone at least twenty minutes. They think it was heart failure."

"I have to see her!" Gordon held out his hand toward the empty recliner.

"I don't advise it, sir."

"She just lay there? For half an hour? Where was Sylvie?"

"We don't know," said Zeke.

Julius set Gordon's drink on the side table.

"They were together when I saw them," he said. "Must have been eight-thirty or so. I was still on the treadmill when I heard the ambulance. That would have been around nine, nine-fifteen. And then driving up to see what happened, I saw her alone on that bench, poor thing."

"Gordon, do you want us to call your son?" Zeke offered.

Gordon gripped the binoculars. Tears ran down his cheeks. "That something like this could happen—" he sobbed, his stricken eyes sliding to Miles. "I want something done. I want something goddamn done!"

The vibrant rose and papaya sunset had dimmed to glowing umber. Very soon it was dark. Cars and golf carts lined the streets around Lake Pearl. At least a hundred people had come to the place where Mavis Hawthorn had died.

Deputy Miles, instead of contacting the state wildlife agency, had called Gator Circus in Naples to obtain the services of two of its handlers. They had put the culprit in a long metal cage after securing its jaws with a belt. Somehow, a Fort Myers TV station had heard about the incident, but its crew was turned away at the gate.

Gordon stood at the front of the crowd supported by Zeke and Julius until a folding chair was brought. He sat staring at the alligator. What he could see of it didn't move. The deputy put his headlights on it, which served mainly to illuminate the bars of the cage.

"God damn gators," said Julius loudly enough to incite conversation nearby. A woman broke into sobs.

The Hawthorns had lived in Casa Verde for more than six years and were active in many of the clubhouse activities. A few snowbirds might not have known them by name, but everyone else did. They were considerate neighbors to folks like the Fishmans, who were slowly adjusting to life in the sunbelt.

Someone in the distance started beating a drum in slow, solitary thuds. It seemed to come from across the lake or even further off. Talking ceased as the flames from a number of cigarette lighters appeared here and there in the dark.

Deputy Miles pulled both a rifle and a baseball bat from the back seat of his car. He propped the rifle against the front fender and stepped toward the cage with the bat. He gave one corner a quick, sharp rap. The alligator made no response.

The officer drew a flashlight from his belt and strode to the edge of the bank. He switched on the flashlight and pointed the beam to the hole in the ground where the mother's offspring were nesting. With his feet firmly planted, he bent over and plunged the head of the bat into the opening—once, twice, three times, six times.

The cage rattled as the reptile thrust its head and tail hard against the top. A forefoot emerged through the bars on one side, the long toes gripping into the turf as all other movement subsided.

The drum continued its solemn cadence on the other side of Lake Pearl. A fish jumped. Traffic hummed back and forth on the Interstate.

Standing, the deputy turned off the flashlight and clipped it onto his belt. Then he walked to the car and took up the loaded two-forty-three. He flipped off the safety.

"Anything you want to say, Mr. Hawthorn?"

Gordon declined with a shake of his head. The deputy put a hand on his shoulder.

"Do you want to put her down, sir? I'll hold the barrel right to her head and you can pull the trigger."

Gordon palmed the tears from his cheeks and tried to sit up straight.

"Where's May?" asked Sylvie. Her eyes were buttoned to Ellen Fishman, who sat beside her on her grandparents' sofa.

"Who?" Ellen squinted over her readers. "You mean Mavis?"

"May!"

"You really don't remember?" Ellen reached for the box of tissues on the coffee table. She dabbed at the lashes of her lower lids and took the girl's hand. "Your grandma's gone, Sylvie. She died this morning—I'm so very sorry—at the lake."

Ellen cringed at having been this direct. She hoped she hadn't just ripped a hole in the delicate fabric of this child's sensibilities. This was the province of child psychologists. Maybe her friend, Dr. Chrone in Yonkers, would recommend a local professional.

A gunshot sounded, faint but clear.

Sylvie slipped her hand from Ellen's and scratched at the place on the old woman's forearm where a dime-sized mole protruded.

"Ouch! That hurt, Sylvie."

On the silent TV, an animated panther playing golf was superimposed on footage of the Casino de las Palmas resort in Port Charlotte. A year and a half after Hurricane Pete, the casino and golf course had finally reopened.

Ellen rose. She opened the sliders to the veranda and looked out toward the street. A three-quarter moon showed over the rooftops. She didn't like this business with the alligator. Neither did Zeke. It was appalling, in fact, and completely illegal. Despite their regard for Deputy Miles, Zeke had called the TV station in hopes that the press would provide some sort of ameliorative presence.

"Jews are complicated," said Sylvie from the sofa.

Ellen suppressed a frown, then a grin. "Who told you that? Your grandma?"

"No. Yes."

The veranda smelled equally of mildew and lemon-verbena air freshener. Ellen switched on the overhead light. Past the little dining table, the space was crowded with flea-market tchotchkes, including a four-foot plastic pelican with a fish caught in its bill. A whatnot just inside the door held Mavis's Nikon D40 and lenses. But it was the sight of a worn beige sweater draped over a chair that turned Ellen back to the living room.

"Your daddy will be here soon," she said, fighting the lump in her throat.

"They're on their honeymooooooon." Sylvie had picked up the heavy binoculars and was aiming them at her lap.

"Not anymore, dear. They're flying up from the Keys."

Ellen examined the bottles of pills on the table by Gordon's recliner. Ambien, Vicodin, Percocet. Gordon had undergone more operations than anyone she knew, some necessary, others to prove a point, it seemed, in the efficacy of western medicine.

"I have a present," said Sylvie. "For Daddy, my dad."

Her sage-green eyes, Ellen realized, always kept the same avid luminosity no matter what she was looking at or expressing.

"Really? That's nice." Ellen resumed her place on the sofa. "What did you get for him, sweetheart? Or did you make it?"

The binoculars swung up so fast that they almost hit Ellen's dentures.

"Where's that Grandpa, El?"

Ellen firmly took hold of the instrument and set it on the coffee table.

"He went to the lake by the entrance, where your grandma had the accident."

Sylvie's face went blank, her gaze dropping as if in contemplation.

"Dirty birdie," she mumbled. "Damn."

She kicked over a stack of *Southern Living* sitting by the sofa, then leapt up and ran from the room.

Ellen straightened the magazines, wondering if Sylvie should spend the night here. Gordon was in no condition to care for this child. Then again, the distraction, however unpleasant, might hold him together until Scott could get there.

Ellen walked to the back of the house. Sylvie was standing in the guest bathroom, staring into the toilet. Her cheeks bulged out as she blew out an angry stream of air.

"What's the matter, Sylvie?"

Pushing past Ellen, Sylvie rushed to the guest room, hunched over, as if following a trail of something on the carpet.

"What is it, Sylvie? If you tell me, maybe I can help."

"Allie, stupid! My present!"

Sylvie lay down on the floor by the bed. Using her elbows for leverage, she propelled herself under the frame inch by inch. She searched the darkness. She thought she saw a pair of tiny eyes glinting. With her left hand, she reached as far as she could. She made a crossbar sweep with her arm.

"Bad boy! Bad!"

Ellen watched her floundering about, just her ankles and feet visible. By the base of the floor lamp lay an empty, white plastic bag.

"What's the present, Sylvie? Tell me what to look for. Is it round? Does it roll?"

"Damn!"

The doorbell rang.

"Goodness," said Ellen, a sudden relief coursing through her. "That must be your daddy. Let's go say hi. We'll look for your present later."

The sound of Sylvie's nails on the carpet startled for its sheer audibility. Ellen leaned over to touch the girl's ankle, but her hand stopped short on reflex.

*

The man on the doorstep was as tall as Gordon must have been in his prime. His brown hair fell to shoulder-length and his blunt, dark eyes were like Mavis's.

Ellen pushed open the screen door. "You must be Scott. I'm heartsick for you and your dad. Come in."

He made the barest hint of a nod, but otherwise didn't move. He wore a western-style shirt with pearl buttons and a pair of saggy dark jeans.

"I'm Ellen," she said. "I live next door. I'm watching Sylvie."

A dark moth fluttered into the house. The man's head drew forward and he looked past her as if to follow the flight of the insect. Then he stood straight, chin lifted.

"This is the Hawthorn residence," he said with an odd declarative tone. "My name is Angel Morehouse, ma'am."

"Oh?" said Ellen. Surprised, she stepped back. "Are you looking for Gordon?"

"If that is Mr. Hawthorn, yes."

She let the screen door shut quietly between them. He was older than she had first thought. A deep crease divided his brow. He might even be fifty.

"We were saddened to hear about his wife," the man said.

Ellen glanced behind her, glad that Sylvie was still in the guest room. "What is it you want, Mr.—?"

"Morehouse."

Only then did she notice that his clothes were wet from his feet—which were bare—to his chest, though his shoulders and hair looked dry.

"Ma'am," he said. "There has been a hurt here." Such a formal way of speaking seemed at odds with his bedraggled appearance. "And a hurt out there."

He nodded toward the back yard and the darkness.

"I have come to heal," he said, standing taller. "To restore the peace between the Hawthorns and the spirit of the swamp."

Ellen whiffed the air for a smell of liquor, detecting beer possibly. Or the musky odor that came from the tamarack barrens at certain times of the year.

"How did you get past Security, Mr. Morehouse? You know the deputy sheriff's right here in Casa, and the men'll be back any minute."

A low hissing noise startled her. It might have come from the patio, it sounded that close. The stranger didn't seem to have noticed.

"Bane to be traded for boon," he continued. "And it must be done on the grounds of this house, where the hurt to *allapattah* will be healed."

He spoke the word reverently, dipping his head as he did so. It was Ellen's first encounter with a local Seminole, if that was indeed what he was. She had done some reading on the history of Florida, some of which

110 | Post Road Fiction

had touched on Native Americans, though she knew next to nothing of their contemporary lives.

"Who gave you this address?" she asked.

He turned his head toward the patio. "Do you hear it, ma'am? The drum? That's my cousin, Tigger, in the woods."

Ellen put her ear to the door screen. She didn't hear drumming. A small puddle, she noticed, had formed on the pavement beneath the man's bare feet. She tried to imagine anyone swimming or wading the canal at night, and on such an outlandish mission. She looked for a hint of guile on his face, in his eyes—finding none. But the smell of beer was unmistakable.

"What do you propose to do here?" she asked.

From his wet jeans pocket he drew out a black-beaded rosary.

"There are words to be spoken," he said. "To *allapattah*. There's a song in our language—"

"Muskogee," said Ellen, pleased to have remembered this fact.

"There is a song in our language and the dance of the marshes. Then a prayer to our Mother of Beasts."

She was almost sure that he was making this up.

"I'm sorry," said Ellen. "You'll have to wait for Gordon—Mr. Hawthorn."

He placed the rosary over his head and carefully freed his hair from its circle. The cross had been replaced with a tiny, carved, wooden alligator. Then he edged away from the light.

"Your sympathies, ma'am, would help to welcome the spirits I call. We need their good will."

Turning, he walked through the patio and into the dark yard.

"Sir? I can't give you permission. You'll have to wait. Please."

Ellen heard Sylvie's voice from the guest room: "*Bad! Bad!*" She couldn't remember if she had drawn the blinds there.

"Mr. Morehouse?" She could hear the drum now, its eerie pulse in the wilderness.

It occurred to her that one rarely thought of wilderness here. People thought in terms of undeveloped land. Yet she did feel at times, walking over the coarse, cropped grass of her yard, that if she closed her eyes for more than a minute, the vines and palmettos and snakes and bugs would rise in one great brambly tsunami and take back their old stomping grounds.

"I'm coming out," she called softly, her heart pounding as she took the steps down.

Ellen stood beneath the patio light, shielding her eyes from its glare. With his dark hair and clothes, she could hardly see him. Above her, a beetle circled the light, its wings in a sonorant whir. She heard his feet in the grass, saw him cut in front of the birdbath. He was humming.

She left the patio and tracked along the side of the house. Recalling the fire ants, she wished she had worn better shoes, though she didn't know if they were active at night.

"Mr. Morehouse?"

Once her eyes adjusted to the dark, she could see him standing by the fence. The humming was directed away from her, toward the forest. His notes shifted from his nose to his throat, each delivered in heavy vibrato. The sound opened to a gentle wail broken by distinct syllables. He sang the same phrase several times and stopped. The drumming accelerated, every fourth beat given emphasis.

Then he started to move, a shadow in shadows. He danced in a crouch from place to place, his broadest motions on the loudest drumbeat. His feet whispered on the spongy turf. He was directly under the guest room window. The blinds were pulled and only the lamplight seeping through them lifted him out of the darkness. Ellen could see his bobbing head, his nose jutting out between the drapes of his hair. A shadow formed against the window blinds. Sylvie must have heard the chanting.

A tree frog trilled from a nearby limb in counterpoint to the drum. As the man continued around the edge of the yard, he fell to all fours and at intervals thumped the ground with his palms. Completing the circle, he passed the birdbath and lay face-down in the grass.

The beetle on the patio was still buzzing there. Ellen thought she heard other wings besides—smaller and softer, making a powdery squall.

The drumming had stopped. Something moved through the brush on the other side of the fence. An armadillo, maybe. Or a pig. Or a panther.

Ellen looked up at the guest room window. The girl's shadow was gone.

"You've got to be going now," she called as quietly as she could. "The men are coming. You won't be safe. And the yard is full of fire ants. Mr. Morehouse?"

Finally, he gathered himself and stood up, tugging his wet shirt from his belly. The fabric was speckled with dirt and cut grass. He came toward her and stopped less than two strides off, his brow reflecting the patio light.

"*Allapattah*," he said, "is at peace."

He bowed his head as a monk might do, then fixed her with a look of almost urgent solemnity.

Ellen caught herself bowing in turn. "Thank you."

The crease in his brow seemed to deepen, his eyes to grow darker, harder.

"Ma'am, what do you think would be fair compensation?"

Ellen stared at him. "What do you mean?"

"For my work." He lifted the rosary from around his neck and gathered it in the palm of one hand.

"Mr. Morehouse." The disappointment she heard in her quavering voice was directed as much to herself as to him. She had believed, if not in his purpose or methods, then at least in his sincerity.

"Fifty dollars, ma'am," he said. "You think it's easy, this magic I do? There is danger involved. Grave danger."

"Certainly not. You should have told me your *fee* to begin with."

"Forty, then? I have to split that with my cousin."

Ellen clasped her hands in front of her and stood as tall as she could. Never had she felt so alone in a place, so captive to the whims of a stranger. Still, the power of moral authority kept her panic at bay. This man was a fake, a shyster.

"You had best be going, whoever you are."

To this, he offered a bemused little smile as his eyes descended the line of her body.

"Your wrist is bleeding, ma'am," he said.

Imperturbable, Ellen kept her gaze on his face.

He shrugged, turned and walked through the patio and the carport, heading in the direction of Lake Emerald and the canal. It would be a miracle, she thought, if the first passing car did not report him to Security. He looked completely vagrant.

"Sylvie?"

Ellen locked and bolted the door. She went to the living room, aware of each footfall, each breath. She sensed the transmission from the silent TV—the shifting spectrum of pixels, the jumps of light and shadow. The noise of the wall clock startled her—the red-winged blackbird chittering the hour.

Remembering what the stranger had told her, she looked at her arms. A trickle of blood marked her left forearm. Ellen snatched up a tissue and daubed at the place, then went to the guest bathroom to wash it. She didn't go in. The contents of the trash bin were strewn along the tiles.

"Sylvie? You're going to sleep over at our place tonight."

In the guest room, the bed had been yanked from the wall and the clothes hamper lay on its side.

"Playing hide and seek, little girl? Now isn't really the time."

Every lamp was on in the master bedroom and the duvet was thrown up on one end of the bed. The master bath wasn't occupied either. Ellen looked in the closet and returned to the living room. The sliders to the veranda stood open and the light was on there, too.

With her pulse starting to sound in her ears, Ellen made her way through the bric-a-brac furniture to the veranda's opposite end. The door to the front walk was neither locked nor latched. She peered out at the street toward Lake Emerald. The rising moon put a luster on the asphalt and the fruit of the pummelo tree in her yard.

"Sylvie!" she called, her voice catching in her throat.

She stepped through the door, but drew back. It would be much more prudent, she thought, to have Zeke call Security than for her to walk out and start searching. She rushed to the living room to get her cell phone. Pressing the speed dial, she noticed that the stack of magazines had once more been knocked over. A few were spread under the coffee table. Had she done this herself unawares? Through the glass tabletop, she saw something else—a long black streak on carpet. She stepped closer, looking over her readers at nothing other than a live baby alligator.

"What is it, Ellen? We're turning the corner. Is Scott there? I left his name at the gate."

The nine-inch reptile started toward her, its stumpy limbs pumping over the carpet. She found herself perched on the edge of the sofa. A crimson streak marked her slacks at the knee. Blood was still seeping from the mole on her arm.

"Honey? You there? Ellen?"

Tiny movements sounded behind her, the claws and tail of the *allapattah* scratching the kitchen floor.

If that was the child's missing present, how on earth, Ellen wondered, had she gotten it? She must have provoked the mother by plundering the nest, and Mavis—poor Mavis!—had intervened?

An arc of headlights hit the front window as a car pulled up to the house. Ellen put her palms to her temples. Scott, too, would be arriving at any moment—Scott Hawthorn, whose daughter was outside somewhere, lost and terrified. Or was she hiding in the house, tucked into some cupboard or crawl space, having a heartless laugh on them all?

On TV, a middle-aged woman in a silver leotard demonstrated the latest abdominal exerciser.

Ellen considered a third possibility—that Angel Morehouse's dubious ritual was rooted in custom, in some sacred, unthinkable magic. *Bane to be traded for boon*, he had said. She heard a car door shut, then two more. She looked toward the kitchen. The alligator sat on a patch of linoleum directly in front of the fridge. Its head was raised and turned back and forth in clearly evident distress. It commenced a series of raspy chirps, like the sound a bird would make if it could bark. ❧

The Backyard
Nicholas Ward

Many nights, too many to count, it was just us.
Paul and Patti and me.
We'd sit in the backyard, in a semi-circle of lawn chairs off the enclosed porch. We'd stare at the rows of vegetables, the old barn, the long-defunct chicken coop, all the details of Paul's old farm house that I will never forget. From inside came the soft folk music from his mom's record player but otherwise it would be silent, the other houses on Paul's street tucking in long before. Patti would hug her legs up to her chest, wild, curly, red hair falling around her while she rested her head against the cool tin of the chair. I'd light a cigarette, scratch my head, teasing out my hair from the gel I over-applied every morning. Paulie would bring out a guitar, passed from his grandfather, and strum. This was June, the summer after our Junior Year of high school, 1999, millennium fast approaching, the heat exploding in Farmington, Michigan.

"Today was perfect," Paul said one night, head bent toward the ground, fingers picking the strings, lips pursed, searching for the right chord.

I smiled, flicked the ashes off my smoke. That afternoon, we'd picked up Patti from her job at the Farmington Bakery for a jaunt to Flipside Records in Clawson, scouring the racks for buried treasure. After we made our purchases, we climbed back in Paulie's white Ford Probe and hopped on the freeway. Paul just drove, a mixtape played, Galaxie 500's guitar drone washing over us as we cruised, well past our hometown through an unchanging landscape of overpasses and rest stations, no destination in mind. We had no commitments, no jobs or dinners with parents to get home to, so Paul kept on driving. Patti sifted through the stacks of magazines he kept in his car, warm summer air blowing her hair all over the backseat. I stared out the window at the fading sun as we played tape after tape, waves of sound crashing around me.

Back at his house, Paul's plucking gained coherence, transforming into Leonard Cohen's "Hallelujah" (or, more accurately, Jeff Buckley's cover).

Patti sat up, alert, lifting her shoulders from their calm repose and hunching over to stare at him. I'd seen Paul play music before: bass in his middle school band, trading guitar riffs in his brother's basement apartment, on the piano at the top of the stairs of that old farm house. But that night, under the bright Michigan stars, the magic that he coaxed from his fingertips circled the three of us, binding us together forever. I felt a fullness overwhelm me, rising outward from my stomach, up through my sternum, exploding in my chest and tingling down, through my shoulders to my arms, my hands, my fingers, shooting into the ground.

That was what I needed in my life and I mourned the sixteen years spent without Patti and Paul together. Maybe I knew then that what we had was fleeting, that none of us could stay in that place, together, forever. I caught Patti wiping the tears that were rolling down her cheeks. Maybe she knew it, too.

Paulie finished out the song and we exhaled together. I hadn't realized I had been holding my breath.

"Wow," Patti said softly.

"Thank you," Paul responded with a nod. "I'm glad you're both here."

Patti smiled. "Me too," she said.

We didn't speak much the rest of that night. Paul, it seemed, had said it all.

Tonight, eleven years later, Patti and I stand together in the same backyard, far enough away from the house not to be seen. We share a bottle of cheap chardonnay and a pack of Parliament Lights as the snow falls in the darkness. The first decade of the millennium has come and gone and everything has changed for us. I live in Chicago now, Patti in Los Angeles, and we're home for the holidays, swigging shitty wine and staring at Paul's old house.

Five years ago tonight.

The night that Paul killed himself.

"You know," I say, passing the bottle back over, "Paul didn't like you when he first met you. He thought you were too familiar, had too much energy, didn't really listen."

"Bitchface," Patti says loudly, invoking her pet name for me, "you never told me that."

I shrug. "Maybe he fell in love with you at first sight and didn't know what to do."

Patti goes silent. She rarely talks about Paul these days. I have to remind myself that we're talking about her fiancé, not merely our best friend from high school.

A lights flicks on inside the house and I take a step back.

"It's fine," Patti says. "Nobody can see us back here. Besides, they're not coming outside tonight."

Paul's parents are probably inside, alone, mourning his passing in their own way. He didn't commit the act in the house itself, but my guess is that the ghost of Paul still lingers there.

"We made a great team," Patti says.

I don't know if she means her and Paul, or me and her and Paul, but I agree.

I met Paul Myers in first grade, when I sat down in Ms. Delaney's class and asked the chubby kid behind me, the one gazing out the window at the playground, what animal he had on his shirt. Without dropping focus from the jungle gym, Paul whispered, "Meercats."

Everything about him illuminated my own deficiencies. He was a great baseball player; I barely made contact. His family lived on a farm where they raised chickens; I lived in a subdivision. He wore thrift store t-shirts at seven years old; I was dressed by my mom.

The first time he came over to my house, he brought a boombox and asked, "Do you like to dance?" We spent the few hours before my parents called us to dinner dancing to Kylie Minogue's "Locomotion" in my basement.

He was my first real friend. As the only child of two working parents, I grew up around other kids, spent afternoons after school at houses in the subdivision. But all those people were thrust upon me. I chose Paul. When Patti came along, we had been friends for eleven years.

Patricia Wheeler—Patti for short—moved to Farmington with her parents and two younger siblings at the beginning of Junior Year, where she hooked up with the Goth kids. Paul and I knew them as a quiet and friendly group, harmless despite the black trench coats, eye makeup, and finger nails. Patti wore flannel shirts but was forever in their company.

It was early December, '98, a Wednesday, when word surfaced about Matt Willer, a sophomore in their group. Matt was a boisterous kid that we'd gone to school with since the second grade. I remember that morning vividly: Paul and I stood at our lockers across from the teachers' lounge. We watched smoke seep out behind the cracks of the closed door, curl around the handle, dance into the crowded hallway.

"What the hell?" Paul asked. Students criss-crossed on their way to first period. Few of them took notice.

"You didn't hear?" I asked Paul. "Matt Willer killed himself."

Paul held his eyes on the closed door. He had shot up past me, dwarfing me by five inches. With his constant stubble, long sideburns, perfectly coiffed curly hair, he looked like a man in his twenties, while I remained a boy in my teens.

The bell rang. We didn't move.

"They're letting them smoke in there," Paul said. "That's smart."

I nodded, thinking that Matt's friends needed a safe space to smoke and cry together.

The door opened and they filed out, clinging to each other as they shuffled to class. Patti, hair pulled back, eyes puffy behind her glasses, saw us and peeled off from the group. I threw my backpack down and gave her a big, silent hug. She moved on to Paul, who bent down to give her an awkward squeeze.

"Okay," Patti said, straightening, wiping her eyes, steeling herself for the day in a manner I would see again later. "Time to go to class."

"Who is that?" Paul asked after she was clear.

"Patti Wheeler," I replied.
"You're friends?" he asked.
"Yeah, I guess. I don't really know her but...she gives lots of hugs."
Paulie frowned. "I think maybe she's in my English class and I've never noticed her."

Later that year, as all the juniors were saying their summer goodbyes, Patti asked me, "Can we hang out this summer? I need new friends." Things had spiraled into chaos for the Goths after Matt Willer's death, fueled by drinking and blaming each other for his suicide. I told Patti she could come along with us any Saturday she wanted, to go record shopping and drive around.

We became a team, a fortress against the outside world and no girls or boys or parents or the future could get past. We were Nick and Paul and Patti, together always: homecoming, football games, parties, the hallway at school, Patti's kitchen floor while I cried about girls, smoking pot in Paul's old barn and listening to his fears of getting older, that all-night diner by the highway where we took Patti for cheesy fries the night she broke up with her boyfriend. We made a lit magazine together, produced two plays, but by the time Senior Year wound down we had our sights set on the Holy Grail: The Talent Show.

"We gotta do something," I told them.

"Totally," Patti said. "I want to leave everyone with a lasting impression."

That was April, graduation on the horizon, three different universities awaiting our arrival shortly after that. I was off to school at Miami of Ohio, five whole hours south of our hometown. Paul and Patti, meanwhile, would be at Eastern Michigan and Michigan State, a stones' throw from each other. I didn't know it at the time, but the talent show was our last hurrah.

We cut AP English that day, our circle in the backyard the best option for hashing out our act for the three-hour spectacle that sent the entire student body nutty with anticipation.

"But what are we going to do?" Patti asked.

We shifted our focus to Paul. He sat silently, one leg crossed over the other, thrift store cardigan hanging from his frame. He was so cool. He smoothed his hands over his forehead, up through his dirty blond hair.

"We're going to play a song," he said. "Patticakes, I will teach you bass; you'll only need three chords. Nick, you have a serviceable set of pipes. I'll play lead guitar," he paused for effect, taking a sharp drag off a cigarette, "and we will leave this town in a blaze of motherfucking glory."

We couldn't achieve this without Paul's guidance. And it wasn't just that he played instruments and we didn't. Paulie had swagger. If he said we could do it, we were gonna do it.

Patti asked The Question. "What song?" Music was everything to us, our language and philosophy, our religion and worship, and Paul was our prophet. While most kids in our high school were discovering Zeppelin or the Smashing Pumpkins, we were guided to bootlegged Prince, to Sonic Youth turned way up. Paul would have the answer. Patti and I tilted our heads to the second floor, as if we could see through siding and insulation, down the hall, and into Paul's bedroom to his records and CDs and journals and scribbled notes.

"Alice Cooper," Paul responded. "'I'm Eighteen.' That's our jam."

It was an odd choice. At that time, Alice Cooper was known more for his absurd cameo in *Wayne's World*, not the anti-establishment rebel of his heyday. But goddamn, that song felt like us. We were eighteen. We were confused every day. We had to get out of this place.

One night after a chaotic and sweaty rehearsal, Paul said, "We're going to transcend everything, this show, this town, our lives. I hope you guys are ready."

The stage at our school was a gigantic proscenium that opened to a 500-person house, packed that night with students, parents, and teachers. We began in total darkness. A spotlight popped center to unveil our trio. I wore skin-tight leather pants and a maroon halter top, my arms held aloft with twin devil horns. To my right, Paulie slouched like a 50s beatnik behind his 1994 40th Anniversary Edition Midnight Blue Fender Stratocaster, a kilt around his waist and pantyhose on his head. Patti posed to my left, suited up for the bass guitar in a brightly-colored apron, worn over a bikini. The lights rose to reveal Tom, leader of the Goths, hunched over a drum kit and Grant, the captain of the football team, on rhythm guitar with a turquoise shirt and painted nails. Before we even began, our fellow classmates went bat shit crazy.

Paulie peeled off a disgusting riff that cruised into "I'm Eighteen" and the rest of us blasted along. I threw myself around like a man on fire, screaming the lyrics with joy; Tom banged the sticks with fury and abandon; Patti preened and pranced; Grant broke a string and fuzzed out for the whole song. And Paul? Deliberately, furiously, purposefully, he ripped off all of the strings on that blue beauty and the stage exploded in noise. To top it all off, there was a fucking smoke machine.

I have watched the performance of this many times on VHS and it wasn't perfect. The mix was a mess, the bass and drums were outta sync, and I couldn't sing nearly as well as I thought. But never in the history of the Midwest did three friends make rock'n'roll more pure, balls-out, and free than we did that night. See it with me: picture the stage smothered in fog, too-hot white lights, Patti and I bouncing like maniacs, play-acting at rock stardom. Then imagine Paul, nylon and kilt, classmates staring up at him in awe, parents in the back in disbelief. Watch him wail away at that guitar, reach way down inside himself to a place he hadn't ever shown anyone. Maybe you won't be able to see it, to understand his struggle with life, with the simple burden of being alive, with confusion and anger and hunger for something, anything, better. Maybe I didn't see it either. Maybe all I saw were three friends making noise.

"Top 5 bands that you discovered since high school that you can't live without. Go."

Behind Patti, Seattle's Puget Sound sparkles in the remarkable afternoon sunshine. I glance at her sideways.

"Bands or individual artists?" I ask. "Am I not allowed to have listened to any of them in high school, but they were around back then?"

She shoves me. "Just list, bitchface, don't over-think."

I over-think everything related to music. Just like Paul. It's been two and a half years now since he died and it's the first time I've seen Patti since the funeral.

"Fuck it," she says, shifting in her seat and pulling her legs up. "I'll go."

We flew in separately to Seattle, rented a car, and are driving to Portland before routing back to the middle of Washington state for a 3-day music festival called Sasquatch.

"Smiths, Silver Jews, Modest Mouse…"

"Modest Mouse?" I ask.

"Oh yeah. My roommates in LA listen to them constantly. I love that band."

Patti lives in Los Angeles now, but before that she lived in Portland, Oregon and before that, she lived in Nashville, Tennessee. That's where Paul and Patti moved after college, where he proposed, where they began their life together. We're driving to Portland today to retrieve some personal items she left at a friend's house.

"Bonnie 'Prince' Billy and…the Arcade Fire."

"Obviously. You know, after Paul's funeral—"

Patti puts a hand on my leg. "I don't wanna talk about that right now."

I clam up. All I want to talk about is Paul.

After his funeral, I came back to Chicago in a cloud. I was waiting tables, a job I hated amongst a series of jobs I hated, floating through a haze, unsure of what I was doing with my life or even what I wanted to be doing. At that point, the haze of uncertainty had lasted almost two years. As of this trip, it's still lasting. I'm starting to think the haze is the never-ending restlessness that will be my life forever.

"Pull in here," Patti instructs and I park in the driveway of a one-story rambler in Portland. There's a man standing out front. He's a little bit older than us, wearing a faded t-shirt and jeans, covered in sweat and dirt.

"Hiya, Patti," he says as we get out of the car, opening his arms for a hug. Patti introduces me and we exchange pleasantries, talk about our journey to Sasquatch, bands we're excited to see, etc.

"Well, all your stuff is back where you left it," he says with a jerk of his thumb. "It's my workstation now, so it's pretty dusty down there. I haven't had a chance to clean up."

We go into the basement, bare but for a couple benches and tools. Every inch is covered in sawdust.

"He makes furniture," Patti explains. She leads me to a small closet in the corner of the room. The door is half open and Patti wrenches it all the way.

"Oh my god," she says.

The stereo equipment and books and duffle bags of clothes and stacks upon stacks of records that we are meant to pack up and ship to Los Angeles, all of it, packed in a rush and thrown here quickly, sticking out of crates with no top, are covered in a fine layer of sawdust.

"Shit," Patti says, hugging herself.

"If we clear this area," I look around for a broom, "I can take out the records one by one and dust them off."

"Those are Paul's records," she says and I stop.

"Hey, Nick," Paul would say, glancing up from his guitar, "when you die can I have your record collection?"

I'd chuckle. I owned CDs. "'Course, Paul. Can I have yours?" His collection—of actual records—tripled the size of mine.

"Oh hell no," Paul would reply. "I'm gonna be buried with mine."

But now here they are. I don't know how or why Patti trekked them across the country with her and she doesn't say. She kneels down and examines the vinyl carefully, pulling out a Beach Boys album to investigate the damage. I wonder what is constantly roiling inside her, what darkness sits on her chest, attacks her at night, wakes her screaming from nightmares. But I can't ask her. Not now.

"I can't deal with this," she says. "Let's just take my clothes and get out of here."

We pack what we can carry in one load, Patti apologizing to her friend, whose name I don't recall and will never see again. We leave behind the music Paul spent a lifetime collecting, relics of a dead man, never to surface or spin again.

We remain silent. We don't speak as Patti drives west out of Portland, into the high desert, vast and open. We follow the Columbia River, curve north through Washington, past Yakima to the Sasquatch camp grounds. In the morning, we awake to a stunning view: miles of brown hills stretching into the distance, eons of blue sky all around us. The amphitheater rests at the bottom of a gorge, a remote and beautiful expanse. For three days we fly from stage to stage, making friends with Canadians, drinking a lot and waking up early with the sunshine. We do not talk. Not really. Not the kind of heart-to-heart that we regularly shared in high school.

We're too close to each other here, sharing a tent, going everywhere together. Maybe we both know that, despite the miles of space and thousands of people, there's nowhere for us to go if one of us says the wrong thing. I am constantly ready to delve into the past, to learn their secrets, but she is not. She isn't the lifelong friend I once had. I don't know why I thought three days in the middle of nowhere would return us to someplace that will never be the same.

After the festival closes, we drive back to Seattle. It's late at night. I have to fight to stay awake while Patti dozes next to me. At one point, she stirs and reaches to turn down the music.

"He got really sick," she blurts out.

"Huh?" I ask.

"Paul," she says. "He got really sick. He wasn't the person we remember. One time, he went after me with a machete, cornered me in the kitchen. Our neighbor broke down the door and tackled him."

"Jesus. Patti, that's..."

"I know," she says.

I wonder if we're both thinking the same thing, that Paul abhorred violence, that if he got violent with Patti, then something dark had snapped inside him. And even though I know I shouldn't ask the question that everyone asks, the question that can't be answered, I do.

"Why? What happened to him?"

Patti stifles a sob but keeps going. "I don't know. Maybe it was always buried inside him and finally burst. Maybe there was a trigger that I'll never know about. Our last Christmas was the best day we ever spent together. Two days later he was gone."

My hands grip the steering wheel tight. This is the first time I've heard anything like this from Before. Patti and I live in the After, trudging through it, picking up the pieces that Paul shattered so that we can somehow move forward. The Before is high school, the talent show, after schools in the backyard, all of the mundane examples of our friendship that I now dissect for clues. *Maybe that guitar riff was a cry for help. The way he narrowed his eyes when he spoke proved he was sick. How about the way he treated me that final summer?* It's futile. I couldn't have saved Paul, no one could. But I wonder always if I could have saved Patti and me and Paul.

I drive through the darkness, saying nothing, towards morning.

Two weeks before we left for college, Patti and I threw a party at her house while her parents were out of town. We invited everyone from high school and made a drink called Hop, Skip, and Go Naked: vodka, beer, and lemonade concentrate.

"You know how you wanna get laid tonight?" Patti asked, bounding out the screen door to find me smoking alone on the back porch.

"Um, yes," I said, taking the drink Patti offered. I was desperate to lose my virginity before college. I was such a cliché.

Patti flicked her eyes to the kitchen, where a pretty girl in all black ladled some hooch into her cup, careful not to spill it on the floor.

"You're not serious," I said. "Megan?"

Patti set her cup down and placed her hands on my shoulders. "Nick, Paul dumped her. You go to college in two weeks. It's a party. Loosen up."

Two weeks before, Patti and Paul and I had sat on the same floor in Patti's kitchen while I cried about girls. Like always. I didn't date in high school, I was awkward and repressed and never knew what to say. We were doing what we always did; if one person is down, the other two helped them stand up.

"What if I never get anyone to like me ever?" I asked.

Patti chuckled. "You will. Some day soon what Paul and I are saying will all make sense." Patti had had sex with Matthew, her first love, whom she started dating around the time she started hanging out with us.

"And if it doesn't?" I asked.

Patti looked to Paulie like, "You gonna help me out here?" Paul looked bored, lying sideways on the linoleum floor, staring up at the ceiling. Maybe he was embarrassed by my neediness. I hadn't even seen him that much lately. At my nineteenth birthday party, he never showed.

He shrugged and said, "We can at least help you get laid." He had lost it back when we were fourteen, when I dreamed of just kissing girls, and slept with every girl he had dated in the interim, including a pretty sophomore named Megan, who—two weeks later—was suddenly not his girlfriend and standing right in front of me.

"Killer party," she said. "You have a cigarette?"

I fished in my pockets for my pack and gave one to her.

"Thanks," she said, smiling up at me. She was gorgeous, tiny with enormous black eyes; smart as hell too, a few years younger but way more self-assured than I was.

"Wanna go sit on the swing set?" she asked. Behind her, Patti nodded her head vigorously.

"Yeah," I said, butterflies creeping into my belly. Pretty girls like Megan never wanted to go sit on swing sets in dark corners of backyards with me. They wanted to do that with Paul. But I was just drunk enough not to think about any of that, about Paul or the party or leaving for college and never coming back.

We sat down and Megan kissed me. A bomb went off in my stomach. She placed her hand on the inside of my thigh. She whispered in my ear, "Let's go upstairs." We waded through the party hand in hand, past the drunk friends and spilled booze, ignoring the turned heads. As we got to the front of the house, I remember this very clearly, where the main door met the stairwell, Paul entered the party with his new girl, blond with heels. We nearly collided with them and exchanged a glance, he and I, quick and furtive.

Megan pulled me up to the second floor. We found an open bedroom, Patti's parents' room. We kissed some more, her lips on my neck, tongue in my ear; her hands moved over my belt, undid each loop, unbuttoned my pants and took them off. "Remove your shirt," she commanded and I did. She pushed me down on the bed and climbed on top. We jostled back and forth, my hands on her waist, steadying myself, moving to a dance I didn't yet know, some rhythm that felt so goddamn holy cow good. And then?

It was over.

That was it? That's what I had cried about?

Maybe there is a code amongst friends, that you aren't supposed to sleep with your best friend's newly ex-girlfriend. But at the time I wasn't totally sure Paul was my friend anymore.

A few days later, he called me at home.

"Well," Paul said. "I guess congratulations are in order."

"Uh...thanks," I said.

Paul was silent. The phone shook in my hands.

"So, Nick, I think that's pretty much it for us. You know, don't call. Or anything. Goodbye."

The next time I saw Paul would be at Patti's twenty-first birthday party. The time after that he was dead.

"Nick, are you sitting down?"

"Um...hi, Mom." I straddled a fire hydrant and pulled my scarf tight. "Why are you calling so late?"

It was my second winter in Chicago, a year and a half out of theatre school, and I waited tables at a fine-dining restaurant in River North. The night was slow, calm before the New Year's Eve storm, and I looked forward to catching a cab home for an early night's sleep.

I had just seen my parents at Christmas a few days before.

My mother took a deep breath.

"Paul Myers killed himself."

I heard her whimper. My mom watched me grow up with Paul, hosted him at our house many times, socialized with his mother at the events in our community.

"Oh my god..." A cab pulled up but I waved it off.

"Patti asked me to call you," she said.

"I haven't seen them in three years." Or spoken, or emailed, or texted.

"Nick...she found him."

I went silent. Numbness crept over me.

"The funeral is Monday. You should come home."

It was Patti's twenty-first birthday party in East Lansing the last time I saw them. I made the trek from Ohio to celebrate. This was a big deal; I rarely left my university bubble with my new friends and killer parties. But it was Patti. Not being there was out of the question.

The party was at her off-campus apartment, a long narrow building with a shared balcony. The cold blistered our faces as we huddled outside smoking, the warmth inside fogging our glasses. People came and went, Patti's new friends in her new life. I played drinking games, downed beer, smoked pot. Patti whirled around the tiny pad, hugging people without stopping to really speak to them. Paul was there, but I didn't talk to him. He had invited me to his twenty-first birthday party the previous summer but after devastating me, hurting me worse than anyone in my life up to that point, I wanted nothing to do with him.

Late, after most of the guests had departed, I had a cigarette on the balcony, wanting everyone to leave so I could crash on the couch and go home. To Ohio.

The door opened and Patti threw her arms around me, her cheek pressed against my back.

"Thank you for coming," she whispered. "I'm sorry we didn't really talk."

She leaned next to me over the ledge. She had replaced her black party dress with pjs and a peacoat, hair poking out under a Montreal Canadians hat.

"So those are my friends," she said.

"They seem nice."

"They are," she said. "I like to be surrounded by people I love."

The door creaked open.

"I have something to tell you," Patti started, while Paul joined her on the other side.

"Actually," Paul took her hand, sliding his fingers into hers, "we have something to tell you."

I remember flicking my cigarette onto the concrete and stubbing it out with my boot.

I remember taking a final swig of my beer and heaving the bottle into the parking lot, where it shattered on the pavement.

I remember laughing. A snotty sneer. Right in their faces.

"Um. . ." It was Patti. "Not exactly the reaction we were looking for?"

"Seriously?" I asked them.

Paul slipped his arm around her waist. "I've been in love with her for years, man."

"Okay," I backed away from them, arms outward. "I should just go."

"No!" Patti said. "We were hoping you'd stay and talk. We want to tell you everything."

"You can't just...drop that bomb on me and expect me to react like everything is a-ok."

You might think that I was in love with one or both of them. You probably think I was in love with Patti. But, in my mind, Patti had a choice to make, between romance and friendship, between Paul and Nick. I know now that she didn't choose Paul over me. She tried to choose both of us and I didn't see it.

"You couldn't have told me this was going on at all?" I asked. "I'm, like, five hours away. It's not like I went anywhere far."

"Life happens," Patti said. "I don't have time to just hop on the phone and make sure you're doing okay."

The next thing I said I would regret forever.

"You would if you were my real friend."

No one spoke for a long time. Patti leaned into Paul's chest.

"Nick, I think you should leave," Paul said.

Tears streamed down my cheeks. I gathered my belongings and spent the night in my car, feeling left out of that once beautiful circle, and empty. When the sun came up and I had sobered up, I drove back to school.

I was early to Paul's wake. A couple of cars dotted the parking lot of the Thayer-Rock funeral home. I took a deep breath, my hand on the door. I opened it.

She was on me immediately, a wave of wild, curly, red hair smothering me in a hug.

For all I know, our embrace took over the small foyer, grief-stricken friends and relatives forced to scoot around us as they entered and exited. I didn't give a shit. It felt good to cry into her again. It felt like home.

"What the fuck," I blurted.

She started laughing. "I know, right?" Music played faintly in the distance, a new song by the Yeah Yeah Yeahs I really liked.

She put her arms on my shoulders and we looked each other square in the eyes.

"Let's go see Paul," she said.

She led me to the casket, past an assembled collage of photos and a laptop playing music. He looked unreal lying there. He'd hanged himself, gruesomely, slumped forward on his bathroom toilet, belt tied to the window behind him. It took force and determination for him to die. To make him look presentable to us, they'd shaved off most of his beard, leaving only a mustache that was so...not Paul.

Standing there felt like years, like we were making up for lost time, communicating in a language only we could understand. I didn't know then that Paul's death would give my life meaning, that since he died I have learned to anticipate the funeral around every corner, tried to fill each moment of each day with a love that buries itself deep in my stomach, explodes in my chest, pulses through my fingertips and out to the world.

Patti interlocked her fingers with mine.

"What's with the mustache?" I asked.

She grinned. "That's what I said. I don't know why they just didn't shave that off too." Her eyes were puffy from crying but she was smiling, her gaze fixed on Paul. "I half expect him to jump up, do a little Paulie dance, rip off that stupid mustache and shout 'Just kidding!'"

We laughed despite ourselves. We needed to.

"When I found him. . ." she trailed off. That story could wait. "But he looks peaceful now."

We stood silent, holding hands. When we exhaled it was in perfect unison.

"I don't know how this is possible," I say, fishing out the last Parliament Light for Patti, while she passes me the bottle of cheap chardonnay, "but you always look the same to me, in my memory or right now. Different hair styles or colors, new tattoos, glasses, contacts, crying, smiling, snow, summer, you're always eighteen years old to me. We could be anywhere in the world, at any time."

"But we're not," she says, with a nod to the old farmhouse, gussied up with a new addition to the back, so that it looks familiar yet unrecognizable in the same breath.

"I want to tell him things," I say.

"Like what?" she asks.

"Little things," I say. "That he'd probably like the Arcade Fire a lot."

Patti smiles. "Yeah, he would."

And you'd probably like LCD Soundsystem too, Paul, and The XX and Janelle Monae.

And I wish you could read what I wrote about you. I wish I could tell you that you visited me in my dreams, talked to me like you were alive, told me everything was going to be okay. I wish you didn't kill yourself and that the three of us—you, me, and Patti—could sit in your backyard as adults and listen to you play music. I'd smoke cigarettes, even though I haven't had one in a long time and maybe your daughter would sit on Patti's lap and your mom would cook platters of vegetables and gossip with my mom and our dads would talk awkwardly while they grilled meat and we could all just be together, one big clan. But you're gone. And never coming back.

I rock on my feet and the snow crunches, the wine twists in my guts. Patti passes our final cigarette and I finish it quickly, stubbing it out on the ground. It's time to go soon, me back to Chicago, Patti to LA where she moved after Portland, after Nashville, after Michigan.

We hug, deep and full, like that night at the funeral home. We're way beyond discovering our friendship again. This time, we will cling to each other and never let go.

She touches my face with her hands. "A month before he died, Paul told me that he missed you terribly, that he thought about you a lot. He felt bad about how things had ended between us. He wanted you back in his life."

"Really?" I ask.

Her gloves grab the lapels of my coat. "He loved you, Nick. And this," Patti gestures to the house but I know what she means. "This is how he brought us back together."

I don't know what to say. I am overwhelmed and overjoyed and tired and full.

"I'll see you soon," I whisper.

"Yes," Patti says. "Soon." ❧

Hogwash
Christopher Robinson

To raise money for our cheer squad
we decided to hold a hogwash.
We put on bikinis even though it was March,
we asked the Shop-n-Save to use their parking lot,
got our buckets of soapy water and washing mitts
and stood there, goosebumped, waiting
for the local farmers to see Kirsten at the corner—
she's a 34 C—and pull their hogs in
for a wash, knowing that we'd miss
a few spots of mudcrust, that one of us
would lose a finger to those teeth, knowing
that we hated and adored the furtive glances
at our cleavage, the not-quite fatherly
nod and smile.

Fullboat

Christopher Robinson

We tried to explain
that we were simply beyond capacity
already, and another cranium
or two could well near sink us. They
wouldn't listen. So here we are,
in the abyssopelagic zone, lungs full up
with lifeless water, keeping
on because a party
doesn't throw itself.

At least they brought
a halfrack of High Life, and shared
their pharmaceuticals.

Now that we're all dead, we have a little
distance on the event. These things
happen, when you live
the good life,

dancing on the water, knocking
about your cultivated personality,
oblivious

to the giant squid
and angler fish, deep,
deep below you.

Three LIVES
Megan Marshall

Although Gertrude Stein's triptych of novellas, *Three Lives*, was always my favorite of her books, I'm not writing here about that cheerfully subversive first work of fiction, with its precocious attention to the intertwining questions of race and class that so absorb us now. Instead I have in mind three works published during the decade before I started researching my first biography, *The Peabody Sisters*, which ultimately claimed twenty years of my adult working life. Looking back, I can see how these three books—Diane Johnson's *Lesser Lives* (1972), Bernard Malamud's *Dubin's Lives* (1979), and Phyllis Rose's *Parallel Lives* (1983)—each with its own seductive appeal for a would-be life-writer, steered me toward that Odyssian voyage; two of them made excellent traveling companions.

I didn't read them in chronological order. Just out of college in the late '70s (two and a half years at Bennington, two and a half at Harvard—yes, I can do the math!) and beginning a friendship with the late great biographer Justin Kaplan, whose generosity to young writers is legendary, I was drawn to Malamud's fictional portrayal of a famous biographer, William Dubin, perhaps modeled on Kaplan in a few respects, and set on a campus not unlike Bennington, where Malamud taught in his later years. *Dubin's Lives* has something in common with Malamud's earlier campus novel, *A New Life,* which Cynthia Ozick described in a recent essay in the *New York Times Book Review* as "one of those rare transfiguring American novels that turn wishing into destiny." As in *A New Life,* the richly observed country setting and elegiac tone distinguish this late-life book from other Malamud novels and stories; William Dubin's "wishing" centers not on advancement toward tenure within the academy, but on mastering the life of D.H. Lawrence in a biography he hopes will meet even greater success than his first prize-winning life of Thoreau. Here's how Dubin talks to himself about his project:

> He had more new material than anyone in recent years and felt he could do a more subtle portrait of the man than had previously appeared. That was the true battle ground for the biographer: the vast available documentation versus the intuition and limited experience of Wm. B. Dubin, formerly of Newark, New Jersey.
>
> Sometimes he felt like an ant about to eat an oak tree. There were several million facts of Lawrence's short life and long work, of which Dubin might master a sufficient quantity. He'd weave them together and say what they meant—that was the daring thing. You assimilated another man's experience and tried to arrange it into "thoughtful centrality"—Samuel Johnson's

expression...The past exudes legend: one can't make pure clay of time's mud. There is no life that can be recaptured wholly; as it was. Which is to say that all biography is ultimately fiction. What does that tell you about the nature of life, and does one really want to know?

Aside from Dubin's dedication to his subject, his adherence to a vocational path already well-worn by previous masters, and his casually ironic questioning of the whole endeavor (I hadn't yet committed to writing a biography of my own), I also envied most aspects of his daily existence: a many-windowed study in a large house, the freedom to work there undisturbed every day, a wife who fixed him lunch and wrote checks for the "cleaning person." Never mind that the "cleaning person" turns out to be Fanny Bick, a distractingly beautiful dropout from the college who will test Dubin's fidelity to his marriage and cause him to wonder "whether he had responded to [Fanny] as his usual self or as one presently steeped in Lawrence's sexual theories, odd as they were." I could see "several million" ways in which Dubin's life would never be mine, and I was enough of a feminist (in fact very much of one) to find the direction of the plot mildly revolting. But I still read the book and enjoyed it the way I did John Updike's *Rabbit* novels—a counterfeit's pleasure in stealing into the mind of the other. I wasn't yet writing, but I was reading like a biographer.

It took Phyllis Rose's *Parallel Lives: Five Victorian Marriages* to teach me some lessons about the varieties of marital experience that were more useful than those offered by Bernard Malamud, and to broaden my sense of what a biographical work could do. It was not by chance that within a year of reading the book I had successfully pitched my own project on three nineteenth-century New England sisters, two of whom had made famous marriages (Sophia Peabody and Nathaniel Hawthorne, Mary Peabody and Horace Mann), and signed a book contract—promising delivery in three years. Rose's book traces the liaisons of Jane Welsh and Thomas Carlyle, Effie Gray and John Ruskin, George Eliot and Henry Lewes, Catherine Hogarth and Charles Dickens, Harriet Taylor and John Stuart Mill. But more than any of the real-life characters in the book (except perhaps Marian Evans, aka George Eliot), I admired Phyllis Rose and her very different style of biographical daring.

In the opening pages, Rose states Dubin's premise, "all biography is fiction," in reverse: "I believe, first of all, that living is an act of creativity." The plan of her book, she writes, "began with a desire to tell the stories of some marriages as unsentimentally as possible, with attention to the shifting tides of power between a man and a woman joined, presumably, for life. My purposes were partly feminist (since marriage is so often the context within which a woman works out her destiny, it has always been an object of feminist scrutiny) and partly...literary." Here was both Olympian distance and intimate inquiry. Feminism and textual analysis. Literature and life.

Three years turned into five, and then seven and ten...Mercifully, early on in my work I had discovered my touchstone book, one that curiously never earned the acclaim it deserved, judging from its author Diane Johnson's decision after writing one more biography (Dashiell Hammett) to give up life writing in favor of social satire as a novelist. *The True History of the First Mrs. Meredith and Other Lesser Lives* begins:

> Many people have described the Famous Writer presiding at his dinner table, in a clean neckcloth. He is famous; everybody remembers his remarks. He remembers his own remarks, being a writer, and notes them in his diary. We forget that there were other people at the table—a quiet person, now muffled by time, shadowy, whose heart pounded with love perhaps, or rage, or fear when our writer shuffled in from his study; whose hands, white knuckled, twisted an apron, whose thoughts raced. Or someone who left the room with a full throat of sobs. Of course there is no way really to know the minds of Lizzie Rossetti, or the first Mrs. Milton, or all those silent Dickens children suffering the mad unkindness, the delirious pleasures of their terrifying father's company—with little places of their own to put their small things away in, with small, terrified thoughts.
>
> But we know a lesser life does not seem lesser to the person who leads one.

Johnson's biography of Mary Ellen Peacock Meredith, daughter and wife of poets, mistress of a painter, who, over a century after her death "survives materially in a lock of hair, a book she owned (*The Arabian Nights*), a green satin dress, another of ecru embroidery, two parasols to match, a dozen letters, a few articles and poems she wrote, and a book of Extracts in which she copied out things that struck her as she read," is the work of a magician. Who else could have spun a true tale out of so little "material"? Johnson's *Lesser Lives* inspired me, even though my materials were of Laurentian "oak tree" proportions. (The three Peabody sisters corresponded extensively, kept numerous journals and books of extracts, and published books and articles by the cartload.) I had begun to fear that I might never finish my book, and yet Johnson's compassionate perspective offered consolation, reminding me of the full spectrum of human experience, the importance of each individual no matter how small her accomplishment: "Mrs. Meredith's life can be looked upon, of course, as an episode in the lives of Meredith or Peacock, but it cannot have seemed that way to her."

I did finish my book recounting the three lives of the Peabody sisters. And then I went on to write another biography of their contemporary,

Margaret Fuller. I will write another, and another, I believe. I have plans for them. But I won't forget the three *Lives* that, one after the other, invited me to write biographically, showed me how, and comforted me when I despaired by revealing something of "the nature of life." Yes, one really does want to know. ❧

Mine Dont Never

J S Khan

Mine *dont never turn out right*, Big J reckons while the Vanilla Gorilla, deputy sheriff in these parts, opens the backdoor of his black Ford pickup-truck to yank out his son, the boy (naturally known as Little J), his guilty eyes protrudin like those of a fish (no doubt some utterly blind, bottomfeedin flathead), n that faint mustache of hisn atwitchin to trigger off incongruent memories of Big J's own deceased father: the always-cleanshaven Marine who fought in two World Wars, who charged the No Man's Land in Belleau Wood under heavy fire n later besmirched a Jap officer's honor on Guadalcanal by tossin the lil yeller imperialist across his mighty thigh to give a by-God whuppin with his own ceremonial *katana*-blade—a colonel with so many clusters on his purple heart you couldnt tell the ribbon's color anymore—n this colossal forebear slain at last by a catfish caught off Cape Fear: the bewhiskered channel cat's poisonous barbels inducin a series of strokes so Big J found him—the former Big J (by then, admittedly, a demented, decrepit octogenarian)—writhin with the fish atop him floppin, n utterly beslimed.

    Big J represses an urgent desire to rip that pathetic scruff off his son's face—but when the boy turns so the Gorilla can uncuff him, he sees half the stache missin already, along with its matchin brow n sideburn.

    Standin outside Big J's Haulers Co., now jes past sundown—which happens earlier hereabouts thanks to the mountains—Little J looks paler than ever under the glow of florescent lights aclickin on overhead, n him jes standin there lookin like he's done given up the ghost caught betwixt the shadows of the trucks with all their motors coolin audibly in the dusk.

    Well, Big J says. Ah reckon one of yall is agoin tell me what happened. Any second now.

    The deputy sheriff—known to his mother alone as Judson Wallace but so-called the Vanilla Gorilla by everbody else (includin his wife) fer his diagnosed gigantism n general lack of melanin-rich skin n hair (which some folks find downright creepy)—explains how he caught the boy with his cousins Hog Leg n Scooter Trash lightin one of Wallace Junot's birdhouses afire: a minor act of terrorism that has been occurrin fer the last four years in Coochland County as if by the stubborn call of an unspoken primal ritual.

    Ah recollect it, Big J says. That eco-whackjob Wally has long envisioned a mecca fer all the nuthatches n loons up there, a downright *avian utopia* despite all God's trees or am Ah right?

That's right, the Gorilla says, noddin in an amiable way. But this year he paid me to stake out his latest in my off-duty hours. As ye might expect, Ah heard their bikes fore Ah saw em, their little scooters' engines whinin up the road. To tell the truth it was an inopportune moment fer me as Ah was just then ashakin my pizzle after waterin the moss to our mutual satisfaction. Anyhow, when Ah got back down to my truck who do Ah see but yer boy n his ridin buddies, though the other two remained on their bikes idlin while he cut hisn off n pranced up to that birdhouse jes agigglin like a schoolgirl on prom night. Well, that was when he fetched out his pocket what Ah reckoned was a Co-Cola bottle filled with gas n stuffed with a rag, but fore Ah could flip on my trucklights he reckoned to light it right there n stick it in that birdhole there n *bab-oon!* shot fire right in his face—why he lost that side-whisker n brow—n he bein lucky as all hell he werent burnt anywheres else. The other two vamoosed ahootin as Ah ran up n tackled him ere he could skedaddle too, n of course the whole time he screamed murder though in truth he was naught but victim of his own dang idjicy.

Well, Big J says, feelin an all-too-familiar hollowness in his gut, in the center of his navel, n what could he possibly call that squalid quiverin of the flesh but shame, or guilt?

Shot fire right in his no-thinkin dumbass face, he says. How about that.

Little J glowers, his weak blue eyes squirrelin away in the furrows of darkness. The scuttlin of junebugs against the garage in mindless swarms causes the boy to fidget anxiously.

Big J scowls, tryin hard not to reckon how it'd been only three weeks since the disgraceful lil turdlin lost his license gittin a DUI: a caper to top even his prior performance gittin fired from the microbrewery *he helped start his own self* fer bein too damn drunk n causin the beer to funk; n ever since he's done nuthin but waste time pissin away his (Big J's!) hard-earned money on booze n gas piddediddlin all over town on that liquorcycle of hisn while at the same time his sister—Big J's only daughter, the beautiful May Pearl—recently cracked up n was bein kept at the local quacksalver's on Airy Rock, n this alone costin him (who else?) a fortune.

Big J mumbles under his breath as he strides back through the garage to his office n unlocks the door. Once inside, he opens his closet to unlock his safe n extract several hundred-dollar bills. He hesitates as he spies an open envelope under a paperweight on his desk shaped like a Napoleonic bust, n carefully removes it n relocks his office. Returnin through the garage, he thrusts a sizable wad on the Gorilla.

Kindly reimburse ole Wally, will ya? he says. An thank ye kindly fer lettin me know fore anyone else, though Ah am damned embarrassed, considerin the boy been out of high-school five years n he's still prankin his old teachers like the feckless dumbshit he is n always will be.

The deputy nods with his frozen smile, placin the money in the backpocket of his khaki uniform. Big J clears his throat fore thrustin out the envelope.

Oh, n when you head back to the Sheriff's office, Gorilla ole buddy, can you do me a favor n tell those jackoffs on the Soil n Water Conservation Board across yer way to stop harassin me n learn ta coordinate their inspections with the local game warden's office? They might learn somethin fer once instead of revealin their own ignorant asses.

The Gorilla looks at the envelope's stamp n return address as he shakes out the letter. His eyes scan the type as his forehead furrows.

Sheriff's office dont handle this shit, J. What you build a dam fer anyway?

Ah aint built no goddamn dam, it's those goddamn beavers that have been ruinin my property n will soon affect my buildin structure in its entirety, n all on account of those goddamn Yankee sonsabitches moved down here Ah caint shoot anymore!

That's a pickle, the Gorilla says, givin a sympathetic whistle. Ah thought the water looked higher pullin in the driveway yonder.

Those beavers threaten the value of my property n my business.

But what's the warden's office have to do with it?

Ah had to apply fer a permit to shoot the critters, but while Ah've been waitin fer the warden to approve the license, the Soil n Water Conservation Board—as ye jes read—has come to the belief Ah have personally *manufactured a structure* to block the creek! An git this: Ah caint even capture the pests n take em off my land, fer if Ah do *that* Ah'll be *relocatin em from their rightful habitat*, thereby actin contrary to laws that protect their—git this—*natural rights!*

Shit, the Gorilla says, affectin a countenance of great sorrow n disbelief. That *is* a pickle to suck.

Damn right. These critters got more rights than a taxpayin business owner.

The Gorilla's teeth gleam purple under the fluorescents as his lips snap into a grin again.

Ah'll talk to their secretary Kimmy, but who knows if she kin help. Ah'll git back to ya.

If someone dont resolve the situation, best believe Ah am affixin to handle it myself.

Believe that, the Gorilla says as he walks around his truck n opens the driverside door.

But dont dwell on it overmuch, he calls back. They dont pay rent fer all that headspace, J.

Dont Ah know it, Gorilla.

The gargantuan officer of the law holds up a gleaming paw as he slides in the interior of his cabin, which appears too small fer his massive build as he crouches n bends his knees to work the pedals. The ignition sparks n the truck spins back up the bend. Big J waves while the boy jes sulks beside him with his uncuffed wrists thrust deep in his blue-jean's pockets.

    Where's the scooter? Big J asks him as the Ford's taillights slip away.

    Up in the Gorge, the boy answers, darin a quick look upward.

    Dad, he says, Ah'm—

    A big fuckin disappointment dont Ah know it.

    Unable to meet his father's aroused ferocity, Little J's eyes flinch away. Big J continues to glare into the boy's profile, where still he discerns in his son's features his own degenerate form. Is it possible? True, Big J got in a fair amount of trouble as a youngster (how could he deny it?) sowing his wild oats as they say n sometimes stealing hubcaps off other kid's cars, but when it came time to put away childish things, well, *didnt* he? Whereas poor lil May always took after his wife—both in personality n physique—the two of em so busy enactin parables of self-pityin self-martyrdom they couldnt see the forest from the trees, n both—Big J reckons it—teched not jes a lil in their purty lil heads.

    He flicks, no, *hurls* his arm toward his vehicle, a '66 Austin Healey he's owned fer at least three decades.

    Get in the car, he says, spittin in the gravel n shakin his head. Right now.

    Mine dont never understand me, Little J mutters to no one in particular as he lies sprawled out abed with his sneakered feet hangin off the edge, jes reckonin to hisself how tired of hearin his parents fight he is, their shouts comin up through the floorboards beneath his bedroom, though he dont even make an effort to drown out their voices or the yappin of his mother's retarded lapdog with his headphones; fer what could be realer, he reckons anew, than his mother's protests all high n hysterical, or his father's bellicose bellows as if he's affixin to shit a fire? Little J lifts from the shot pocket at his waist a soccerball to launch overhead n watches as its pentagon-stitched pattern spirals lazily backward up to the ceilin fore fallin back in his hands. He wonders which of the two is more self-righteous: Dad, with his need to control people with money n the family business, plus his murderous hatred of the beavers (which all of his rants return to nowadays), or Mom with her crazed church causes n Biblical societies where people lay hands on you to heal you of demonic infirmities or somesuch bunkum while sayin *Ah'll be prayin fer ya* in tones so black you'd reckon their distaste fer each n everone else must be proportional to the love they professed to feel fer baby Jesus—

    You've done spent too much money on this already, his mother cries out. All that electric tape n wire fencin, n whattayoucallem *beaver deceivers*? Ah dont want that man around here no more—

Ah swear the boy set to conspire against me with those beavers n those idjit bureaucrats downtown! What, *you* too now?

Who cares about the beavers? Cain't we talk about Little J? We should pray as a family!

The car-ride home had been no less entertainin, though Little J had not dared speak as his dad threw his lame-ass sportscar in gear as soon as they were off the gravel road—this abrupt acceleration knockin his small frame against his seatbelt while he fumbled with the belt's latch—n all the while his dad hollered to call down God's wrath somethin about Granddad, n *jes how would he reckon ye you lil ungrateful shit*, though in truth Little J does not give a *rat's ass* what that hackneyed ghost might reckon him or anythin else, his few dubious memories of that lopsided giant consistin only of the brown spots of skin around his faded eyes n how those eyes affixed on hisn one evening with a demented glare in his fifth year as the ole senile bastard rambled about how *Someday They will come to take away yer Bibles n yer guns, so you must be ready, Littlest J*, though he never specified who *They* were, n this terrified the boy equally as the old man's obsession with right angles, which—him bein a former Grandmaster of the Teutonic Lodge—he also felt naturally obligated to impart, so the twisted codger traced that legendary vertex across their porch or along doorsills, even in the grooves between the yellow linoleum tiles of their kitchenfloor—

It is the right-angled triangle that unites man with God! Granddad wheezed, havin worked hisself up into an inexplicable sweat. He would prod Little J with a blunt finger to trace the lofty figure as he lifted a scuffled loafer n stomped it. *The base measured by the number three, the Deity n Divine! The perpendicular measured by four, the Earth its square! The hypotenuse measured by five, the union between em! Git it? Simple as one, two, three!*

Clearly Little J did not *git it*, havin gone on to flunk geometry in middle school n again in high school, n from there to receive an *Incomplete* in trigonometry at Ginny Tech thanks to his *Episode* (to borrow Mom's high-toned jargon), which saw his inglorious return home n brief self-employment at the brewery, where he'd attempted to start a legitimate business out from under his father's shadow, though all was to end in disaster.

Little J fires the soccerball like a basketball again. His sister—herself lost adrift her own *Episode* (to stick with the popular script)—reckons herself a Wiccan Princess or somesuch bunkum, n this horrifies Mom worse than her goin crazier than a shithouse mouse, but what was *that* compared to Mom's kooky church or dogwhisperin or Granddad's sacred math? Not that Dad was big on spirituality, him bein consumed with nuthin but what he called the *hardline*—

You aint even in high school anymore, his dad fired at him in the car only minutes ago, throwin a dangerous look that cut through his thoughts, then as now. *Hellfire, you aint even in college! An what the hell am Ah goin ta tell Em?*

Stick to the hardline, he almost whined. Couldnt the old man leave him alone?

Boy, it is my godgiven right to make certain none of yall expose yer asses where they dont belong! If you can't abide by my rules, kick rocks, kiddo! The boy wouldn't be such a loser if he wasnt always hangin out with yer sister's abortive brood! Dad's voice rattles through the floor. Hogwarsh n Peckerhead or whatever they call theyselves—

Poison is what they call Little J—never Little J (a name he naturally despises)—n this proud moniker he earned after swingin off a vine near Walelu Creek whereat, missin the water, he crashed into a bed of poison ivy. He'd done so on a dare launched by Scooter Trash (who earned his own alias wreckin his scooter into a dumpster-bin) while they's fishin in Hog Leg's skiff, *jes chasin them damn channel fish,* as Hog Leg always put it, n bein whiskied to a most exquisite degree Little J had attempted the feat only to suffer a violent rash, his fortuitous degree of drunkenness causin him to go limp when he hit the bramble n happily break no bones.

They're not bad boys, his mother protests. *They're just misled, with no work since ya fired em! An you won't even hire yer own son—*

Ah caint have em workin with the cranes or rigs if they are drunk from sunup or sippin weed in the trucks! Say what you want about Wall Street Jews—they may wanna work us all nekkid in the rain, but at least they're hardworkin. At least they're *fuckin* ethical!

Now, honey, you cain't talk thataway, the Jews prepared the way fer Christ Our God—

As if he would ever stop hangin out with his own bloodkin! At least as long as he was trapped in this tiny town between blue ridges that seemed to hedge in the sky like a natural prison. It was true Mom's folks were all a smidgin teched, moonstruck ye might say, maybe a lil too in love with playin the hazard n losin hard, but they's all so down-to-earth, descended from bootleggers n moonshiners—somethin Dad should appreciate, or in the very least respect, such as his admiration fer his other deceased grandfather, who all (even Mom!) called Frank—

Frank once had me light his crackpipe with a blowtorch, Hog Leg's father, his Aunt Cissy's husband Roy, told em while he sat on his porch sippin a Coors, *so Ah reckon it goes without sayin he liked ta party hard…*

Or could he, at the age of twenty-four, simply turn off all his memories of the times they spent together since only knee-high, say, catchin lightnin-bugs like Zeke Jones taught em, stuffin the incandescent insects in the bores of their b.b. guns so when they cocked n fired the bugs burst from their flimsy muzzles in a spray of showerin phosphorescence? Or what about all the times they's spent since his return from Ginny Tech, jes the three of em fishin, floatin, n talkin, though Little J *scratch that* Poison would never let a channel fish do *him* in since he knew well enough to grab the slimy bitches bellyside up, his thumb n middle finger atop they pectorals so they cain't git at his knuckles—at least *that* knowledge he proffered from his predecessor's demise—unlike what he never learned from Frank's, Frank bein the first person in all Coochland County to pop positive fer HIV n die of AIDS years before his own birth. Yet even better, Little J reckons, is to wear heavy leather gloves when ye handle em like Scooter Trash does, fer thataway their finicky whiskers caint tech ye atall.

Please jes shut yer mouthole, Em! Ah'm ringin up Loomis n that is all there is to it!

But honey what about Little J? That's the real problem we need to discuss, n *together*!

It's done past quittin time with that dipshit!

Poison *scratch that* Big Poison sets down the soccerball to stare at his walls covered with his old Star Wars toys, his gaze affixin on Boba Fett in his glossy, still-luminous package. Loomis Shank: the Varmint Vigilante—how ridiculous! At least *he'*d exhibited *some* ambition when he began his microbrewery, havin gotten Dad to invest in him n Zeke Jr.'s dreams, with their own beer in ever tap in ever bars downtown: a fine yeasty strain aged on bourbon oakchips he named *Banshee Fever*: a fine healthy concoction tastin just like everthin in life should taste, robust but chased by purest smoothness, takin you jes to the edge with a few glasses (ABV 6.66%) but never plumb over.

Ah jes wish fer *one goddamn time* someone in this family thought about *me*, how much work Ah gotta do take care of all this horseshit!

Had Dad *really* expected him to graduate with a degree in Business, or had he only been settin him up fer expected failure? Fer when the prodigal son suffered his *Episode* durin his sophomore year, flunkin out n simultaneously losin his position as goalie on the soccer team, he certainly conceded there had been *some* lil drinkin involved, sure, *some* lil sippin on the brew he secretly was concoctin in his dorm's closet till caught out—bein mid-Episode n overdrunk n hollerin about the bug in his ear n all—but had this not been a natural part of the process, that of *becomin a brewmaster*? Had his parents never heard that, in bygone eras, alchemists in their attempts to forge purest gold often went insane waftin their own chemicals? Little J knows all about this historical fact because he is well-versed in conspiracy theories—which he knows all about from countless hours on the World-Wide-Web jes studyin websites n Youtube videos that expose the Illuminati's secret plots (well, between surfin fishin blogs or bukake pornsites). Plus, his father always put too much emphasis on the bottle as the cause of his breakdown anyhow, overlookin altogether the very real invasive insect that wiggled its way deep in his left ear to cause an awful wormin sensation in the lower chamber of his whattayoucallit tympanum that had his folks (even sweet lil May!) rollin their eyes with disbelief after the Dean called home, though the doctors *did* later prove the insect no figment of his alcohol-addled imagination, since a tiny but very real junebug had squirmed in there only days ago—possibly while he slept—so he really *had* felt somethin makin its way into that waxy hole toward the honeycomb of his brain—

Even later, when he was released from Airy Rock—n still bein fearful larvae deep in his ear were hatchin a horde of quiverin pupae—had Dad really been supportive of his efforts to found Cragstown Brewery? Fer the money his dad loves to throw around to solve problems so he can bemoan em—*like a real man who creates solutions instead of fallin victim to his ever situation*—had that particular act of faith n goodwill not been more about pity n shame fer his mockery of his son fore he saw the doctor remove the beetle from his ear n hold it forth with mechanical tweezers? To dumbfound all, n his mother nearly faintin—though May thought it was pretty cool. Naturally, the beetle had been crushed by his irresistible fingermooshin, as well as the tweezers snaggin n extractin it—though *most* of its head still hung to its twisted thorax alongside a few spasmin limbs.

But reckonin on the pupae possibly splittin their creamy eggshells in his left ear—the newborn bugs breathin his brain's air (though the doctors assured him no such eggs could exist after removin the original offender)—he tries consciously to think of somethin else, fearful *They* might be listenin (who exactly, despite his online research, he still caint reckon rightly—sorry, Granddad). Possibly since he was thinkin of his sister earlier, he thinks of her n him as children instead, consciously conjurin scenes of her n him aged five n nine pluckin blackberries in a thorny wicker patch behind their home, or catchin salamanders in the springs, but allowin his thoughts to trend overlong in *that* direction only makes him more upset so his throat constricts, gittin all hot n salty, n he reckons he should go visit May in the ward fer suicide watch, though he figures he'll have to avoid talkin about what he's been up to since he saw her last, such as hangin with Hog Leg n fishin, since the thought of *that* pastime n sport only makes her cry like a dang child whenever she imagines the ugly buggers danglin wide-eyed n hooked or floppin in the belly of the boat, though he'd tried numerous times to explain that fish dont feel no pain atall—she of all people should git this since she conceives herself such a science whiz—cause fish dont got enough whattayoucallem special nerve receptors n hence not enough brainpower to experience death's pangs (which is luckier than most of us, he reckons grimly), though when he told her this recently it only made her cry harder, her n Mom bein so dang soft beyond all reason whenever it came to animals.

But thinkin on his younger sister up in Airy Rock where he suffered the worst of his *delirium tremens* only makes him more finicky still, fer beneath these thoughts lurks what he alone among the family knows (besides May): that something between her n Hog Leg happened at Myrtle Beach a few weeks ago when they were stayin at the Knotty Pine Motel, n jes after he passed out after drinkin too many growlers of his own beer, only jes *what* exactly he still caint reckon, though his sister's acted fearful of ole Hog ever since n begged him not to hang out with their cousin anymore, to the point finally—after she started to cut herself n got all bulimic again—he finally girded up his loins enough to approach Hog Leg on the subject—

Jes what did you do to May in Myrtle? he asked when Scooter Trash was away pissin, his head floatin above old furniture dumped in the cove near the falls at Fizzlebottom's Folly. *Did you try n tech her? You know that haint right.*

Why not? Hog Leg replied with a wink. *You aint her keeper, are ye? But if ya dont know it already, yer dad used to jump my mom's bones back in the day.*

Horseshit.

Horseshit yerself. Jes ask yer Mom, you lil cocksucker.

The steps that lead to his room outside creak softly, followed by a knock on the door.

Speak of the Devil.

Mine dont never realize how blessed they are, Emma Gwen thinks sadly as she knocks on her son's door n hears his grunt beyond the threshold so she turns the knob n pushes her way in, seein him jes asettin there on his bed halfdrunk n glowerin at a soccerball restin at his feet, n when he finally looks up at her with eyes clouded over with too-much hurtin she sees too his halfburnt mustache with its lost symmetry as if—like a small caterpillar—the whole dang thing done inched too far to the left of his mouth, n all at once she sees too superimposed over her son's feature Frank's spittin image (God bless his soul!), fer one time long ago while showin off her daddy lit his crackpipe with a blowtorch n accidentally scorched away one of his whiskers—which unlike her son's were gloriously thick n most Burt Reynolds-like—n as she ruminates about this n May Pearl's Episode she is simply whelmed so her soul commences to shudder deep inside her chest, her fondest wish even now to wail like Moses a prayer of deepest profundity n thereby achieve at least a fractional forgiveness fer this stiffnecked tribe her people, fer as any of her churchfriends could witness (a hundred times over too!), Emma has tried mighty hard to be merciful n gracious n longsufferin with her kin, but she also knows the Bible teaches the LORD our God visits the iniquity of our fathers on our children even unto the third (or was it fourth?) generation—n it is precisely *this* unhappy knowledge that draws uncontrollable tears to her eyes as she looks at her firstborn n she wonders if there is no way atall to break the shackles of all this useless generational suffering. Fer is sin alone our birthright, O God, or what about the anointin of yer own Son Jesus? Could that lil Lamb have learned kindness n forgiveness from *You*, really, or could one as all-knowin as Yerself still learn somethin from yer offspring, peculiar as that may seem?

You alright? she asks. You didnt get burnt?

No, he says in a hoarse voice. Ah dont want to talk about it.

It was Laz, wasnt it? Him's the one put ye up to it.

Ah said Ah dont want to talk about it.

Em hesitates before speakin again, wonderin how many times she's been stuck in a similar quandary (or was it quagmire she meant?), wantin desperately to absorb her children's pain into her own bones but unable to n sometimes jes feelin *downright awful*, like the two of em nuthin but open wounds she carried about in ever cell in ever organ of her body: the mysterious stigmata all mothers must feel rippin open anew ever time their babies fall in harm's way n they are helpless to assist em. LORD have mercy, but Emma has lived long fer her relatively short years on this earth (forty-eight, though she'd never tell) n known many strange tragedies n sordid travesties—not only the divorce of her parents when her n Cissy were just lil things, or Frank's drug abuse n relatively early death, sure *all that*—but also bein lanced by a cottonmouth once at the age of nine in Hal Burke's pool n once too in her teens bein *literally struck by lightnin* while swimmin in a pond with a goose n her gostlings—ever one of the lil birds so precious—n after she realized what happened she woke up shocked n fearful but okay without pain but glimpsin all the gostlings jes *disappeared outright*, though the mother goose floated dead atop the water. Gone up to our LORD, if animals are so lucky, but on this the Good Book speaks not. Did the lil uns explode like her cousin Ivan when he blew hisself up after drinkin a whole draught of ether bought off some Pollack drunkard, fer after he swigged the bottle down he lit a cigarette n *boom!* the fiery liquor blew out his guts in bloody smithereens, which certainly outdid her son's escapades with fire (or her daddy's fer that matter), but still Little J's n May's troubles hurt her worse than *anythin* else, save maybe the stillbirth of her third child, whom she'd named Natalie since her due-date was set so close to Christmas n *Natalie* in one of her name-books was said to mean *Christmas-child.*

LORD knows a body ought not complain, but what sort of world do we live in if the people we love most hurt us more than anythin else can, n again n again too, n even seem to resent us fer wantin to protect em—n *even more* seem to relish the evidence of our guiltiest remorse? Like when she visited May jest yesterdee on Airy Rock, bringin her some strawberries she knew the willful girl would vomit noways, n when the girl told her she was a Darwinist after she tried to get her to pray with her, she said: *What, May, you wanna live like ole dang Jane Goodall with a bunch of smelly apes?* n the lil witch fired back: *Be bettern livin with our family.*

Why, that just about clove Emma's heart in two.

She considers mentionin to Little J the legend of Frank's incinerated whiskers so as to lighten the mood a lil, but then decides to let sleepin dogs lie (or die?), seein as how her daddy only suffered addiction problems more dark (that accursed generational sin!), n she recollects the only thing her husband ever said kind about her daddy, n this in regard to May's askin one night over supper how Frank had contacted HIV after she took a sex-ed class Emma had not approved, though the fresh lil brat was already quite the forge-artist—

Well, you know Frank, J answered (though May didnt, obviously), so Emma set down her cutlery n cleared her throat, castin a nervous eye on her daughter n son whose shiny cheeks were stuffed with okra. *It's not like he was queer or nuthin, he jes couldnt stop havin sex.*

Not that Little J's addiction problems were parallel in *that* regard, though Emma figures (LORD how she wishes she didn't!) he has his own struggles with *that* abusive demon n not jes booze, her havin spied on accident the undeleted history on the internet browser which shows how many hours he's spent in their study since acomin home from Ginny Tech with a screen awash with sordid filth so when he's asleep he must dream of nuthin but buckets of dead fish n naked women frothed in slime—simply awful to think! But how were their children to respect *anythin* when her husband's wicked tongue was always twistin *everthin* up?

Well, tomorrow is Sunday, she says, so Ah'm agoin ta church. You are more than welcome to join me. Brother Jimmy, the new preacher, he's real smart—he went to Tech like you n is purty young. Yall would git along fine. He plays soccer n the fiddle too. Folks say New Day Baptist is ablossomin under his fresh guidance.

Ah dont think so.

Ah'm visitin yer sister afterward too. She'd like to see you.

Well, he says with a sigh as he flops back on his bed. Maybe Ah'll come.

Alright. Emma holds the doorknob in her hand, pausin.

Ah'm here if you need me, son, she says, her eyes misty again. If you'd like, we can pray.

Ah dont think so.

Alright.

She steps out to leave him to his solitude but hears suddenly in an urgent whisper: *Mom?*

Yes? she opens the door again n smiles at him bright as she knows how.

Did Dad date Aunt Cissy fore he married you?

Her smile freezes.

Well, yes, she says. Why? Did Cecilia tell you that?

No. Hog did.

Well, she says. She nods n presses her lips together thoughtfully.

That was back in high school, she says after a moment. Aunt Cissy n yer daddy were in the same grade. How we met, actually. Anyhow, that's ancient history. Jest one of those funny facts of life—it bein such a long n windin road n all.

Yeah. Real long n windin like.

Emma closes the door to walk back down the stairs toward the kitchen, her mind like a hive of waspers abuzzin up a warpath. Why was she so mad?—that wasn't like her! To distract herself, she commences to wash several dishes in the sink fore she sees her hands are tremblin so she inserts the last dish in the rack n closes her eyes, reckonin *Ah'm agittin more heted about this than Ah should, why Dear God should such things even matter, bein over thirty years gone?* but sometimes she feels she must protect her children from *everthang*, knowledge itself always vergin on sin, it seemed, n of course she also reckons Cecilia has always been jealous she ended up with J while she got stuck with dumb ole Roy, fer at least *her* husband runs his daddy's ole business even though sometimes he's meaner than Mr. Mustard n hires hitmen to kill endangered critters, 'cause at least he supports his wife and kids unlike Roy who is nuthin but a dang drunk.

But why should that make *me* upset? she wonders.

Could it be, dear Jesus, Ah myself am jealous of Cissy bein with *him?* *Still?*

Well, nary tis the main point, fer likely Laz jes saw some old photos of J n Cissy at the racetrack all young with long hair both holdin each other in front of one of those lil Sprites J used to race up that track on the mountain where they shot that movie about the Cherokee nation. But if Little J is not paranoid already, this sure won't help—*that* is the main point, she tells herself, her children's mental wellbein—fer she recollects how when Little J got back from Airy Rock he appeared to be gittin better at first till she found him in the attic one evenin bent over Big J's daddy's ole books, one of em bearin the silliest puttin-on-airs title, something like *Commentary on Morals and Dogma of the Ancient Accepted Rites of Scottish Freemasonry* or somesuch bunkum about as sensible as those Catholic rituals she knows are nuthin but the devisin of fiends to create confusion n lead people astray from a true-to-life relationship with Christ Our LORD, fer truly when she bent to look at the pages in that book her son stared at in the attic she saw a drawing of an Egyptian beetle jes alookin like the one freakishly wormed its way in his ear while he was stark mad on booze (which May identified as a *scarabaidae*), n her boy tapped that pagan symbol with his finger n said: Mom, Ah've seen stuff like this on the World-Wide-Web. Ah think they are remote neurally moniterin me.

Say what?

Mom Ah think that bug was an Illuminati plant. Ah think they are readin my thoughts.

Suddenly her Lhasa Apsa Mr. Bojangles (Bo-Bo fer short) begins to bark in the front hall, jes yappin it up like a lil beast n sayin in dogspeak (which Emma understands perfectly) *Strangers, Mommy! Here come strangers!* n at the same time trucklights wash into the window above the kitchensink so she winces n blinks, lookin up to see a beatup old pickup-truck pullin in their driveway, n she sees too her husband's been settin out on the porch with his lil internet device, likely lookin at truck routes fer his truckers or checkin tomorrow's orders fer his riggers, puttin his stubborn mulishness back into his work.

Loomis Shank, a tall lanky blonde boy n shady-tree pestman, steps out the truck to shake J's hand. They converse in muted tones, conjurin up conspiracies to assassinate the beavers, fer likely this time Loomis'll jes shoot n bury em somewheres since none of his more so-called peaceful methods have worked thus far. At least May Pearl aint here to see this sad scene, Emma reckons. She watches as Loomis pulls out a packet of Skoal n packs it fore pullin out a wad of tobacco to shove in his front lip. Her face wrinkles with disgust as he commence to squirt juice out his mouth onto her flower garden, jes spitting freely like some foul fountain atop her yeller rhododendrons n pink bloomin bleedin hearts which bear her most cherished blossoms this time of year.

Let me git em, Mommy! Bo-Bo keeps barkin, so she goes n hushes him. She bends to straighten his pink bowtie atop his furry face n then lead him into their bedroom. Seein how she is already in her nightgown, she glances at herself in the mirror, wonderin jes what happened to her looks, then slips in bed n allows Bo-Bo to hop up n rest atop the blanket betwixt her legs. She considers flippin on the television but decides against it, figurin as she does that J will come in fore much longer— his stern orders of execution handed down—n git in bed beside her to watch his Hitler documentaries on the History Channel, a ritual he has observed so long she finds it hard to believe he has not seen em all by now. LORD knows those fascists loved their spectacles, but how much new footage n propaganda film could they possibly unearth? As if watchin bombers in black n white drop payloads on unexpectin citizens or studyin the faces of concentration camp victims lookin holloweyed n ghostly from behind barbed wire was the best way to relax the mind fore slippin into dreams!

She glances at her bedside table, where she sees settin there in its usual place her Ryrie Study Bible (which contains, tucked in at Corinthians 13 unknown to anyone but she, a photograph of her ultrasound of Natalie at eighteen weeks) n atop that another slimmer, glossier volume about Josephine, Napoleon's first wife, n all the roses n violets she helped to cultivate n spread across Europe. Fer while Emma is familiar with her husband's appreciation fer the Corsican upstart (which is why she bought him that paperweight he keeps in his office), she herself tends to sympathize with Josephine more in their toxic (but royal!) romance, n while Emma would never cheat on her own husband—bein a right godfearin woman an no Catholic whore neither—nevertheless Napoleon always struck her as nuthin more than a cold n administrative lil toad.

She hears the front door close down the hallway. All at once Bo-Bo raises up his cute lil nose to bark suspiciously, *Who's that, Mommy?* She holds the book on Josephine's garden open to study a picture of gorgeous hybrid roses, the whole while reckonin what will happen next. J will enter, likely share a few vulgar witticisms about their son—now that he's in a cheerful mood after orderin his beaver hit—n then he'll go in the bathroom n urinate louder than a horse while brushin his teeth at the same time. Certainly he will kick Bo-Bo out of the bed (who will growl n rustle out to the living room to sleep on the couch) n then most certainly he will watch a good forty minutes of his mindless war documentaries. If she is lucky, he'll be tired n shove off right afterward, but if not he'll prod her with his lil pickle n git her to roll over fer a quick bump or two, though she'll certainly comply, n with a strange n sad tenderness, too, tryin hard not to think on these lofty visions of heaven that haunt her so, n them her folks here down below still so very far beneath. ❧

Goodnight, Moon

V. Hansmann

The storm blew itself out before dawn. There had been no sleeping through it, so around six o'clock, you decided to go in search of a coffee truck. A cup of hot coffee would distract and reassure. Enterprising New Yorkers would never let a little rain deter them, you thought. Surely there was commerce in caffeine and crullers. So, armed with an umbrella and a heavy little LED flashlight, you opened the door to the stairs.

The cold, blue puncture of its beam made the darkness even darker. The watery incandescence of an old failing flashlight would have assuaged, but the harsh light only compounded the trepidation. You took a breath, clicked it off, and slipped it into your pocket. Reaching out your hand, the measure of the stairwell felt familiar, the banister and the tread. Nevertheless, the descent was black on black on black and full of the suction of foreboding.

A branch from the nearby locust tree blocked the front door, a tangled obstacle to toss aside. Spattered across the sidewalk, its leaves winked like ghostly thumbprints, then vanished. The wind had moved on; the blackness in its wake was dense as tar, but the air felt thin and tattered.

The only illumination came from the headlights of the occasional automobile and a posse of police cars on slow patrol. It was impossible to discern much of anything. A person coming toward you could be detected only if they moved in front of a light source. Specters. Your eyes were as dilated as they could possibly be. The shimmer of obsidian wetness threw distortion like mylar confetti. Such discombobulation was thrilling.

Looking north up Broadway, the crown of the Chrysler Building radiated perfect consolation through a diffusion of ambient orange light, while downtown, a few unidentifiable buildings merely glowed. The two NYU towers that housed faculty shone brightly, while the third one of the set, home to people of low to moderate income, stood lifeless.

Along Astor Place, a formation of massive shapes hulked like military vehicles in mute readiness. You could not get a fix on their true dimensions or purpose, or read the writing on their sides, but after a few moments the details coalesced—a convoy of street sweepers.

You turned right down Lafayette Street and walked beneath an arcade of scaffolding. Hugging the foot of a building, a long row of large, soft humps. After a hiccup of speculation, they became human habitation. Weathering an elemental assault like this with no real roof overhead seemed incomprehensible, and on you went.

The atmosphere shifted from infinite night to denatured day. To the east, in the bleak undercarriage of the sky, a seam of the palest blue opened over the Puck Building. There was no coffee, nor had the world ended. You put your key in the lock and trudged the four flights to home. From your window, you beheld people out and about conducting due diligence on their new day. The walkers of dogs took care of the basics. Your apartment was on the fifth floor corner above the intersection of Bleecker and Lafayette. Mulberry Street terminated there as well, creating a lively five-corners juncture. The Lexington Avenue subway ordinarily stopped at the corner, but service had ceased twelve hours prior. Yellow hazard tape blocked the entrance stairs.

The coffee imperative reasserted itself. Every morning, without fail, you brewed a pot to start your day. Down to the street again, only this time turning west, you reconnoitered Bleecker to Sixth Avenue. Nothing. On the way home, you noticed people milling outside a darkened bodega. Peering in revealed the availability of hot water and fried egg sandwiches. Their gas was working. You filled a large paper cup with hot water, which they waved away graciously, walked it home, and coaxed some Earl Grey into being. That, and a blueberry scone, felt like a reprieve of some kind.

You managed to make a couple of cell phone calls on that last foray. Reception was nearly hopeless, but you reached your parents, who somehow maintained you would soon appear on their New Jersey doorstep. "We're the only street in the whole town with electricity!" said your mother, "I'll make up your room." "I'd have to walk," you said. They're very old and it's a recurrent formality to disabuse them of cockamamie notions like this.

Clearly, downtown was kaput. But it was unclear just how far north one had to travel for life to resume. You recalled the night's telltale atmospheric sheen and hazarded a guess.

After teatime, it was naptime. You had not really slept during the hurricane. Something had wrenched loose at the construction site across the street, causing sonic booms from wildly flapping sheet metal.

Sometime before noon, you awoke to knocking at the door. The family from the floor above, returning from their first trip outside, inquired as to your wellbeing but bore no real news. That started you thinking like a Boy Scout: what could be done with the materials at hand? On one trip home to New Jersey, your mother had forced you to take an old transistor radio.

"Here, Bob, you never know."

You knew.

Never.

You took it anyway, because it was a 60s artifact in a leather carrying case with dials and a telescoping antenna. And because acceptance was always the most effective tactic with your mother and the onslaught of her benevolence. You recalled where you'd put the thing, which bureau, but not which drawer. Several remotes had to be cannibalized for batteries. Static, and suddenly—news. Chatter from distant precincts.

Lunch! Food will restore tattered equilibrium. You rescued two cooked chicken breasts from the fridge. A potential sandwich. Daringly, you swiped some mayonnaise across two slices of rye, but really, it would have tasted so much better on toast.

Somewhat later, more knocking.

What the fuck!

"It's Greg," said Greg from the stairs. You opened the door with a grin, "How the fuck did you get in the building?" "I have keys," he said. Of course. That's what neighbors are for.

You offered him a Diet Coke, chilled with the last of the ice, and the two of you sat and gabbed about this and that: the huge fire at Breezy Point, the extent of the power outage up to 34th Street, and the massive storm surge that had overcome the East Village and Chelsea to the west. Soon he left. He had a dog to walk.

The remainder of the afternoon you spent fussing—trying to organize stuff, trying to read, trying to conjure up cell phone reception. Finally, you found a spot, a random, susceptible location where, if crouching, you could hold a weak signal. You got in touch with your folks again, reiterating the impossibility of trekking to Jersey and spoke with both daughters and your ex-wife, who's in Connecticut without power for the third time in a little over a year.

Daylight fades from the room.

It's a quarter to eight. Candlelight and a concerto grosso from the transistor enfolds you. The turbulence has passed; the rain and wind, the confusion and anxiety, and the dissociation that comes with calamity. Soon we will know what exactly happened. You step to the window and look out at other candles flickering across the street, catching a glimpse of the devil moon as it ducks behind a flying scrim of clouds. There, sailing above the warm, glowing rooms of others, the implacable planetoid that had pulled tumult over the city's seawalls and into its tunnels, exploding transformers, and drawing this blanket of black velvet silence over your neighborhood. ❧

THE LEARNING TREE by Gordon Parks
Katherine Karlin

When *The Learning Tree* was published, in 1963, its author, Gordon Parks, was already a famous photographer; his pictorial essays for *Life* magazine humanized his African-American subjects in the context of the early Civil Rights movement, and he was fashion lensman of choice for Chanel and Dior. *The Learning Tree* was Parks's first work of fiction, and the significance of its publication coinciding with the historic March on Washington was probably not lost on the author, who drew from his experience of growing up black in 1920s southeast Kansas for his coming-of-age story. Parks, who died in 2006 at the age of ninety-three, was yet to enjoy even greater successes—as a chronicler of the Black Power movement, the portraitist of his good friend Muhammad Ali, and the director of the 1971 Blaxploitation hit, "Shaft." In fact, "Shaft" was his second movie; in 1969, he adapted his own book, *The Learning Tree*, shot on location in Kansas—it was the first Hollywood studio film to be directed by an African-American, a distinction that has faded as fast as the movie's sun-drenched Technicolor palette.

The moment of *The Learning Tree*'s appearance is best appreciated, though, if you read the book in response to the cultural juggernaut of *To Kill a Mockingbird*. Harper Lee's novel came out in 1960, the classic film two years later; there's no question that Parks was writing *The Learning Tree* as the nation was under the formidable spell of Atticus Finch. You can see it in the very structure of the story. Like *Mockingbird*, Parks's novel has at its center a feisty young protagonist, Newt Winger—a sensitive, highly intelligent boy (he is twelve when the book opens, nearly sixteen at the end) whose imagination extends beyond his hometown of Cherokee Flats, based on Fort Scott, where Parks grew up. *The Learning Tree* reaches its climax with a dramatic courtroom scene that echoes the prosecution of Lee's Tom Robbins. And, of course, *The Learning Tree* is underpinned by the historical complications of race relations.

The key difference, of course, is that *The Learning Tree* is about black people, who play, at best, a functional role in *To Kill a Mockingbird*. And while Tom Robbins and the loyal Finch maid Calpurnia must bear the burden of representing their race, Parks's diverse cast of characters show the range of black experience, from the inquisitive Newt to his hard-working parents, Jack and Sarah, his aspirational girlfriend, Arcella, and the vicious town drunk, Booker Savage. Encompassing a village, Parks does not always succeed in avoiding stock personalities, like the lip-licking pastor who happens to show up at suppertime, or Newt's gang of interchangeably mischievous scamps. Yet there is genuine empathy in the depiction of Newt's nemesis, the drunk's hardened son, Marcus Savage, who is raised in conditions barely better than those of the Wingers' livestock. We also get a glimpse at Newt's light-skinned cousin, who must decide whether she will pass as white, and a fleeting mention of a tormented gay man which, while not exactly probing, is certainly not dismissive, and speaks to the breadth of Parks's photographic eye.

The Learning Tree departs from the *Mockingbird* narrative, too, in that it is about Kansas rather than the south; indeed, it's a story that could unfold only in Kansas. (Parks's decision to open both novel and movie with a scene of a destructive twister yokes his story to yet another beloved classic.) Freed blacks settled in Kansas after the upending of Reconstruction in the late 1870s, reasonably expecting that a state founded on the very tenets of anti-slavery, that was ground zero for the Civil War, would offer sanctuary from the organized vigilantism of the Ku Klux Klan. In the rural southeast portion of the state, black farmers purchased land with the hopes of a peaceable existence, the state borders buttressing them from the rabidly pro-slavery traditions of Missouri to the east, and the lawlessness of the Oklahoma Territory to the south. To say these hopes were dashed is to reduce the byzantine history of race relations in Kansas, nuances that Parks appreciates all too well. Early in the novel, after the twister cuts its swath of ruin, Newt's father climbs to the roof of the A.M.E. Church to repair its dislodged steeple. From this bird's eye view, Parks describes, in his sharply visual prose, Jack's panoramic view of Cherokee Flats:

> The stone courthouse and jail (squatting smugly, medieval-castlelike, in the square) stood out strong and unscathed in the bright Saturday morning sun. But the secondary business area, lying a block to the west behind it, had suffered the brunt of the storm. Talbot's harness shop was flat on the ground, its crushed sides jutting out from under the broken roof. Comstock's store front, peeping from beneath two huge maple trees, sagged, cock-eyed and windowless, against nine two-by-fours. Blake's general store, Davis' bakery, Carson's drugstore, Sam Wong's laundry, Mack's hamburger shack, snuggling together when the storm struck, were now hopelessly tangled in a half-block pile of crumpled roofs and smashed walls. Sam, the village's only Chinese citizen, was dead somewhere in the rubble of broken bottles, shattered plaster, torn clothes, spoiled hamburger and baking dough, pots, pans, hardware, ladies' accessories, and such.

As Jack surveys the situation, he reflects on Kansas's peculiar brand of racism. He "had mixed feelings about this place. Like all other Kansas towns, Cherokee Flats wallowed in the social complexities of a borderline state. Here, for the black man, freedom loosed one hand while custom restrained the other." The contradictions of Kansas racial politics are registered not only in one small town but within individual characters: we see Newt's classmate Waldo in one scene bravely defending Newt's right to service in a drug store, and then casually calling his cousin "a nigger" in the next. Newt's mother works for the town judge, who is liberal-minded and generous, but who never lets Sarah forget that she is his servant.

Whereas *Mockingbird* gives its readers, presumably enlightened white people, the opportunity to feel superior to Depression-era southerners, *The Learning Tree* affords no such distance; the binaries of racist versus non-racist are not all that polarized. Moreover, it has at its center no heroic white savior, no Atticus Finch. If anyone inhabits the role of hero, it's Newt's indomitable mother, Sarah Winger. Any fan of "Shaft" will tell you that Parks is not the subtlest delineator of female characters, but he has created in Sarah perhaps his most admirable woman. With a couple of scenes deleted, she might have been reduced to an archetypal matriarch, holding the family together at all costs. But we also see her leading a fight to integrate the schools, questioning her faith, and briefly recalling both the rape she survived and the lynching of her brother. It is Sarah who encourages Newt's intellectual curiosity and artistic impulses, and it is she who speaks the title words, extolling the hidden benefits of Cherokee Flats.

The Learning Tree is not a rebuke to Harper Lee's classic. Rather, I think it's an attempt at a discussion, a gentle reminder that those who suffer have voices, too. And it is an astonishingly complete survey of a community that history has forgotten, for all its paradoxes. (Interestingly, the dramatist William Inge, the bard of Kansas, was born a year after Parks and grew up in the same corner of the state, but his sociologically astute plays manage to erase the black population.) As *To Kill a Mockingbird* goes into its bazillionth printing, *The Learning Tree* has tumbled into obscurity. It is in print. You can order the Fawcett paperback, the only version available, and I urge you to do so. But as soon as you get it, crack the spine with your elbow so you can read the text at the micro-margined gutter, and keep the book out of the humidity so the cheap paper doesn't disintegrate. This book deserves better. ❧

Our Town

Wesley Rothman

for Sabato Rodia and his Watts Towers

In our town, our small city, sunken precinct, shots
do not ring. In our phantom kingdom, shots are not

speedy lead bells. Every chapel of the Southland
chimes at noon on Sunday. Bell towers jangle

one another from Gardena and Bellflower,
Compton and South Gate, jolting the haze—

this cathedral city's vaulted ceiling—raising
prayers like skyscrapers, one beam at a time.

In our town, faith is the heat that hovers
over asphalt, thin and scorching. And here,

in our town, the toll of shootouts volleyed
at dusk, dust shaken from roof shingles

and the tiers of these towers, shaken
by sirens, volleyed by warriors, this toll

is the blueprint of society. Cops and bangers.
Bang! Bang! Bang! bumps blood of the curb

and flesh of the street. Every block is Holy.
A hammer falls. Shoutouts and fingers fly,

inscribe a prayer in the air before hands dive
deep into pockets, into the Holy water

of a brother's open ribcage, a baptismal font
of terror. The rhythms drive by. Noon, night,

then never again, we wake to build ourselves
a Holy house, we bind and build the towers.

Sinnerman

Wesley Rothman

I can gas a mile in the time
it takes Nina to run down a sinner.

Down to the dark tides
of deep notes, she calls up

cacophony to stun
her suspect, the totaled conscience

wrapped around a tree, that tree
branching veins of memory. The future

stolen by the sinner, plucked
like a gleaming ruby. Running from the siren

of her voice, back pocket bulging with red,
with easy riches. The sinner murders choices

in the street, and I'm praying at the fat base
of the memory-holding oak. I'm rapt

by prayer, its desperate whisper.
No whisper or faith will fell the tree

so I run. If I can run the rock right up
and over the hill I can keep on running,

running down another possible me. Chasing
the me that knows a thing or three

about redemption, about breaking less
of the world. But the rock runs me back

to this busted up belief: I come
from where I come from

not anywhere else. How can that mean anything
for redemption? I'm bent around a tree

that only the jaws of death can wrench
away from me. And I run to the river

pockets full of rocks.
In the current I ask the rocks

to keep me still. Still the whispers, still
the roaring waters, the piano crashing,

and sirens in the cathedrals
of my ears. The power of doubt

and the glory of sound run me down
as I run, run, and run. They prop up a dark kingdom

where I'm the king and the jester, the preacher
and the rundown sinner.

The Pass
John O'Connor

The defining moment of my adolescence came during a junior high school gym class when I pirated a behind-the-head-no-look-pass from a basketball prodigy named Eric Portis. The pass was an upgraded version of the behind-the-back-no-look-pass, with radically diminished accuracy. It was just one weapon in an arsenal that Eric Portis used to demoralize lesser players like myself, including a hypnotic crossover, a torrential three-pointer, a fifteen-foot rainbow floater, and even—again, this was *junior high school*—an occasional fingertip dunk. Only the behind-the-head-no-look-pass, however, belonged to Eric Portis. As far as we knew, he had invented it, so he held the copyright, and it was not for sale. Were one of us to attempt it, it would've been like Kurt Rambis dishing Magic Johnson's patented no-look-ball-fake-pass on the break to James Worthy. That is, unimaginable.

I hadn't consciously planned to co-opt the behind-the-head-no-look-pass from Eric Portis.[1] In fact, until that very moment I hadn't dreamed I was remotely capable. Prior to the seventh grade I'd logged about four minutes on the basketball court, and it became instantly clear that I had no feel for the game. My father had press-ganged me early into baseball, and while I had no feel for that either, it accommodated failure far better than basketball. In the latter, as one of only five teammates on a congested, over-lit court, your incompetence is instantly forthcoming, which is why basketball is an apt metaphor for life: in few other realms do one's wilting self-image and bankrupt dreams converge with such swift and horrifying clarity. In baseball, it's possible to hide. You can pass entire games, I discovered, by melting into the outfield greenery, fading to a speck on the horizon, and hardly ever touching the ball. But that only works for so long, and although it nearly killed my dad, I switched to co-ed soccer. In the coddling, anesthetized world of the American Youth Soccer Organization (AYSO), you didn't need to hide at all because incompetence was not only tolerated but feverishly promoted (nobody liked a showoff in AYSO). Unfortunately AYSO's hippie ideology didn't apply to real life and didn't help me one lick in basketball.

What might've been a simple undertaking for others—a wide-open lay-up, for instance—became for me an unconquerable abstraction. It wasn't that I was uncoordinated. My body moved like it grasped the

---

[1] Charles Barkley has pointed out, rightly I think, that the premise of a "no-look" pass is disingenuous. After all, how can you pass to someone without *ever* having looked to see if they were there? But I'll stick to the nomenclature.

physics of the game. It was even said, to much head-scratching, that I *looked* like I could play. I could jump okay for a white kid, move laterally, was taller than most players. I possessed the basic machinery: eyes, hands, feet, etc. But the ball simply would not enter the basket. Whenever I drew near that contraption, something inside of me slackened. It was as if I entered a kind of dream-state where my mind was swept clean and I lost both my fundamental dexterity and my sense of where I was and what I was doing. I became claustrophobically transient, scurrying away from the basket, unable to make it register up close, taking cover wherever I could find it, wedged between a teammate and the sideline, say, or parked on the center circle, reddening with fear.

I had, in other words, right up until the moment I stole Eric Portis's move, no expectation of ever becoming a real athlete, let alone one capable of deploying a behind-the-head-no-look-pass, or reliably inbounding the ball for that matter. I figured I had about as much chance of duplicating the pass as I had of performing a vicious tomahawk dunk.

This was during Reagan's second term. Gym class at South Junior High School in Kalamazoo, Michigan began with twenty minutes of "open gym," which for boys meant full-court, five-on-five basketball. It was a crucial social arbiter at South, where notions of cool, at least for pasty white boys like myself, were defined by the black kids. Sucking at basketball—not exclusively but especially for whites—torpedoed your stock to near-unrecoverable depths. Some days we ran full-court the entire class hour. You had no choice in the matter. Good or bad, mutant athlete or hopeless freak, unless you were a girl, you played.[2] This was a radical departure from elementary school gym, where we had played kickball and four-square and capture the flag—indulgent, ego-bolstering games in which everyone had a role and individual success was minimized. Basketball, by contrast, was trench warfare. After games, I was shell-shocked, stumbling through the halls muttering to myself, textbooks clutched to my chest in cold, white hands, fingernails chomped to bits.

The thing was, I loved the game. It was the Bad Boys era in Detroit, with Isiah Thomas and Bill Lambeer and Vinnie "The Microwave" Johnson and Dennis Rodman before he went off the rails. Rick Mahorn, the Pistons' bruising power forward, was in my mind the greatest man who'd ever lived. And the ruthless accountability of the sport appealed to my budding Hobbesian: with nowhere to hide, you either performed or you forfeited your right to exist. Competence was the leveler. Without it, you

---

2 *The girls' and boys' sides of the gym were separated by an accordion-like partition that was maybe two-stories high. I don't know how, ten years after Title IX, a public school class could be segregated by gender, but it was, and the girls were yoked to the iron-fisted reign of Mrs. Washington, who oversaw a gruesome battery of calisthenics and rope-climbs.*

were irrelevant. The trouble was, I was on the wrong side of the divide. In this world, there are guys like me and guys like Eric Portis. The former are put here so the latter can achieve glory. Actually, we serve an undervalued role, for without us hacks there can be no heroes. But knowing this doesn't make our lives any easier. On the contrary, this kind of psychic forfeiture, I found, can exact an ugly toll.

    I felt myself to be carrying a burden sports-wise. My dad had been a decorated ball-field hero growing up in Indiana, a varsity letterman in basketball, baseball, and football. His trophies loitered in our basement storage area like a dusty shrine to athletic prowess. The centerpiece, "Best All-Around Athlete," won during his senior year, was a good three-inches taller than I was. During the summer between his sophomore and junior years, my dad had pitched for a semi-professional baseball team in Seminole, Texas, where his mother's family lived. He drove down from Bloomington to work on his uncle's cotton farm during the week and pitch nights and weekends in Lubbock, Amarillo, and Hobbs, New Mexico, freezing batters ten years older, men who worked in the oilfields or played college ball and drank themselves numb after games. My dad went on to pitch and play tailback on scholarship at Dartmouth; though, in a turn that ate at him deep into middle age, he failed to make the cut in basketball.

    As my Little League coach, his past glories sometimes reared-up in practice. Loping around on the mound, he'd unleash these meteors that yelped and slashed past my teammates as we took turns swatting at them, losing our bats in the trees. I remember once when he took his t-shirt off and the hair rose like smoke from his shoulders. Even at that distance you could see a crosshatched scar running along his left shoulder from clavicle to armpit, the remnant of a torn rotator cuff and botched surgery that had ruined his pitching arm. Eventually he'd ease up and let us hit. But I preferred to see him going full-tilt, with that crazy martial wind-up followed by the hard slap of ball in leather.

    My baseball career was brief and disgraceful. Had I not been the coach's son I wouldn't have lasted as long as I did. We played on meagerly watered fields out by the highway, with an outfield of low scrub mined with treacherous, career-ending divots, and an infield not much better. I tried catcher at first but proved inadequate to the task and was exiled to right field, where my skill as a backstop emerged. Not once but *thrice* I lost a fly ball on its descent—a feat which forever attached infamy to my name—and amidst the stunned, terrified hush of spectators, stood there shrugging in the sunlight as the ball crashed into my sternum and knocked me flailing to the ground. I was given a batting helmet to wear, which seemed extraordinarily cruel. Then I realized I could disappear for long stretches, quietly slipping beyond the range of batters, nearly to the parking lot, until my dad shouted at me to move back into position. If I concentrated, I could even will batters to hit the ball elsewhere, or shallow enough so that the second baseman could beat me to it. My poor father witnessed all of this. He never gave up on me, though. I loved him for that. He hoped I'd blossom into a real player, which might've been his greatest act of self-deception ever. I couldn't wait to be done with the game. I took it for two years, then quit with hardly a word passing between us. It must've been a blow when I started soccer. I knew in his secret heart he hated that game that had no danger or beauty in it. But he was at every match, pacing the sidelines.

Anyway, by junior high school I had come full-bore to the crushing realization of countless 12-year-olds: I wasn't cut out for sports. I wasn't just bad. I was toxic. Despite my pedigree, I was doomed to toil in the gravel-pit of inferiority, to endure the relentless, dispiriting subjection of the athletic underclass. And there was nothing I could do about it. There's a platitude about sports teaching youth the virtues of hard work and fair play, how "sportsmanship" rewards patience and resilience, instills respect for others, prepares one for life's trials, etc.

There might be some truth in that. But for most of us, most of the time, sports teach only bitterness and despair. The field of play isn't a proving ground of redemption or personal betterment. It's Hell. A dungeon of ritualized failure. A perverse laboratory where misery is splayed-out, dissected, microscoped, the results boxed and inventoried in the warehouse of self-loathing. What it teaches us is that there are times in life when you are nothing, when you are naked and useless, your body a mere toy for others' amusement. And that one of those times is gym class.

Our teacher, Coach Lipschultz, who naturally we called Shitlips, was a Vince Lombardi doppelgänger with a prominent gap-toothed overbite and several kaleidoscopic plaid trouser-tie ensembles. Much of the time he remained rooted to a crumbling swivel chair in his office, fiddling with a Rubik's Cube, which I never once saw him solve. For twenty minutes a day, we had the run of the gym.

Fourth period gym class at South Junior High in 1986 held a remarkable pool of basketball talent. There was Cedric "Snapper" Jones, whose nickname came from the sound the net made after his shot cracked through it; Darrell "Touché" Simms, as ruthless a twelve-year-old post-up man as there ever was, who also considered himself something of a wit; and Robert Taylor, a stick-thin African-American with a feathery moustache that he was very proud of, and who, nine years later, received two life sentences for a grisly double murder of local video store employees. But we knew Rob merely as a cunning mid-court tactician. (Perhaps an early sign of Rob's path came on Halloween that year, when he'd arrived to school dressed as J.R. Ewing from "Dallas" in a gray three-piece suit, cowboy boots, ten-gallon hat, and carrying a brown leather briefcase. This didn't sit well with the other black kids, some of whom rode Rob about it all day, until he finally snapped. I don't recall what happened, only that Rob was suspended and someone else carted off in an ambulance.)

Eric Portis was the best. His game was more complete, his style silkier, more pliant than everyone else's, and it seemed wholly his own as opposed to having been cribbed from some NBA idol. Portis was laboratory-engineered for the game, with hands large enough at age twelve to palm a basketball, shoulders like hillocks, the muscles announcing themselves in crests and vales across his back; he had a deceptively tall six-foot frame powered by some kind of ghost chemical. His 15-foot jumper—a lost art in today's game—was a miracle: time seemed to decelerate as he squared his feet and elbows, his body effortlessly triangulating with ball and basket to conquer Euclidean space. Sometimes, in the midst of this, he'd glance at his Swatch, as if incredibly bored. To top it off, he wore immaculate white leather high-tops with tubesocks yanked to his knees like Pistons' swingman Adrian Dantley, a sleeveless t-shirt, gold necklace, and a single earring of Christ on the Cross, all complimented by a neatly trimmed jericurl. He was my idealized basketball-self, minus the jericurl.

I practiced at home, shooting around in the driveway, watching shot after shot smash into the backboard and plop to the ground. I was too ashamed to tell my dad what was happening. Our baseball experiment was still warm, and besides, I was beyond help. We lived in a white middle-class neighborhood close to downtown, and our hoop was the only one on the block. An elm tree cast looping branches in front of it, harassing my shots. The driveway was a sloping grassy paddock broken here-and-there by little asphalt ranges, and depending on where I stood, the basket height could fluctuate by a foot, so shooting was essentially a parlor game. But I could play alone, without judgment.

In gym class there was marginal improvement, but it came in such excruciating, baby-step fashion that the minutest achievement seemed only to highlight other deficiencies. A small victory in-bounding the ball would be followed by an ill-considered jumper being emphatically swatted into the bleachers (and the postscript chorus of laughter). Then, impossibly, I got worse, regressing twelve years in spatial intelligence. The very sight of the basketball bewildered me. *What, mind you, is this sherbet-orb doing in my hands?* As I got worse, I got dangerous. Ineptness in basketball inevitably spawns the desperate man's recourse: ghastly, almost lethal fouls. I'll never forget the dying chimp-like yowl of Bill Baker as he writhed on the baseline clutching his mangled ankle, which came courtesy of a shove in the back I'd given him on a lay-up. He recovered, but never quite went to his left the same.

Things spiraled. I sulked and swore through games, launched one-handers down court, played sham defense, punted balls to the rafters. My most forbearing teammates began to glare at me, their former pity swinging towards hate.

It was no use. I was a sideshow. A peril to myself and others. A lost cause. So, after half a term of soul-rending humiliation, I quit. If I remember correctly, as I strolled off the court I made an emphatic hand-wiping gesture to signal the finality of it. My departure meant an odd number of players and the scourge of subs. But nobody tried to talk me out of it. They were relieved. I didn't blame them.

I was glad to be moving on. Retreating to Coach Shitlips' office, I assumed water-cooler duty and fiddled with the combinations to old padlocks while waiting for Christmas. Shitlips abided me as long as I was quiet, and since I wanted nothing more than to disappear, I happily obliged him.

It was a mild winter that year. Snow failed to materialize in the driveway, so I shot around some. Now and then my dad joined me. He and my mom were separated and he was living down the road in a new condo development, but sometimes he stayed with us. Dad was having a second-act as a marathoner and triathlete, traveling to races across the Midwest, giving himself over to it so intensely—running, cycling, and swimming nearly every day—that a scarf of loose skin hung around his neck. We'd trade shots, or he'd sit cross-legged in the yard with a beer, looking on as I rifled balls into the garage, disemboweling leaf bags leftover from the fall.

I had this driveway routine where I'd roll the ball off the roof and catch it and shoot, wait for the clang and clatter, then chase it down. My dad did the same, though he usually connected. Then one afternoon he started mortaring shots from the side yard, from out in the street, from behind my mom's Vanagon. At some point he lost the ball over the roof. He wasn't drinking heavily but there was a Coors in the grass. Our dog Brutus knocked it over and the suds bled into the ground. My dad drained what was left, rolled the ball off the roof, caught it, pivoted, and rainbowed it right back up there. On the way down it got stuck behind the basket. I poked it out with a rake.

"Nice one," I said.

He did the same thing on his next shot.

"You're heatin' up."

We kept shooting and missing. Eventually, by statistical decree, I had to connect. But that day I don't think I did. Not once. Even standing under the basket. Maybe I was trying to miss. My dad must have wondered. Brutus got a kick out of the rake-poke and went wild when the ball came down. It had slobber and grass all over it. Darkness was on us when I snatched the ball up and stared hard at it a moment. My dad waited, fingertips spidering. In that expanse of night the ball seemed a sudden absurdity, something that existed only as an instrument of luck, a flame of wild possibility that remained forever out of reach. I wound-up and punted it away. We watched it splash into the compost pile. I brought it back, stomping and swearing across the yard, wiped it off and handed it over. My dad looked at me, his face hidden in evening shadow. He seemed about to say something. I saw his hands, the nicotine-stained fingers, bare and fibrous, turning the ball over and over until the seams flowed into each other and I felt the beat of skin and leather inside of me like an invisible pump. Then, palming the ball Statue of Liberty-style, my dad rolled back on his heels, softly stutter-stepped, feinted, and swung the prettiest Kareem hook straight into the porch shrubbery.

I don't recall much else. But for some reason it was then that the value of the behind-the-head-no-look-pass dawned on me. In four months I'd seen Eric Portis pull it off maybe a half-dozen times, which meant it had about a five-percent success rate. Its virtue was also its principal failing: it tended to catch people off-guard, including the recipient, who occasionally received the pass with his face. The other 95% of the time it sailed out-of-bounds or pinged off a kneecap. It was the kind of play that drove coaches nuts, and among an older demographic Eric Portis would've been mercilessly ridiculed. But for us, the point of the pass wasn't its efficacy; the point was that it looked good. According to our fringe adolescent logic, successful execution was so fantastically improbable that failure didn't rest with the passer but rather with the fickle hand of Fate. The few times when Eric Portis *did* pull it off—in traffic, the ball shrieking through a thicket of limbs to its rabbit-eyed target—lived in our minds forever. Like all flashy plays, the-behind-the-head-no-look-pass was, at root, a psychic gambit calculated to stun, to disquiet, to augment legend. Whether or not it worked was an afterthought.

When winter break ended, I returned to Shitlips' office. Things continued, until one afternoon Mrs. Washington's shadow flooded the doorway. A large African-American whose polyester slacks contained porpoise-like thighs, Mrs. Washington had a way of moving her eyebrows that communicated the entire human emotional range, a kind of eyebrow sign language that was awesome to behold.

"What's this boy doing in here?" she said, an eyebrow crawling up one side of her forehead while the other crawled down. Shitlips and I gaped at one another.

"He's working," Shitlips said. I waved a padlock at her. Mrs. Washington's eyebrows executed an impressive figure eight.

"This isn't right, Bernard. He should be out there playing."

Shitlips chewed on this. He swiveled towards me, shrugged, and set down his Rubik's Cube. Rising, he slunk around the desk and gently seized me by the forearm, hoisted me up, and to my horror, shoved me out the door. I stood there a moment blinking as the sneaker-and-wood squeak of a game drifted over. When I glanced back at Shitlips, he was in his chair, his head slumped to one side, staring at his hands while Mrs. Washington said something to him. I went and parked myself on the bleachers, glowering at Mrs. Washington, shooting cancer-daggers into her meddlesome heart. Eventually I got bored and joined a game. Nobody said a word. It was like I'd never left.

Except that as soon as I stepped onto the court something was different. Tiny pockets of energy suddenly resided in the soles of my Keds. I felt lighter, less shambling than I'd been before, like a hand was pushing me from behind. The ball, that dumb orange Spalding, which had always been unwieldy, molded easily to my palms. Without anyone telling me, I realized the importance of creating space for myself to shoot, and I saw the ball going through the net before I released it. More incredibly, my tunnel vision faded and my claustrophobia disengaged. Things appeared as they never had. I knew with shocking clarity where to go, what to expect. An alien sensation—confidence?—crashed over me. In an instant, my conception of the world and my place in it shifted. I was a new person, unrecognizable from my former self.

I can't explain it. Perhaps it was osmosis or a dormant synapse was sent firing, or all of that headlong fear and torment finally popped and my ego put its foot down. I suppose this might be called "learning." But it was more than that. I'm talking about wholesale psychic transfiguration, a seismic realignment of brainwave tectonics that allowed me to see and feel what I hadn't before, so that what had been static and immovable in me became fluid, variable, alive.

Whatever the reason, things started to click. Before I knew what was happening, I'd scored eight points, equal to my previous semester's total. I'd also picked Snapper's pocket and flown out-of-bounds for an errant pass. I ended one series with a menacing post-move: Rob Taylor was on my back like a marmot when I spun and floated a hook-shot into the supple, beckoning net—payback for an earlier play when Rob had given me a mouthful of forehead on a ferocious drive.

Then, without thinking, I unfurled the behind-the-head-no-look-pass. It began innocently. After receiving the ball at the top of the key, I dribbled left, was stonewalled, backpedaled, and went right as the defense collapsed around me. Out of ideas, I glanced to my right, closed my eyes, and with my right hand, hooked the ball behind my head, zinging it left. Nobody saw it coming. The ball whizzed past a half-a-dozen noggins and slapped into the chest of a teammate hibernating in three-point land. When he realized what had happened, he lined up and snapped one home.

Everyone froze. Eric Portis was my teammate that day. He shot me a look. I'd made a huge error, it seemed to say. A rule had been broken, unspoken etiquette transgressed. For which payment would be dear.

Inexplicably, his face broke into a grin.

"Nice pass," he said. As we turned and trotted down the court, he raised his palm and—Oh, sweet joy!—high-fived me. Things were never the same.

I said earlier that guys like me and guys like Eric Portis occupy two complimentary sides of the athletic rift. I should've mentioned a third way: mediocrity. Some of us, contrary to the natural order of things, through pure luck or synaptic reshuffle or remembered past-life or I don't know what, end up here. It's not the hokum that coaches and sideline orators spew—triumph over adversity and so on. It's an accident. That's all. Though perhaps one that makes it easier to crawl out of bed in the morning.

To be sure, my game was still full of holes: unpardonable turnovers, defensive meltdowns. But I could compete. I had passable defense, a semi-reliable jumper, an intuitive sense for the game. For a while, I could hardly keep from smiling. I figured I'd have to contend with Eric Portis for possession of the behind-the-head-no-look-pass, but he soon dropped it from his repertoire, so I inserted it into mine. I didn't rely on it too often, lest an astute defender catch on. It failed more often than not, but I used it to perfection a handful of times and on each occasion it ratcheted-up my status a notch. The fact that I'd stolen it from Eric Portis was forgotten, as were the circumstances of my hasty erudition.

When I explained all of this to my dad, I didn't think he believed me. "Why didn't you say something?" he asked.

How do you say, it was like a dream, everything was far-off and murky, as if I were seeing it from the top of the stairs, until I wasn't?

This was my final burst of accelerated development. Some days it seems to me like I've never improved at anything else. Like I've been coasting ever since. I'm forty. How embarrassing would it be at my age to aspire to more when you've proven that second-rate is the best you can do?

Years later I bumped into Eric Portis, selling popcorn at a movie theater in Kalamazoo, his jericurl replaced by a crisp flat-top, the crucifixion earring by a diamond stud. We talked about Rob Taylor, who was in prison down the road in Jackson. How crazy was that? Eric mentioned a pickup game I should come play in, which we both knew wasn't going to happen, but it was nice to think about.

It was around then that my dad injured his foot while running, a repetitive stress fracture that never seemed to heal. His second wife had left him and he was living alone in a big house on Lake Michigan with an

Post Road **Nonfiction** | 167

enormous stretch of grass. He moved onto the couch, forged a spiritual acquaintance with Johnny Walker Red, and swelled several pant sizes. His face went limp and pink. He came down with what he thought was the stomach flu and was so numbed by Scotch that it took a few days before he realized it was bigger than that. I was living in New York. One night my sister Katie called to say that dad's appendix had burst. Apparently it'd been a close call. He bounced back pretty quick, but he quit the triathlon/marathon business cold turkey. Hasn't run a mile since. Or touched the booze. I've talked to my dad about this. Maybe it's grief or maybe it's fatigue. You want to carry it inside of you, to continue to see clearly in the real world, the old voices from that dry West Texas town fanning your blood's desire. But once it turns off, it can't be reclaimed. No matter what direction you've chosen it can lead straight to the heart of regret, though you keep going on with things, dreaming and learning, waiting for another epiphany to strike the confusion from your life. ❧

Glenn Gould

Wang Jiaxin (translated by Diana Shi & George O'Connell)

A pair of hands invisibly
touch the keyboard, and slowly
you step into Canada's knee-deep snows.
I'm listening: is this still the vast winter day of North America?
No, the scope of silence itself, the music
peacefully rising, entering my body
the moment it stops for breath.
This is the rhythm
set by your trek, each step
longer than a man's life. This the song
to ears inaudible; only the skull can hear.
A murmur rolling toward us,
played by you, irresistible,
carried off on the fitful shadows of these notes.
Between us, an immense sheet of snow outstretched;
on the scores, your scrawls illegible.

Back from a noisy party, I think of you
in the deepest solitude, not ready yet
to listen. Jammed on a Beijing bus,
or standing forever in a foreign twilight,
wanting to go home,
not knowing how,
you come to me. Who can say
what music's sought me always?
I hold back, knowing what took you
in the end takes me. Not ready
for death, I hold back as you did,
my angel on its stool, counting silence,
yet still I'm ecstatic, loving life
yet alone. Now that I sit
at last in darkness, is it you there
playing Bach's fugue—

yes, no, yes,
yes, no.
Such moments startle me,
as if someone uttered "hush"
while the piano's black bird vanishes, you vanish,
the road to winter vanishes.
This in the end is the music I hear,
arriving like gray hair, or a child born at dawn.
This is winter's vault, rising in magnificence,
a mother's love sculpting fog in bitter cold,
a landscape glimpsed en route to the sea and a dead volcano,
the story that begins after all stories end.
This is the pulse of joy,
the forehead burnished by death.
This is the endless telling—you find at last
the one to whom you'll speak.
This is hymn, in silence the song
loud and resonant,
how I enter a future suddenly broad, open,
crossing the deep snows of time.

Winter, 1997, Stuttgart

Meeting Rain, Wutai Mountain

Wang Jiaxin (translated by Diana Shi & George O'Connell)

After five hundred *li* of dusty road,
we drove through a red canyon
as thunder boomed over the mountain,
rain right on our heels.

Mist rose,
the mountaintop temple veiled in the shower.
It came so indulgently, luxuriously,
my teeth chattered.
I recall my parched thirst on the way,
and later, the strange wooden fish in the monk's hand,
in my dreams a rush
of streaming water.

Awake, last night's fruit pits tossed out the window
already beaten into muddy earth.
Rain clears, the day's trees,
the rocks, the temple shining.
Then morning's windchime,
and across the mountain slope,
a drift of chanted sutras.

An Altered Book by Cara Barer
Alexandra Chasin

Although it has no visible story, characters, setting, premise—no beginning or end—and not even any legible language, Cara Barer's *PDR is* a book. As such, I recommend it. *PDR* is a book about books, no matter what else it is, or used to be, about. It is a paradigmatic example of a contemporary trend toward "altered books." Like other altered books, *PDR* is a piece of sculpture. It is also a photograph. Magritte's famous painting of a sentence about a pipe asserts that the sentence is not a pipe, and neither is the accompanying picture; conversely, the word, the picture, and the idea of pipe suggest that all three *are* pipes (or the negation would make no sense). Likewise, *PDR* suggests that a book may be many things in addition to being a book.

Like a book, *PDR* works symbolically, through visual and material modes, re-presenting abstract ideas (or *meaning*) as well as embodying physical principles and enacting social values. Also like a book, *PDR* is three-dimensional and designed to be apprehended through visual more often than auditory and tactile senses. But Barer's book complicates the issue, calling attention to the materiality of books, their physicality, objectness, manipulability—qualities that inhere in all books—though we rarely speak of Literature in these terms. With Literature, you can't tell a book by its cover; with books, the cover is the thing itself.

Like Literature, Barer's photograph presents itself as Art, demonstrating that books function differently in different contexts. The book's new state as a work of art is clear in its framing by the artist, including her description of her work, but also her rendering of the re-presented book in the idiom of art photography, its exhibition in galleries, etc. The location of the object, its value, the way people talk about it, all of these situate Cara Barer's altered books, as well as her photographs of them, as art objects.

As an art object, *PDR* strips the literary values out of the book partly by making it impossible to read as written and published. Conventionally, Literature transcends the book form—after all, no ideas could have been harmed in the production of this art object, could they?—but this sculpture and photograph foreground and enhance the value of the mere vehicle of whatever ideas had been contained therein. Here, aesthetic value is re-placed in the lowly physical object that is the book's carcass, from which the literary spirit has departed. Thus Barer's book sculptures represent, for some viewers, a kind of violence. I, for example, was raised to view dog-earring pages and writing in the margins as sacrilegious, offensive *to the content* of a book. Breaking a spine had moral implications. Barer has more than broken the spines of the books she has altered. She has called into question the status of the book at this moment in cultural history.

For other viewers—the dog-earers and margin scribblers?—the book's non-literary uses are commonplace; books support small children on adult chairs at the dining table, or hold doors open, provide hard surfaces on which to write, press flowers, hide secret documents. In this way, Barer's book sculptures have an affinity with the use of U.S. flags to patch the seat of your jeans. These relocations of sacred objects call forth strong reactions.

As sacred objects, books cannot be altered without calling values into question. Altered books cannot *not* raise questions about the meanings and uses of the book in this particular historical moment, a moment in which digital technologies are challenging long-held assumptions about reading, writing, and their media. For hundreds of years in the West, since long before the emergence of the printing press, the *codex* has been the dominant reading mechanism. The codex is the form of the book in which many pages radiate out of a central spine; it has proved to be a particularly versatile technology of reading, as against the tablet and the scroll (earlier modes of text delivery), and so far still works better for long-term storage than newer technologies. Durable though it is, the codex itself is undergoing a challenge in the digital era. Some readers feel that the development of new media—the accelerating proliferation of new technologies of content delivery—commits violence against the book as a form, with grievous aesthetic, cultural, and moral consequences...

For my part, I appreciate the way in which *PDR* pictures the codex in crisis. It is unknowable just yet precisely what this crisis is producing, what new meanings, forms, and functions will emerge with the new technologies, and what will be lost. It is too soon, too late, and too simple either to lament or celebrate. The democratic promise of the new may never be realized without being appropriated or contravened, and the loss of humanism is a superstructural effect that can hardly be laid at the foot, or feet, of electronics.

Look at your electronic reader. Is it a book? Does it house a book? Is it a delivery mechanism for a book? Is it the future of the book? The electronic reader certainly has some kind of primary relationship with the book—the designed similarities, as with page turning/swiping and the familiar aspect ratio, are the least of it. Much more fundamentally, the idea of a material object as the arbitrary delivery mechanism for some content that transcends the materiality of the medium—that idea is preserved in the reader. Because or in spite of this, the electronic reader cannot help but call the question of the form and function of books.

What is knowable is that many current alarms use the same terms as the alarm over cheap paperback printing in the 18th Century. For

18th-century men of letters, mass printing threatened to feminize, and thereby bring about the end of, Literature. For many critics today, the Literature that survived that new technology of the 18th century is under siege again with the newer digital technologies. I appreciate the way *PDR* begs the question while—or *by*—obscuring any literary values. The old book could have been *War and Peace* or it could have been the *Physician's Desk Reference*—the photograph doesn't display any content.

Even though Barer has made significant changes, the original state of *PDR* as a conventional book, in codex form, remains visible and legible. I recommend looking at this image—and at altered books more generally—as an invitation to rethink the book, to think through the continuities and discontinuities between codex culture and digital culture, their social and political concomitants, the historical problems of literary and aesthetic value, literacy itself, and the multiplicity of manifestations of bookness. Certainly, corporations and courts are thinking through these things. Readers and writers must engage these questions—or be engaged willy-nilly. I recommend suspending certainty about the aesthetic and moral implications of current changes. Now that it's too late, it's time to re-read the book, with—and without—reference to Literature. ☙

Swapped

Kate McMahon

My mom calls and invites me for sushi.

"Have you ever even had sushi?" I ask, glancing at the clock on the microwave. My son's nap will be over soon.

"No, but the new place by the train station has a lunch special. And Linda from my women's group says a Japanese diet does wonders for your figure." She's been going to this women's group. I think I hear my son stirring on the baby monitor.

"Alright. I just have to wait for Jack to get back."

Jack is at the grocery store because it's Saturday and he wants to make omelets for us to eat on the porch. He gets home twenty minutes later with eggs and mimosa fixings, but I have that look on my face and I tell him I'm going to meet my mom. My dad left her five months ago, and I have been running out like this a lot. The rustling on the monitor turns into a full-on wail.

I grab the keys from Jack and get in the car. It's a station wagon, and the sour smell of breast milk and spit-up hangs subtly in the interior. This isn't the car I thought we'd have when I imagined moving out of the city, just as I hadn't expected I'd one day buy a house in the town where I grew up. But this is how things are now, and when I arrive in the restaurant parking lot I sit there for a few minutes just listening to the end of a song that reminds me of another one I like better. Then I join my mom out front.

The restaurant has a neon-green sign and grand-opening raceway flags. There is a massive fish tank in the window, which our hostess seats us right next to even though there are a lot of open tables. The giant goldfish look prehistoric. There are too many of them in one tank, and they keep bumping into the glass.

"Teriyaki! Is that like frajitas?" She always says *fra*jitas, and I don't bother correcting her anymore. Her face is rosy, her hair darker than usual. She's got a big bauble necklace on over her linen shirt, like she's on vacation. Lately she goes one of two ways, and the necklace is a good sign.

"You look good, Mom. I like the necklace."

"Thanks. Linda made it." She thumbs animatedly through the laminated menu. "I think I'm going to get the number forty-three."

The Japanese waitress comes over and smiles blithely. I order number seventeen with brown rice because my body is just not what it used to be since pregnancy. Mom enunciates her order loudly and with arms, like she is training a dolphin. She asks me at the last minute if I want a bowl of wasabi. I realize she means edamame, and we get some for the table.

When the waitress walks away, we are silent for a second, and I'm afraid she is going to ask me about Dad. He is living on the other side of town now and stops by my house once a week to leave gifts for the baby, usually when I'm not around. There's another woman. I haven't met her, but Jack saw them last month walking out of the movie theater.

"So, I'm thinking about taking a trip," Mom says breathlessly, laying her hands flat on the table for effect. "To Costa Rica."

"Wow, that's fantastic," I say, with effort. It is fantastic. I'm just tired. "By yourself?"

She smoothes her napkin unconsciously. "No, with the group. They are plugging into a yoga retreat, right on the beach. Some of the girls went last year to the one in Mexico, and they just couldn't stop raving about it."

"But you don't do yoga," I say reflexively, as the waitress drops the bowl of edamame onto our table.

I immediately regret saying this because Mom visibly stiffens and her face breaks a little.

"Well, I know that. But I want to start." She splits a shell with her hands and carefully places the soybeans into her mouth.

"Well then, I think it's a great idea," I offer, with more effort this time. "Really." It's not working. I reach into the bowl, deftly pop the soybean shell with my teeth and suck off the rock salt. One of the goldfish is not swimming; it's motionless, glaring right at me. The mood has shifted.

"Anyway, it was just an idea. Nothing set in stone."

We don't talk about much more before the waitress brings the food. Mom hasn't ordered sushi after all, and her chicken lunch comes on a steaming cast-iron platter that is still spitting hot oil. It actually looks just like fajitas.

I dig into my plate of flavorless steamed vegetables as Mom waits for her meal to cool down. I wonder if Jack is feeding the baby cheese, or chopped-up mushrooms. He's always pushing it with the solid foods, and it makes me nervous.

"Did you know I was engaged before?" Mom says, out of nowhere. I put my fork down because it seems like the right thing to do. "Before I knew Dad. I don't know why I would have ever told you that."

"No," I reply blandly, at a loss. I am instinctively queasy, as I am whenever I am caught off-guard. The goldfish is still fixed on me, its black eyes unblinking like fossil coins, and I shudder. "To who?"

"He was a widower. Louis. I was in my early twenties, and he was my doctor." Her untouched food still sizzles beneath her on the table.

I grab onto the first thing I can think to say. "So, he was old?"

"Not really. Early thirties. He was married for a year and a half when his wife wrapped their car around a tree. He was very young at the time."

176 | *Post Road* Guest Folio

She picks up her knife and stabs at the chicken. Still too hot.

"What happened?"

She sighs, largely. "We met a few years after that and eventually decided to get married. We even planned this big wedding in South Carolina, where his family was from. Grandma wanted a big to-do, me being the first daughter and all. Grandma *loved* him. He was very smart, very handsome. Very kind. Would you believe it—she didn't even mind that we started living together when we got engaged!"

This last bit is considerable. Before my Catholic grandmother died, we couldn't even tell her that Jack is half-Jewish.

"He was a good man. And I was so in love with him." There's a bittersweet wistfulness in her voice that sends a knot to my throat. She is not looking at me anymore, but at a spot in space just to the left of my head.

Mom goes quiet, and I'm flashing to an old photograph of her at her wedding to my dad that used to be on their mantel. Her hair is done up in baby's breath, and he is grinning in a wide-lapel brown suit. The wedding was small and simple, on a boat off of Jersey City, and the Statue of Liberty's torch is visible behind them in this picture. I've been angry at my dad for five months, but my anger at him in this moment is overwhelming.

"Why did he break it off?" I ask, unable to stop myself.

She unhooks her gaze from the spot next to my head and looks right at me. "He didn't. I did."

She takes a half-hearted bite of her chicken and frowns; I knew she wouldn't like Japanese food. She goes on:

"His first wife was named April. He told me about her right away, and I didn't mind. I swear I didn't. I saw how sensitive he was. I think I actually liked him even more because of it. But then, once we decided to marry and moved in together, she was everywhere. . .Every song on the radio, I'd think, was this their song? Every old friend of his I'd meet, I'd think, how well did they know her? Did they like her better? I pushed it away for months and planned the wedding, with this panic building up little by little. I remember hiding the kitchen calendar in March so I wouldn't have to read her name every day for the next month. Can you imagine?"

"No," I say, dutifully. I can't imagine any of it.

"But I never said a word to him. Just went on like everything was fine. Grandma had a shower for me that summer, two months before the wedding. I remember I wore a yellow dress, with a white belt, and ironed my hair straight. Just two of Louis's family made the trip up from South Carolina, his mother and one of his sisters. We were opening gifts and then, all of a sudden, I couldn't breathe. I remember just where his mother was sitting, in the corner by a pair of bay windows. The whole time I'm opening gifts, I just remember thinking, Christ! She's watching me, and all she's thinking is I'm not April."

Post Road **Guest Folio** | 177

She shakes her head now, re-smoothes her napkin.

"It's foolish to me now, but I couldn't get this image out of my head. The three of us—April, Louis, and me—in some cemetery someday, all in a row."

I don't know what to make of it, my mom having her own whole past out of my view. For all its obviousness, this realization strikes me with an unsettling force; just this morning, half-asleep while nursing the baby, I myself glanced at the clock and marveled that in my former life I might have stumbled home at such an hour. "What happened to him?"

"I saw him once, years later in an airport. But he didn't see me. You were there. We were on our way to Aunt Jean's right after she had the twins. He was looking at magazines at the news stand with three young boys that looked just like him."

I remember that trip. We had a layover, and I threw up in the bathroom.

"I've thought about this a lot. Looking back, I realize it wasn't enough for me that he loved me. I think all I ever wanted to hear was that he loved me the most." She pauses here, gravely, then indulges a sad smile. "What did I know?"

I don't know what to say. I pick up my fork again and push the vegetables around, buying time. I have never given any thought to how or where I might be buried. Next to Jack, I assume. And what about the baby? Will his body one day be laid out in soil somewhere far from Jack's and mine? It occurs to me for the first time that my mom won't be buried next to my dad, let alone next to Louis and April. Suddenly, her bauble necklace is breaking my heart. I want to rip it right off.

The waitress arrives to save us, and I push my plate to the middle of the table and ask for a to-go box. Mom does the same, though I know she is just being polite. She will offer me her full container as soon as we walk into the parking lot.

I give the waitress my credit card, and when she returns, I scratch Jack's last name quickly across the receipt. After three years, it still somehow feels like a small betrayal, asserting my new last name in front of my parents. My mom fidgets with the top of the take-out container, and all I can think is how hopelessly stuck she is to my Dad's name like a regrettable tattoo. I swapped it out, and now she is alone with it.

"Have you ever had a mimosa?" The question lands awkwardly, because there are no other words to match anything I mean—that I'm sad, and I'm sorry, and I'd rather be anywhere else.

She shakes her head no. Mom drinks after-dinner liqueur around Christmastime and Sam Adams beer during her yearly vacation to Hyannis, and that's about it. "Linda loves them, though."

I stand up and grab her purse from the back of her chair. "Jack's making omelets," I announce, leading her towards the door and away from the leftovers we have abandoned on the table. ☙

The Sleeping Kingdom
Caitlin Keefe Moran

I measured my life by summers then.
That was the first line of the story I wrote about Laurie and the summers we spent together on Little Moose Lake. Not a good sentence, really—better in my head than on paper—but it was true. Laurie and I are cousins, born five months apart; her mother and my mother are sisters, born ten months apart and more like twins than just siblings. She was my first and last best friend. And any day my parents packed me and Gram, my mother's mother, into the car and followed Laurie and her parents two hours north up Route 28 to Little Moose was the happiest day of the year for me.

We went to the cabin because of Gram, who couldn't stand Syracuse during the heat of the summer. She grew up in Québec, in the little city of Trois-Rivières. The only thing she ever told us about Trois-Rivières was that its residents were called Trifluvians, which tickled me and Laurie; we had a bit of Trifluvian inside of us! Gram took her roots much more seriously. Every summer her father had taken her and her siblings up north, to a lake she would never name ringed with silver-barked pines, so they wouldn't forget that his people, the Atikamekw, belonged to the land. She grew up boating and hiking and fishing in the summer, snowshoeing and skiing in the winter, but when Grandpa had to move to the United States for work, she bundled up her two almost-twins and left Québec forever. Bullying my mother and my aunt into driving up to a cabin in northern New York every summer was her way of reclaiming pieces of her childhood, bringing her almost-twin daughters and almost-twin granddaughters as close as she could to her past.

Our routine was always the same: when we arrived in Old Forge, we loaded up on supplies at the Big M—bread and meat for sandwiches, baby carrots and string cheese, juice boxes, ice-cream bars, pancake mix, sunscreen, bug spray, Band-Aids, water shoes and sunhats. Mom and Aunt Michelle took care of most of this, while Laurie and I trailed behind, trying and failing to sneak extra candy into the cart. Dad and Uncle Stephen went ahead in our car to open up the cabin, to shake the dried husks of dead bugs out of the screens and throw away the occasional mouse corpse before we saw it and squealed for hours. The only thing Gram ever bought was a gallon tub of pistachios. She ate them by the hundreds at the cabin, leaving the shells lying about on the porch, on the dock, on the floor of the pontoon boat, even in the bathtub. I stepped on one at just the right angle the summer I was nine and sliced the back of my heel open.

"Next summer," Dad grumbled at Mom as he drove me to the hospital, my foot swaddled in Laurie's Power Rangers beach towel, "we're getting your mother a wastebasket." I needed nine stitches and couldn't swim for weeks.

But even with the hazards to our feet, Laurie and I always waited for the nights when the pistachio bucket suddenly appeared, because that meant Gram was about to tell a story. Gram had lots of macabre tales up her sleeve. Mom and Aunt Michelle never came out to the dock with us—hunger for Gram's stories of the "old country," as she called Québec, had skipped a generation. She set up her lawn chair on the dock as the sun set and told us tales of witches who ensnared French traders in Manitoba by singing to them and then cursed them so their skin burned off from the inside. My favorite was the story of a lumberjack who bought a flying canoe from the devil in exchange for not speaking any of the holy words for a year, but of course, because he was a Trifluvian, like Gram, he couldn't help throwing a *tabarnouche* in every other sentence, and so the magical boat crashed into a copse of pine trees and he was never found. But Gram's favorite—also Laurie's—wasn't connected to Canada particularly. That's why it haunted us so much, I guess, because it could have happened anywhere, even in Old Forge. Even by the shores of Little Moose Lake.

"Anywhere there lies a body of water wide enough to exhaust the good swimmer, and deep enough to block out the rays of the sun, there you will find the sleeping kingdom."

That's how Gram always began the story, while Laurie and I sat side-by-side on the dock, shoulders touching. By the middle of the summer, her skin was tanned darker than the planks we sat on, while my pale back had crisped up red and crinkled like onion-skin paper, and my milky blonde hair looked pink from the sunburn on my scalp. That was how people knew we were cousins and not twins. Sun and Moon, Gram called us sometimes. *Le soleil et la lune.*

In a sleeping kingdom, Gram said, there were two types of creatures: the snatchers and the sleepers. No one knew much about the snatchers. Some said they were scaly and green, some said they shimmered like the sun on a churning river. A small contingent—those with no imagination, Gram said—thought the snatchers were invisible. But everyone knew they were bitter. They were jealous and greedy and angry that when the world was made ("By who?" Laurie always asked, and Gram said that it didn't matter), they were stuck under the water, unable to rise to land.

Laurie and I wondered if there was a sleeping kingdom at the bottom of Little Moose Lake. Neither of us had been down deep enough to see if the water blocked out the sun. A man had come one summer, an Englishman, who had swum across almost all of the lakes in the Adirondacks for some kind of record. He hadn't looked exhausted when he climbed out of the water in East Bay, which was connected to Little Moose Lake, but he might have been too good a swimmer to count. When our families went out on the pontoon boat, I often caught Laurie leaning over the edge with her bright red bikini bottom sticking up in the air, as if hoping, by staring hard enough, to catch a glimpse of the bone-white head of a sleeper.

The snatchers believed that if they brought enough land-dwellers with them to the bottom of the lakes and seas, they could make a deal to be released from their watery prison.

"A deal with who?" Laurie asked.

"Whom," I corrected, "and it doesn't matter. A story is a story."

That was the difference between Laurie and me then. She wanted facts—names, ages, whether the person in question would go to the Nicks Lake Diner for coffee and a plate of eggs and hash, or if he would pick up a greasy egg sandwich from the Dunkin Donuts on South Shore Road to eat alone. I thought those kind of details were a waste of time for everyone, the teller and the listeners. If Gram said snatchers were evil and grasping, I believed her. Laurie wanted to know how they had become so. It didn't surprise me when, years later, Laurie declared herself an atheist in front of our entire religion class because no one would answer her questions.

"The snatchers," said Gram, "dragged as many humans down with them as they could. They weren't picky, anyone would do. Trappers, merchants, infants, ministers' daughters, loggers in the prime of their health." She leered at us. "Little American girls."

This was my favorite part of the entire story, when I forgot about the splinters in my feet and my waterlogged ears and the scrapes on my knees and felt only the disconcerting pleasure of goose bumps over a peeling sunburn.

"But?" Laurie prompted. She never let the moment last long enough.

Gram grinned at Laurie's impatience. "But soon the people of the towns and villages along the Hudson Bay, and the cities that lay along the St. Lawrence, began to realize that their kin hadn't drowned, but were held, immobilized by the dreck and the seaweed, by the snatchers. And they decided to get their kinfolk back."

I imagined what it would be like to lie at the bottom of Little Moose Lake, seaweed coiled around my arms and legs, silt creeping up the back of my neck, staring up into the blackness, knowing that somewhere above me my mother and father were crying about my death. Knowing that they whispered about me at school, the little girl who would haunt the water forever. It might be worse than drowning.

"The snatchers anticipated this, and saw another opportunity to increase their power." Gram paused here, always, to select another pistachio from her bucket. She cracked the shell open neatly and sucked long and hard on the nut before finally crushing it between her molars. As Laurie and I grew older and became wise to her routine, Gram drew out the munching even longer, until the wait became an exercise in agony.

"The snatchers decided they would allow people to sacrifice themselves for their loved ones," Gram continued. "An exchange. Once a year, on Midsummer's Eve, the queen of the snatchers, an old crone rumored to have magic powers, rose to the surface of the water and cried out the names of those trapped below. The people of the towns and villages, especially those who suspected that their loved ones were lost to the snatchers, gathered along the shore to listen. If they heard the name of someone they loved, they could offer themselves up, to sleep in the place of the other."

Even though Laurie and I knew what was coming next, could quote it word-for-word by the time we were seven years old, we sat so entranced that we forgot to swat at the mosquitoes that landed and feasted on our legs.

"So the minister slept for his daughter. The logger's wife, who knew she was dying, slept for her husband. Fathers slept for sons, mothers for daughters, brothers for sisters and sisters for brothers. Once, a man in Montréal was so in love with a woman engaged to be married, he gave himself up to sleep for her captured fiancé."

Laurie loved this part—the noble sacrifice driven by melancholia and love. The first story she ever wrote took place on the final day of this man's life. No one was surprised, when the St. Boniface drama club put on *A Tale of Two Cities* our freshman year, that she won an award for her portrayal of Lucie Manette.

There were abuses of this system, according to Gram. People blackmailed into sleeping for strangers, to pay for debts or to save their families from scandal. There were even accounts of travelers abducted at gunpoint and forced to give themselves up. People learned quickly not to travel on Midsummer's Eve, even to the next town.

"So how were the snatchers defeated?" Laurie asked once, the summer before fifth grade. Gram had never gone any further than a failed attempt by a group of sailors to rescue their lost captain by force. It was a grim way to end a story, but Gram always said the Québecois liked it grim.

"Have they been defeated?" Gram responded. "How can we know for sure?"

Laurie made a face. "People don't go to the lake on Midsummer's Eve to sacrifice themselves anymore."

"Your face will freeze like that, stinker," Gram said. "But all right, since you asked."

People realized they were being had, Gram said, and the tradition fell out of use. The snatchers began to target specific people—the families of the rich and influential, of local magistrates and politicians. They always wanted power, after all. And then some outside factors contributed to the decline of the snatchers, more banal stuff. Factories began pouring chemicals and waste into the lakes. Motors were invented for boats. People wore life vests. The Canadian Coast Guard was founded.

"But they're still out there, girls." Gram leaned forward, and it seemed that even the waves lapping against the shore went still to listen to her.

"Always be vigilant. Take care of each other."

The summer before ninth grade was the last time we went to the lake. The following year, Gram died suddenly in April, of her heart just calling it quits. Mom said it was a blessing, what with her arthritis being so bad and her diabetes beginning to act up. It rained on the day of the funeral, and earthworms stippled the drive of the cemetery even though the last of the winter's brownish snow had yet to melt from the base of the trees. Later that night, while the rest of our family sat around cheese platters downstairs, swapping memories and drinking the funeral from their minds, Laurie and I spent hours spread out on her bedroom floor, writing down Gram's stories.

Some we knew were lost forever—we could only remember the first line or the main character's name, and we didn't know if we could find them in a book of Canadian folktales in the local library or if Gram had just invented them on the spot. Even if we could look them up, though, they wouldn't have Gram's voice, and Gram's voice was the magic. But we remembered "The Sleeping Kingdom," beginning to end, almost verbatim. We wrote out two copies of the little storybook, one for each of us, and though we both agreed that we should show our mothers, we never did.

The following summer, Laurie's parents divorced and my dad lost his job. We called it the Great Unspooling; when things unraveled in our family, they unraveled in a hurry. The next fall, when Laurie and I should have entered tenth grade together, I switched to the local public school, since we couldn't pay tuition anymore. I didn't mind it so much—I hated wearing a uniform and saying prayers before class every day, and the only person who had wanted me to go to St. Boniface in the first place was Gram. It wasn't that I didn't like religion—there was something about Mass that got to me in a good way, and I always cared more about all of it than Laurie did. I just didn't want it mixing with calculus tests and Spanish and Homecoming—once God got tangled up in every part of my day, God wasn't special anymore. Laurie thought all of it was crap, of course, but she grudgingly stayed behind; Uncle Stephen paid her tuition as part of the divorce settlement.

I made the cross-country team at my new school. The coach told me I was a solid middle-of-the-pack finisher, but had potential. It was a blessed relief to be compelled out of the house to train; I couldn't stand watching

Dad sit at the dining-room table leafing through job listings while Mom added up the bills in the kitchen. Laurie joined me on my long runs; if she stayed too long in the same place, Aunt Michelle would corner her and begin complaining about Uncle Stephen. We went out regardless of the weather—in fact, the gloom of a rainy day made staying inside the house even worse—which was why we were out on a cheerless raw Saturday in early November, a day that wasn't fit for man or beast. The drizzle was light enough that we only felt it in dribs and drabs, depending on which way the wind blew, but somehow that just made it worse. My breath smelled like damp socks as I ran. Laurie loped along next to me, her feet barely touching the ground. At St. Boniface, she was a starter on the varsity soccer team; college coaches were already coming around to scout her. She ran with a midfielder's tetchy gait, always alert for a soccer ball rolling past her feet; a tap, and she was gone in a different direction, like a spooked rabbit. I plodded by comparison, the long-distance runner with one goal and one way to get there. It amazed me back then that we didn't shove each other into traffic on these runs.

We reached the top of the hill and pulled up, bending over to adjust our sneakers and jacket sleeves and Under Armor, which was really just a cover for the need to pant like dogs. The city spread below us, or so I assumed—the fog strangled all but the church spires and a handful of apartment complexes. For a strange moment, the only sound between the ghostly gray sky and the ghostly gray fog was our breathing. It felt like we were on the moon.

"What a crap year it's been," Laurie said suddenly. She cupped her hands around her pink, wind-licked ears. Uncle Stephen had a new girlfriend, one of the ladies who worked at the bank. She was, as my mom put it, many moons younger than Aunt Michelle.

"Yeah," I said. "It really has been."

"Your dad found a job yet?" Laurie asked. She leaned on the guardrail and extended her leg behind her to stretch her calf. A gust of wind rolled up the hill, and a surprise spray of rain lashed my face. Laurie didn't seem to notice.

"Nope," I said. I joined her at the guardrail. "But he's in better spirits. Mom got a promotion at work, so that's taken some of the pressure off."

Our breathing had slowed to almost normal; we faced each other, our hands on our hips.

"Ready?" Laurie asked. I grunted in assent. "Hey listen, Tay," Laurie said suddenly. She grinned. "We'll make it, you know? We'll be all right."

"Sure," I said. "Sure we will. We have each other." It seemed like the right thing to say, but it also seemed powerful: a verbal talisman, a binding declaration before the world. A promise.

We turned together and started back down the hill, submerging ourselves in gently rippling waves of fog.

*

Chérie arrived the following spring.

Chérie was Laurie's harlot-red '97 Chevy Cavalier, a gift from Uncle Stephen for her sixteenth birthday. In our family, that was an unheard-of extravagance—the very mention of it sent my parents into fits for months—but Uncle Stephen's attempt to one-up Aunt Michelle worked out for Laurie and me. We named the car Chérie, Gram's nickname for both of us when we were babies, and though we knew on some level it was a piece of junk—the bottom was rusting, the muffler kept falling off, the radio worked only when planets aligned just right—to us, it was the most beautiful machine in the world.

Ostensibly, there were limits to where Laurie could drive. She still had a curfew, and she was only allowed to take it out on weeknights to go to work. We both worked at Upstate Adventure Island and Magic Waters Theme Park Resort, which was just as soul-crushing and tacky as it sounds; I took tickets at the entrance, while Laurie manned an ice-cream stand by the waterslide lockers. We were constantly sunburned and grossly underpaid, but we felt strangely free. Sometimes after work we would buy jumbo iced coffees with whipped cream and drive around with the windows down, Chérie clanking loudly in protest any time we neared fifty miles an hour. That summer we began to talk about going back to Little Moose Lake.

"Didn't your parents sell the cabin after Gram died?" Laurie asked as she pulled out of the gas station, her coffee balanced between her legs.

"Yeah, no one wanted to take responsibility for the upkeep," I said. "But we could find a motel or something. There might be good rates the weekend after Labor Day. You know, rent a couple of tubes, float around."

Laurie grinned. "Just me and you and the snatchers."

Then, at the end of the summer, Laurie didn't show up for work for two weeks.

Since she was my ride, this was a problem for me. She didn't answer my texts or phone calls the first morning, while I stood by the mailbox in my uniform waiting for Chérie to come swerving into view, and by the time I convinced my mom to drive me to the park on her lunch break, I was an hour and a half late. As I left that night, I saw a text from Laurie: "Sorry about this morning. Been sleeping a lot. Mono's a bitch." I texted her back that she should rest and not worry about me.

For the next two weeks, I dropped my mom off at work in the morning and took her car. This was sufficiently annoying to her that she grumbled about it to Aunt Michelle, who said this was the first she had heard about Laurie having mono. I realized Laurie and I had been in a fight without me even realizing it, and I let myself stew in righteous anger for another week before finally cracking and showing up at Laurie's apartment with a box of donut holes from Tim Hortons and a Coke slushie for each of us.

Aunt Michelle was shucking corn in the kitchen when I arrived. "She's in her room," she said, without looking up from the corn. "I think she's having some boy trouble."

Laurie's room was inhumanly hot and smelled like half-eaten dinners were percolating under the bed. She had the radio turned up at full volume and made no attempt to turn it down when I came in. She looked like she hadn't showered in days.

"Hey," she said.

I handed her the slushie. "Hey. So are we good? I thought you might be mad at me."

Laurie shook her head. "Not mad at you. I just needed to go away for a little bit. Everything was a little too overwhelming."

"You probably know you got fired."

Laurie shrugs. "No loss there."

I handed her the last paycheck she would get for the summer and sat down on the end of her bed. "Your supervisor gave me this." She nodded. "So remember that guy Tom?" Tom went to my high school and sold neon-colored fisherman hats and "funglasses" at a stand near the park entrance. He was vaguely clammy and smelled like pretzels, but occasionally told a good joke.

Laurie nodded.

"Well, he asked me to get pizza with him. But not in a, you know, date kind of way. It sounded like there might be other people there. But I don't know, it might not be nothing. What do you think?"

Laurie didn't have any insight into what "get pizza" meant. She tried for a few sentences and then fell silent, picking at the strings of her blanket. I stopped trying to make conversation and opened a window, just for something to do. I felt myself beginning to sweat through my shorts.

"Tay," Laurie said after a while, "do you remember 'The Sleeping Kingdom'?" Her voice was wobbly and soft, not her voice at all.

"Course I do," I said. "Why?"

She nibbled on a donut and shook her head. "Nothing. Just thinking about it."

"Is there something going on with a guy?" I asked finally. "Aunt Michelle thought that maybe . . ."

And then Laurie burst into tears.

My first thought, when she told me about the assault, was about where I could get a gun. I seriously considered it—I knew that Uncle Stephen had an antique hunting rifle sitting somewhere in his new house. It didn't matter that I didn't know how to shoot it—I could use it as a club if I had to. It was just some guy, she said, at some soccer party. He went to the private boys' school that was the brother school to St. Boniface.

No, I didn't know him. Yes, she had been drinking. No, she hadn't gotten a rape kit. That was the end of the questions I knew how to ask, and the questions Laurie would answer.

We met after school every other day at Laurie's favorite café, Cristo's, on Walton Street downtown. Each time she ordered a bagel drenched in butter, a hot chocolate and a plastic tub of jam. I drank tea and sometimes ate a muffin. Laurie chose a public place because it made her go out and prevented her from crying. I went along with it because I thought those were the two main problems we had to address: going out and not crying. When we first sat down, she always lined up two rows of five straws in front of her, and when she finished stripping off the paper and shredding it to bits and bending all the straws in so many places that they were useless, she gathered them up in a neat pile and threw the mess away. That's how I knew it was time to leave.

This lasted through October and November, and into a dreadful Syracuse winter. I signed up for SAT prep classes, and Laurie waved away my concern when she said she hadn't and didn't care. I listened and nodded as Laurie talked, though she didn't talk much—she preferred sitting in silence to discussing the assault. I didn't push her; I let her wrap herself in muteness. I was there, if she needed me. I thought that was enough.

The guidance counselor looked at my résumé before winter exams and told me that I didn't have enough extracurriculars. Cross-country wasn't enough, she said. Colleges want well-rounded students. Like I was a misshapen blob that had to be aggressively remolded and sanded smooth. That's how I ended up in an after-school writing workshop, in a room off the gym where the wrestling team stored mats during the off-season. My clothes, my backpack, even my notebook smelled like sweaty underwear when I left. I approached the class with the least amount of enthusiasm possible. Writing had always been Laurie's thing, though not so much anymore. She never said she had stopped writing, but the new journal I bought her for her birthday sat unopened on top of her dresser, still wrapped in cellophane, for months.

The story came pouring out one night, after a disastrous afternoon with Laurie when I began to realize she wasn't getting better but I was getting worse, and if something didn't change we would both sink down to the part of the water that the sun couldn't reach. I wrote about the sleeping kingdom as if it were real, as if Laurie and I knew that Gram was stuck down there, though no one believed it. In the story, Gram talked the queen of the snatchers into bringing her to the surface so she could give Laurie advice. I took Laurie down there, handed her off. Laurie kissed Gram's slimy, puckered forehead, and after that she was healed. It was a fantasy of unburdening. A fairytale solution. But I should have known better. Even in fairytales, quick fixes have a price.

When Mrs. Carson handed back the story, marked up with edits, she pulled me aside. She said it was quite good. It showed vision, emotion. The university was sponsoring a short-story contest for high-school students. She encouraged me to submit. A writing award, she said, could add some diversity to my college application.

I changed all the characters' names, moved the setting to Colorado, and signed the submission sheet without reading it. Two months letter, I received a letter telling me I had won first place.

The Problem came a week later, when the university committee printed my story, with my name attached, in the Syracuse *Post-Standard*. When I asked Mrs. Carson about the Problem the next day, she seemed surprised. Hadn't I read the rules of the contest? I looked up the submission guidelines online and read over and over again the sentence that said the winning story would be published in the *Post-Standard*.

Aunt Michelle saw it first and called my mother, who hadn't even read it. Michelle had suspected I knew something about Laurie, and she connected the dots. Mom picked me up from track practice and marched me straight into the dining room to interrogate me like a spy apprehended behind enemy lines.

"Did you know about—about Laurie?" Mom asked. I nodded. "And you didn't tell anyone?"

"Laurie didn't want me to."

"Not even a teacher, or a police officer?"

"She didn't tell me until weeks after it happened. And I didn't want to go behind her back." In the end, of course, this was exactly what I had done. That's why it was a Problem.

Mom sighed. "It was a mistake, of course it was, but it's not unforgivable. It's good for Laurie in the long run, she'll get into counseling now at least. You know how histrionic Michelle is. We'll give her some time to cool off."

Laurie showed up a couple of hours later. I was sitting on the back porch, the uneven wooden boards digging into the backs of my thighs. I heard Chérie's distinctive wheeze in the driveway, a slammed door, and then Laurie materialized in the dimness of the porch light. She had been crying in the car.

"Hey," I said. I couldn't say anything more.

Laurie said nothing for a moment. I looked at the ground, at the toad hiding by the edge of the bushes.

"My mom's saying it's my dad's fault, for giving me the car," Laurie said quietly. "My dad's saying it's my mom's fault, for not watching me closer."

"I'm really sorry—" I began.

"The only thing I had," Laurie said over me, "was that I got to choose when to tell my story. I got to pick the people I told."

"I didn't know they were going to print it," I said. The house was silent except for the thud of moth bodies against the light. Laurie wouldn't sit down with me. "If I had known that, I would have never sent it in."

"Doesn't matter." Laurie's voice was toneless. I had expected her to rage and swear, but she was so calm we could have been talking about the price of gas. "It wasn't your story to tell."

The obviousness of what she said stopped all my excuses in my throat.

"It was a good story, though." Laurie was crying again. "You really found your writing voice."

"Laurie, please—"

"Take this." She tossed a package on the porch. It was the journal I had given her for her birthday, before she stopped writing. "You've got a lot of good material now."

Mom had been listening at the kitchen window. "She's just like Michelle," she said when I came back inside. She nodded at the unopened journal. "That flair for the dramatic."

And then our mothers stopped talking, too.

Stories are tricky. If you don't watch your words carefully, they'll wiggle away from you and say all sorts of things you weren't even thinking. Gram knew how to tell stories, and tell them responsibly. I didn't have the same gift; my gift was in the appraising and weighing, the measuring of moments, but in trying to preserve and sanctify them, I crushed them. Laurie had the words. I had no business trying to make them do my bidding.

I wanted to tell Laurie that I would drive up to Little Moose—make a deal with the devil for a flying canoe, if I had to—on Midsummer's Eve. I would stand on the dock, littered with Gram's pistachio shells. I would feel the splinters in my feet and the sunburn on my shoulders, under a shining white moon. I would listen for the queen of the snatchers to rise to the surface and cry out the names of those sleeping at the bottom of the lake, and I would call out my name, loudly and clearly, as a sacrifice. I would wait for the queen to lift her into the still night air, limp and pale but still breathing. And a hundred times—a thousand times, if I had to—I would sleep for her. ❧

The Disappearing Wife

Simon Savelyev

I was at a cookout with my wife, Darlene. This was an annual affair hosted by one of my college buddies, Rick Jr., who had a sprawling green lawn he liked to show off every few months. I was standing around the food table with a few of the women, who were commenting on a couple across the yard. Darlene and I knew the couple from some of Rick Jr.'s previous parties. The husband's name was Shep, and his wife was Trish.

Everyone was talking about how great Trish looked. "Would you just *look* at her!" one of the women said. "She looks *terrific*."

"She's really slimmed down. And that skirt! Doesn't she look great, Vlad?" Darlene said, and touched my arm.

I agreed that she did. In the past, Trish had always looked sort of frumpy and swollen. She was young—we were all fairly young, most of us under forty—but she had never had a particularly healthy look to her. But here she was—thin, somehow taller, sun-dappled under the summer trees. Her posture was fine-lined and elegant. She held her cigarette wrist-up, like models in old magazines.

We walked over so Darlene could tell Trish in person just how beautiful she looked. While the two women fawned, Shep nudged me and said, "I know what you're thinking. What's my secret, right? Let me tell you, I had nothing to do with it. Hell, I *like* a little meat on my bones. But Trish—she gets an idea in her head, and there's no stopping her. She's on this new regimen. One of them deals where you have to put everything in plastic baggies and drink through straws."

"Well, she looks great," I said. I was afraid of being too complimentary, since I didn't want to imply that Trish had looked bad to begin with.

Shep popped the tab on a can of beer and let the foam run over his fingers. "Shoot. At this point I'm saying give it a rest. Take a load off. You look good, woman! Now watch some TV, for chrissakes. Eat a cheeseburger. I don't want you wasting away to nothing."

All of this put my wife into a happy mood. On the way home that afternoon, she cranked up the radio and smiled out the window. The sea breeze blew our hair in crazy circles. She turned to me and said, "Boy, Trish looked great. I'm really happy for her. Good for her, right? Don't you think?"

"Absolutely," I said. "Good for her."

That night, as we were getting ready for bed, she brought it up again. She was massaging moisturizer into her legs when she suddenly looked up and laughed. "*Trish*. I just can't get over it. She looked so *great*."

I was watching a TV program I liked, a reality show about men in the arctic. I looked at Darlene and smiled. "She looked really good. Are you coming to bed?"

"I have to brush my teeth," she said. She scooted off the bed and went to the bathroom, but I didn't hear any water running. I could tell she was looking at herself in the mirror. Finally the faucet came on, and she began scrubbing rapidly with her toothbrush. Then she spat, and over the water called out, "Hey! Maybe I should try out that diet. The one Trish was on?"

After a minute she came out of the bathroom, drying her hands. "Well? What do you think?"

The show had gone to a commercial, so I looked at her. "What are you talking about? You don't need to go on a diet."

She stood sideways to the mirror on the door and lifted her t-shirt. She sucked in her belly. Then she raised her arm to flex her biceps, and poked it with her finger. "I wish I had better arms. Don't you love it when women have strong arms? Mine are all flabby and soft."

"Your arms look beautiful," I said.

"But you have to admit they're a little thick. That's just a fact. I was born with thick arms. If there's one thing I'd change about myself, I'd have to say it's my arms. I'd like to have nice toned arms and a toned butt."

"Your arms are perfect, and your butt is perfect."

She rolled her eyes at me and then turned back to the mirror. "Well, I think I could stand to lose a few pounds, and I'm not too proud to admit it. I'd like a nice tight belly and a toned butt and strong arms." She turned to look at her backside. "I think I should do it. Imagine how great I'd look! You know it only took Trish a few months to lose all that weight?" She said, "Well? Wouldn't you like me better if I thinned out a little?"

"No," I said. "I love you just as you are. I wouldn't love you any more than I do now." But then I wondered whether I was being unduly dismissive. I'd felt that even the slightest show of uncertainty on this issue could only lead to recriminations at some later point. It'd come back to bite me. But then it occurred to me that I might be overthinking things. Maybe Darlene wasn't seeking my approval, but merely my support—just as if she'd said she wanted to change jobs or start going to church. Maybe all she wanted was some husbandly encouragement. I said, "I wouldn't love you less, though, either. If you want to go on a diet, sure, go on a diet. I think that's great. I won't love you any more or less. I'll love you the same."

At first, the diet seemed like a good thing. Darlene foreswore all processed foods and stocked the fridge with baby carrots and spring water. She filled a basket with apples and nectarines and let them ripen on the table. She bought books on dieting and exercise, on holistic approaches to nutrition and spiritual wellbeing. She bought herself a tracksuit and woke up early for walks around the neighborhood. Every night after dinner she went down to the basement and put on an exercise video, and I could hear her hopping around and grunting in the dark. Despite all this, Darlene didn't seem to be losing any weight. I told her it would take some time, but it was heartbreaking to watch her step on the scale every morning, day after day, with no change.

She bought different books, different sneakers, a different tracksuit. She read pamphlets that promoted the consumption of nuts and seeds and raw meat, that encouraged drinking urine as part of a purification cycle. She bought protein shakes and spent hundreds of dollars on dietary supplements—seaweed extracts, hot-pepper capsules, micro-engineered fat-burners, on and on. She switched to videos on tae bo, kick-boxing, and Sudanese erotic dance.

After a while, I noticed that the fruit she bought was rotting in the basket. The baby spinach in the fridge had turned into a gelatinous green goop. I was afraid she wasn't eating enough, but she insisted she was fine, she'd eaten plenty—look at her, she was a freaking balloon.

"Well, I'm going to start packing you a lunch."

"Fine, great. Pack a lunch," she said.

"I'm serious. You need vitamins."

"Perfect. I'd love a lunch."

As time went on, Darlene grew morose. I could see she was losing hope. Every night she went downstairs to do her videos, but to no effect. Sometimes she would emerge hours later without a lick of sweat on her, and I had to wonder whether she was even exercising anymore or just watching TV in the dark. Sometimes she came back upstairs with mussed hair and a puffy face, as if she'd been sleeping.

Around this time I started smelling smoke on her, subtle but unmistakable. It was in her clothes, in her hair. I found ashes on the rim of the toilet and in the kitchen sink, spent butts floating in a bottle on the porch. One day I came home from work to find her lying on the couch in front of the TV, tapping a cigarette into a coffee mug on her belly.

I put down an armful of groceries. "Since when are we smoking in the house?"

She sighed loudly. Finally she said, "Vlad, I really don't need this right now. I have a splitting headache."

There was an empty carton of ice cream on the floor by the couch, with a salad spoon sticking out of it. "Did you go to work today?"

She didn't answer, just picked up the remote to change the channel.

"All I'm saying—"

She sat up quickly. "Jesus Christ! Will you relax?" She put her hand to her forehead and closed her eyes. "Oh man. I think I'm coming down with something. Will you get me some aspirin, honey-baby? Please?"

"Are you okay?"

"Please, Vlad! Some aspirin. My head is about to explode."

And then, out of nowhere, she started losing weight. Just a few pounds at first, but then more substantially. I could see it when she got ready for bed at night—her body was getting leaner, more shapely. People, men, began to notice her on the street. What worried me was that this change was occurring alongside a complete abandonment of her exercise routine. She had quit her morning walks and dance videos. Every day I would pack her a lunch and cook her dinner, but usually she would just pick at her plate and leave the table early to watch television. Most nights I was just cooking for myself.

"You need to eat," I would tell her.

"I do eat," she would say, tapping a cigarette into her salad.

"You need to eat more. You're getting too thin. You don't exercise. You're leaving ashes everywhere."

"Vlad, please," she would say, covering her forehead. "My goddam head is killing me."

As summer turned to fall, things got worse. The weight started to really drop off. Her face became pallid and sunken. She was up at all hours of the night, and sleeping late. Sometimes at work I'd get a call from her boss at the cannery saying she hadn't shown up for work. I'd come home in the afternoon to find her still in bed.

Eventually, her boss had no choice but to fire her. I couldn't blame him, but I was also worried about what she would do for work. I suspected that she might decide not to take on a new job, that she would content herself by lying on the couch all day, with the shades drawn, watching TV.

But I was wrong. She got a job as a waitress the day after she was fired, at a sports bar the next town over. She worked five nights a week, and sometimes didn't come home until dawn, reeking of booze and cigarettes. When she snuck into bed on those mornings, I could feel the boniness of her body, how thin she had become, and a feeling of disgust would pass over me.

In October I got a call from Rick Jr., who was planning a party the weekend before Halloween that he wanted Darlene and me to attend. "I don't know, Ricky," I said.

"Why not?"

I couldn't think of a plausible excuse off the top of my head. Finally I said, "I'll see what Darlene wants to do."

When I told her about the party, she said, "I know just the costume!"

I explained that it wasn't a costume party, it was just a party in October, but she insisted. She went out and bought a little devil outfit for herself—red stockings and a black corset, and little red horns she could wear in her hair.

As I watched her get ready that evening, I found myself suddenly aroused. I went up behind her and started moving my hands over her body. She had become so thin I could actually feel her ribs through the corset. Lately things hadn't been going so well in the bedroom—Darlene usually had a headache or was tired or just in a foul mood. But this night, when I touched her, she turned to me with a look that was almost menacing. She pushed me back onto the bed and started sucking on my Adam's apple, feverishly unbuckling my pants.

When we got to the party, it was like one of those moments from the movies when the record suddenly zips and the phones stop ringing and all the faces slowly turn to stare.

Darlene was the only one in costume, of course, but it wasn't the costume everyone was talking about. Rick Jr. was the first to say it: "My God, you're *skinny!*"

Darlene smiled radiantly and allowed him to kiss the back of her hand. As more people came over to tell her how great she looked, how thin and how utterly fantastic, I could see a change coming over her. She grew expansive and sarcastic. She chain-smoked, lighting each cigarette on the ember of its predecessor. A small cadre of women formed around her, and they all seemed set on impressing her—by telling a racy story or offering some juicy bit of gossip. It was like they were suddenly all catty high-school girls again. At one point Darlene broke off the conversation and asked someone's husband to go fetch her a G&T—a G&T, she called it—and for the first time I felt a stab of jealousy. I was right there—I could have easily fetched the G&T.

Finally somebody mentioned Shep and Trish, and Darlene said "Where are those two, anyway? I've been looking for Trish all night."

"Didn't you hear?" said one of the women. "Shep was in an accident. He was out for a walk or something when all of a sudden this bus came out of nowhere and smashed right into him."

"No!"

"Yeah. Supposedly he flew like thirty feet and then landed in a *tree*. Fractured head, broken ribs, arms, all sorts of internal damage."

"No!" Darlene's eyes were wide. She puffed on her cigarette. "When did this happen?"

"Just a month or two ago. He's lucky he didn't die. He's in a full body cast now. Poor Trish is taking care of him, nursing him back to health. She's an angel, that woman."

Later on, I had to use the bathroom. When I came out, I couldn't find Darlene. I looked around the house for her, and then went onto the back deck. I asked Rick Jr. if he'd seen her. He hadn't. I began asking random people, people I'd never met, if they'd seen my wife. They asked me what she looked like. "She's thin," I said. I tried to think of other details, but none came to mind.

I finally found her in the back yard, standing in the shadow of the boathouse with three or four men. They were all smoking and laughing, but when I came closer, they went quiet.

"Almost ready, hon?" I said. Nobody looked at me except for Darlene. Finally she came forward, dropping her cigarette and delicately grinding it into the lawn. As we walked toward the car together, my hand gripping her elbow, she looked back to the men and grinned.

One day I noticed a charge on my credit card for an airline ticket to Las Vegas, and another for a reservation at the MGM Grand Hotel. When I asked Darlene about it, she said, "Didn't I tell you? That's my Vegas trip. Vicky and I are going next week. I'm sure I told you."

"You didn't tell me. Who's Vicky?"

"Vicky from the bar. Why do you look so mystified?"

She was sitting at the kitchen table, eating a steak-and-cheese sub. A cigarette smoldered on the rim of her Coke can.

"When is this happening?"

"Next week. What's the big deal, can't I ever go on vacation?"

I went to the refrigerator, suddenly hungry, and scanned the shelves for something to eat. "Well!" I said. "I guess you can do whatever you want!"

She frowned and said through a full mouth, "What's that supposed to mean?"

I had lost my train of thought. "How come we never have anything good to eat?"

"What are you talking about? You're looking at a goddam fridge full of food."

I closed the refrigerator and went over to the table to sit down. I felt I was being taken advantage of and should be angry, but I wasn't. I was confused, and my head hurt. I was extraordinarily hungry. "I think I'm coming down with something," I said.

Darlene leaned back in her chair and put the cigarette to her lips.

I closed my eyes and started massaging my temples. When I opened my eyes again, I found myself staring at the uneaten half of Darlene's sandwich. I leaned across the table and picked it up. "How long will you be gone?"

She smiled. A weekend, she said. Friday to Monday, tops.

It was eerie, how quickly I became accustomed to her absence, the quiet of the house. She left on Friday morning, and by the time I got home from work, it was as if she'd been gone a year. I went from room to room, displeased with the mess, and decided to do something about it. I vacuumed all the floors and then mopped. I wiped down the stove, scoured the bathroom, disinfected every surface. I did loads and loads of laundry. At night I took a bath and watched television and drank beer. In this way, the weekend passed.

Darlene never called, but this didn't particularly bother me. Not until Sunday, when I used her car to run an errand and was almost knocked over by a foul smell coming from the back seat. It was a sharp, almost painful odor, with the ammoniac punch of a dead animal. I searched around, but didn't find anything. Finally I realized the odor was coming from the trunk. When I opened it, I found bags and bags of uneaten lunches, lunches I'd made for her over the summer. There must have been forty or fifty of them, sagging with mold and rot.

That night I woke sweating, short of breath, my stomach cramped, and by morning I had the terrible sense that I'd lost Darlene forever.

I was supposed to pick her up at the airport at four o'clock, but I got there early to be safe. After her plane landed and she failed to show at baggage claim, I called her cell. She didn't pick up. I tried her hotel, but they'd never heard of her. I was suddenly seized with panic, and I had to go outside and sit on the rim of a huge potted plant, collecting my nerves.

I stayed at the airport until nine o'clock, calling her phone every twenty minutes. Finally, I left a message threatening to call the police. A bluff, but it worked. Darlene finally called back.

"Jesus fucking Christ!" she yelled. "What the hell is the matter with you?"

"Where are you?"

"Vegas! Where do you think?"

"I've been waiting at the airport for six hours."

"Well, whoop-dee fucking doo! I decided to stay another day—so shoot me! Why the hell are you calling the cops on me?"

"When are you coming home?"

"Ah, Christ." I could hear her breathing on the other end of the line "Okay, you know what? I have to just come out and say it. I'm going to be staying out here for a little longer than expected."

"What do you mean? How long?"

"A few more days. Probably a week or two. I don't know—look, I can't talk now, Randy's looking for me."

"Who's Randy?"

"Randy's—never mind."

"No, I want to know."

"He's a guy, okay? A really famous magician."

"A magician? What are you doing with a magician?"

"Nothing. He's got this place out here, like a kind of compound. Randy's really rich, and he says he can get me a job at one of his shows."

"*What?*"

"A job."

"Doing what?"

"Like as an assistant."

"Assistant *what*? I thought you were only talking about a couple of days. What do you need a job for?"

"Look, Randy is big time! You're not listening. This guy *levitates!* Over *buildings!*"

"I don't understand. Are you moving in with this guy or what? You're my wife, right? Are you my wife or aren't you?" I waited. "Hello?"

I stood there listening for quite a while, listening but not hearing anything, because the phone had cut out. Whether it was hers or mine, I didn't know. But I felt a need to make a show of listening, of having a conversation, of being dealt a particular fate and accepting it. So I kept that phone up against my head, pretending to be the recipient of some kind of news, nodding, *Yes, yes, I understand.*

I didn't want to go home. Something about its cleanliness, its newly minted order, frightened me. So instead I went to a college bar not far from my house. My wife was gone, gone with a magician in a land in which, it was said, things stayed. I just wanted to sit there and get drunk and not be seen by anyone.

The place was quiet except for a group of young men making noise at the end of the bar. I ordered a G&T and let my eyes adjust to the dark. And then I saw him, sitting at the bar just a few seats away. It was Shep, who had recently been hit by a bus.

He looked terrible. Both of his arms were in casts, propped up at shoulder height. It was unclear to me how he was physically able to drink, given this lack of mobility. He also had some kind of scaffolding connecting his head to his shoulders. He hadn't seen me, and I was tempted to slip away unnoticed, but something compelled me to stay. I went over and placed my hand gently on his back, and he glanced at me stiffly.

"Vlad," he said through his teeth, almost smiling.

"Shep." I sat down next to him. "How are you?"

"Truthfully, I've been better." He eased his face down low to the bar and stuck his tongue out to find the two mixing straws in his drink. Then he sucked down his bourbon in three long sips. He sat up again and said, "How's Darlene?"

The bartender brought me a drink, which I tipped back smoothly. "Vegas. She met a magician."

Shep didn't look at me, didn't speak.

"She says he can levitate...I don't know."

Shep sort of hissed through his teeth and said, "Vegas." He motioned for a couple more drinks and said, "I'm real sorry to hear that, Vlad. Real sorry. Go on and keep talking, if you want to. Or don't. Just sit there and keep quiet, if you want. You do whatever you need to right now."

And you know what? I did. I went on. I told him everything, because that was what I needed. I told how Darlene had seen Trish and decided to go on a diet, how she'd struggled and failed and then took up smoking and drinking. How she got inexplicably thinner. How her whole personality had changed, and how I'd stood by and watched it happen. I went on for a long time, and Shep sat there quietly listening.

When I finished, Shep didn't say anything. At the end of the bar, one of the college students was trying to teach his friends a trick with a brandy snifter. He tipped the glass sideways to ignite the brandy with his lighter. The glass glowed and flickered with blue flame, and for a second I thought he was going to drink it like that. Instead, he put the glass on the bar and clapped his hand over it. The fire blinked out. When he lifted his hand, the glass was stuck to it, and his friends all whooped and cheered.

Shep was still looking in the direction of the college kids when he said, "Want to hear something depressing? Trish left me, too." He glanced at me as if uncertain how I would take this. "She moved out to Los Angeles three months ago. I only tell you this because of what you just shared with me. She said . . ." He swallowed hard. "She said I couldn't satisfy her anymore. I couldn't satisfy her *sexually*."

The bartender came over with a fresh drink, placed it on a white napkin. For a while we were both quiet. Then Shep said, "Would you believe it if I told you she went out there to make adult movies?" He turned to face me, to see if I believed him.

I tried to make a face that said, *I do believe you, yes.*

Shep turned back to the bar.

I said, "I didn't know that, Shep. I had no idea. I thought with the accident and everything, I thought Trish was helping you out. Nursing you back to health."

"Ha. Not even close. She was out the door long before that happened. I'll tell you something, if you want, that I've never told anyone. Do you want to hear it?"

I didn't, but I nodded.

His voice was quiet, almost hoarse. "Would you believe it if I told you—" again he turned to face me "—if I told you I did this to myself on purpose?"

Meaning: he had ruined his body, he had thrown himself in front of a bus, on purpose. I looked down at my drink. When I looked up again, his face was wet. Even if he'd wanted to hide himself, what could he do? He had no arms, at least none that worked.

I put my hand low on his back and patted him gently, and together we watched the students at the end of the bar, who were all trying the trick with the flame now. None of them could reproduce it. The first student had become the instructor. "It creates a vacuum," he said. "That's the secret. That's what makes it stay." This didn't help anyone—the glasses kept falling, rolling off the bar. Liquor spilled everywhere. "You can't be afraid of it," he said. "You have to seal that shit up, right to your skin. That's the whole trick. Make it stick; feel it suck."

More people were coming into the bar now, in from the cold, and the place was getting noisy. Everyone jockeying for space at the stools. The flame trick becoming a real attraction. People giving advice to the students, but the students, try as they might, just not getting it. At one point, for a brief second, one boy's hand was completely enshrouded in blue flame. He looked at it and screamed, then ran off to the bathroom. Everyone laughed, and someone else took his place.

When I looked back at Shep, he was bent down over his drink, making kissing motions with his lips and tongue. "Wait, wait," I said. I reached over and took hold of the glass. Shep sat up and smiled, sort of. I lifted the liquor to his lips, eased it forward, watched it go down. ❧

Dandy

Ricco Villanueva Siasoco

In the summer of 1972, I beat a man and left him—pinstriped shirt bloodied and eyes swollen to purple slits—on a bank of the Muddy River. He was a man I had met in a bar, and he'd given me a blow job. I had never laid hands on anyone before that evening, and never have since.

Years later, teaching English in the same urban university where I'd completed my undergraduate and post-graduate degrees, I called the roll for the first meeting of a composition class. The man I left for near-dead beside the Muddy River sat at the far end of the folding table. He made a striking figure, with his shiny hair pomaded and his crisp pinstriped shirt. He was tall, and though he appeared to be my age—in his late 50s—he had the slouching posture of a young man. I don't know if he recognized me then. When I called his name, Oliver Neal, he raised his hand and dangled a yellow handkerchief at me as if he were waving a tiny dinner bell.

I extend the same invitation to my students as I do to my colleagues in Comparative Literature—that is, to call me by my first name, George. Our department chair, Sandra Lockwood, a small unassuming woman with blonde streaks in her hair and raisin-like eyes, asks me for more formality. I disagree. In order to command respect, after all, one must also bestow it.

Now I consider myself neither overly masculine nor blithe and effeminate. I wear black shoes with black belts and own stylish, unusual ties that I wear to department gatherings or late-summer evenings at the Symphony. I am single. I like a full-bodied Cabernet or Shiraz with my dinner, a vintage port (second-label) following dessert (if given the choice between fruit and pastry, ordinarily fruit), and each January, in the month-long holiday between terms, I retire to the same vineyard north of San Francisco to escape the brutality of the New England winter. My parents died more than a decade ago, and my 19-year-old daughter Maggie is my only family besides a few aunts and uncles, second cousins and the like, scattered through the verdant Green Mountains of Vermont.

Oliver Neal, on the other hand, was nothing less than flamboyant. Flamboyant in the manner of Quentin Crisp, complete with witticisms and caustic remarks. One morning I recall that he appeared in class dressed in a tangerine shirt with petal-like frills at the end of the sleeves. It was a "Fight Ugliness" morning, he announced to the class, who, *en masse*, chuckled. And in a strange way, I found this flamboyance a comfort. Because despite my years of teaching and Sandra's complaints of my overfamiliarity with students, I retained a certain nervousness when speaking to them. I'd sit in my office before class and jot down notes on lined cards: *Take attendance. Tell joke.* Oliver, in his carefree way, provided a contrast to my nervousness. If I faltered or said things that seemed inane, I would never be as ridiculous as this man.

The first assignment I gave the class was to write two pages about the most frightening event that had occurred to them. It was the same exercise I assigned at the beginning of each term; I found it useful in assessing skills.

As a windy rain clinked the flagpins of the pole outside our classroom, the usual parade of 18-year-old woes were read aloud: the loss of a sporting event, mutilated romance, the sudden death of a grandparent. Oliver had titled his essay, "The Irreparable Loss of Mr. Cat."

How to be gentle about a dead cat. I placed my bifocals on my forehead and praised the detail of Mr. Cat's sleeping bag, its connotations of warmth and intimacy. It was the easiest part to extrapolate in the essay. I talked about the compassionate tone, how Oliver made the detritus of his tragedy compelling, how he evoked loss without idling in love. Then I commented on the need for organization, several dead metaphors, and a page of description that might be cut.

After I dismissed the class, Oliver remained. He sat with his head erect and hands clasped atop his leather notebook. I was the first to speak: "You're a returning student, Oliver?" This term I'd learned from Sandra. It was a polite way of referring to an older student, the middle-aged housewife or one of a dozen senior citizens in the department's Evergreen program. Oliver smiled. His tanned face seemed to breathe in the sunlight that had displaced the rainstorm and now cast the room in a bland yellow haze.

"I wrote another essay," Oliver said. "The most frightening event that ever happened to me. It was the night I was nearly beaten to death."

He stared at me across the table. I gathered my notes and neatened them like a deck of cards. Was he playing games? Did he recognize me? The morning after I deserted him on the Muddy River, I remember clipping an article from the *Globe* about the incident and carefully stowing it in a desk drawer. When I discovered it later, I stuffed it in my pocket and brought it home, shredding it with a leftover cassoulet in the garbage disposal.

Outside my classroom, a young man with a bullhorn extolled the virtues of his fraternity to the entire quad. The day had brightened considerably. I encouraged Oliver to bring his essay to a future class, speaking with the breezy, non-committal tone of a teacher. (Granted, a part of me was intrigued to see his account of that night.)

Oliver stood. His chair scraped the tile floor. With one hand, he carefully smoothed a lock of white hair that had fallen across his cheek.

Post Road Guest Folio | 201

As he closed the door of the classroom, I could have sworn that he winked at me; it seemed as intimate and as flagrant as the handkerchief that he always held in one hand.

I often assign my students Homer and Dante or the Heaney translation of *Beowulf*—Faulkner or Hemingway if they seem particularly earnest or unread. In the eighth circle of the *Inferno*, for example, Dante is both repelled and fascinated by a pair of disembodied heads, the soul on top making a banquet of the one beneath. It seems an apt metaphor for this life: conquer, or be conquered; eat, or be consumed by a voracious beast. Never to this extreme, of course, but I do believe much can be gained from assertiveness.

I follow a Tuesday-Thursday schedule for teaching, and thus slot my office hours to coincide with my days on campus. After our tense conversation, Oliver left a copy of his essay about our Muddy River encounter in my faculty mailbox. A note written on elegant stationery with the initials O.N. embossed at the top accompanied it.

Dear George,
Attached is the story of the most frightening night of my life. I think you will find it revealing. I plan to attend your next office hour and look forward to your reaction.
Respectfully,
Oliver Neal

There was no mention of me in "Under the Bridge," simply the fact that Oliver had never found his assailant. And though the essay's overall tone was one of anger, it was the quietness in his prose that shocked me: the persistent need for closure; the gentle hint of a refrain. There was a natural cadence that seemed to repeat, *Tomorrow I'll understand, or the following day, or the next.* I was sure he knew my identity and this essay was his method of confrontation. *Come out with it,* I wanted to say, correcting his grammar in red ink.

On Tuesday morning, Oliver waited in the dim hallway outside my office. He was dressed in a button-down shirt and a gaudy pink tie. I unlocked my door and offered him the chair opposite my own.

"Did you read my essay?" he asked.

I nodded and placed my satchel on the floor.

"It was you. You were the one, George."

I sat quietly and forced myself not to speak.

Oliver leaned forward, elbows on his knees. "That part about leading me out of the reeds? Do you remember that? When we went under the bridge. Me crouching at your waist and undoing your belt—"

"What do you want, Oliver?"

He leaned back, crossing his legs and staring at me. He was pleased with himself, a crooked smile indicating the distance between student and teacher had been breached. He stared at the floor, and I noticed the shiny gloss of scalp beneath his thinning hair. His fingers were pressed together at the tips, resembling an A-frame. Another moment passed, and he reached for his briefcase—a rigid brown box—and placed it on his lap. The lid snapped open. Papers, I thought, a lawsuit or some other form of extortion. This, I realized, would please Oliver Neal the most.

He handed me an ordinary file folder with five or six papers inside. I moved my bifocals from my head to my nose and opened the folder. At the top of the first page was the logo and address for Random House Publishers, New York. Below, a letter to Oliver from an acquisitions editor named Marilyn O'Connor.

"I received $15,000 up front, because they loved my proposal. The rest of my advance is contingent upon acceptance of the manuscript." Oliver gently closed the lid of his briefcase. "They think it needs structure. Ms. O'Connor suggested I find an editor, someone with experience. She mentioned a grammar Nazi or some college type."

He placed his elbows on the armrests of the chair. My chest felt constricted, my teeth unnaturally clenched, but I would not reveal this to Oliver. I often denied that this was the year 2001, that society had entered a new, uncharted millennium, and a part of me began to understand Oliver's motivation for reentering my life. It had been decades since I had studied Walter Benjamin in graduate school, but his theory of history seemed manifest in this man seated across my desk: the angel of history, with eyes turned to the past. Even as his wings propelled him forward on the progress of Paradise.

I leaned back in my desk chair. It creaked loudly: a single, rust-corroded hinge. Oliver was silent, his mouth curved into a thin smile. I imagined both squealing with delight.

Retribution has always held more interest for me than redemption. Dante? The great poet didn't make lemonade from his lemons. Rather, he squeezed every last drop of acid from the experience and, through his unholy *Inferno*, splashed it on the open sores of his persecutors. Twenty-eight years ago, I had committed a crime that had yet to be paid for. Now Charon—in the form of a middle-aged dandy—had arrived to ferry me across the river.

Several days later, I sat in my office and reread Oliver's manuscript. He had written approximately eighty pages of his life story, a description of his childhood in a wealthy Boston suburb up to his melodramatic 16th birthday, when he entered his family's parlor in white bloomers and his mother's strapless sundress. His father, a staunch New England Brahmin, smacked him; his mother locked herself in their solarium and wept. *"How could you do this to us?" Father fumed. He yanked Mother's beautiful sundress off me and I stood before him in the parlor, naked as the wind.*

"You don't understand," I yelled back, piercing him like a razor-sharp blade. "And you never will. I'm not like you. I will never be so old." (Did Oliver mean "bold"? or "cold"?)

That was the last time I spoke with Father. Like a fragile bouquet that has bloomed and lost its fragrant scent, my dear Father died later that same day.

Oliver's manuscript was riddled with this florid prose. I'd read better descriptions of bat mitzvahs and seventh-grade dances.

We discussed revision strategies and new ideas for the manuscript on a weekly basis. In the beginning I wrote minimal comments on the manuscript and dreaded the endless recall of that evening. I wanted to refuse him altogether, but Oliver had intimated that he had no qualms about contacting the police. One cold October morning, we talked in my office, the high-pitched clanking of the radiator a counterpoint to our quiet conversation. Oliver had written a description of our fateful encounter that paralleled the tale of David and Goliath.

And there went out a Goliath that lured me carefully into the reeds. I was enthralled by this monster, being but a young and defenseless David, and I would have followed him anywhere. I was portrayed as a vicious, one-dimensional beast; Oliver, as the noble, though disadvantaged, David.

I handed him a sheet with my comments organized in a bulleted list. "Can't we tone down the aggression a bit?" I asked. "Make the monster more human?"

Oliver snorted. "The entire story hinges on your aggression, George."

"But you *asked* me to hit you." There was a surreal quality to our conversation, as if we were discussing gardening rather than a violent encounter. I tapped my shoe restlessly on the floor beneath my desk.

"That's irrelevant, isn't it? I want this to be fierce, to embody the wild terror I felt that night. It must be epic, George! 'He who desires, but acts not, breeds pestilence.' Oscar Wilde said that."

Of course Oliver chose to identify with Wilde. I didn't tell him the quotation sounded more like William Blake.

I swallowed and straightened my dark tie. "The reader has to feel sympathy for *both* characters, Oliver. You need to prepare us for the confrontation. It will only make the story more resonant." I looked him directly in the face.

Oliver made a constipated expression, his upper lip touching the end of his nose. For a moment I considered suggesting a composition handbook I preferred that emphasized the audience as a focusing force.

"I know what you want me to say, George. But this is my story." He grabbed his manuscript from my desk. "I'm going to tell it the way it happened."

The second week in October, my daughter Maggie phoned. She was in the process of selecting spring classes and had to declare a major. I asked which of her courses interested her.

"I really like Cultural Studies. Don't smirk, George. Somebody needs to deconstruct hip-hop lyrics for old white guys like you." I laughed. In the background, I heard the sizzle of a lighter, and I imagined Maggie in her dorm room smoking a cigarette. It pleased me that I was privy to a few secrets that her mother did not know.

"I'm thinking about teaching after I graduate."

"But you have so much potential, Maggie."

"I'm a social justice freak," she said. "Education is power. Could I sit in on one of your classes?"

My daughter is bright and genial, "not gay, but gay-friendly," I heard her remark once, the kind of young woman who prefers listening to all sides of an argument before making a decision. I imagined her leading an NGO in Eastern Africa someday.

"Let me think about it," I said. I heard the click of her telephone and returned to the dozen or so essays I had yet to grade.

Maggie loves literature as much as I do; she has always been a reader—solely my influence, I'd like to believe, but her mother, my friend Pamela (to whom I donated my sperm, but with whom I have never been romantically involved), is a devotee of Shakespeare and Yeats, Trollope (to my chagrin) as well as the Romantics and even the Beats. Pamela has been a devoted friend since our undergraduate days, when she and I worked for a research lab that studied attention-deficit disorders in children; now she is "Dr. Pam" to our friends and practices internal medicine at Brigham and Women's. She has always supported a close relationship between Maggie and myself, explaining to Maggie when she entered junior high school that I was her birth father. The timing couldn't have been better: Maggie asked me to Sadie Hawkins dances, and to lend an impartial ear when her mother would not. But our time together had become increasingly limited during this, her difficult freshman year. A few days after our phone call, Maggie told me she had purchased a plane ticket to Boston. I immediately began to buy her favorite junk foods—yogurt pretzels and caramel rice cakes—as well as thick fashion magazines.

Our lesson the Thursday of Maggie's visit was on the persuasive essay. Oliver's manuscript, of course, had usurped much of my time, so I offered up the usual suspects: King's "I Have a Dream" speech, a thoughtful essay on migraines, a brief excerpt from *Notes of a Native Son*. Only two-thirds of my class were in their seats when we arrived.

I introduced Maggie, and she sat in a desk chair apart from our table near the window. She produced a reporter's notepad and a pen and sat poised in her deliberate way. Did we both sense that she wasn't going to learn anything from my class? Her attentiveness—the very effort of it—emboldened me and reminded me of a child seeking approval. Over breakfast, we had argued about her education and her staunch refusal to accept my financial support. In her gravelly voice she repeated, *I'll pay for it myself, George, or I just won't go.* Last spring she had entertained the idea of working on a fishing boat in Alaska with her deadbeat boyfriend rather than entering Princeton. Pamela and I tried to be gentle in our disapproval, but it was her boyfriend's inertia that ultimately changed her mind.

Oliver, of course, volunteered to read his essay aloud. Ostensibly, the topic was the formative years of the homosexual. "Nature or nurture?" he began, and I felt the physical attentiveness of my students as a musician intuits his audience from the lighted stage. Maggie, too, leaned forward in her rickety chair.

"The homosexual has always been oppressed in society. This essay seeks to understand why this oppression occurs—but more importantly, the roots of homosexual desire." I recognized the passage from the end of Chapter 8, which we'd just revised in conference.

Oliver gestured theatrically. I caught Maggie's eye, and she shrugged. It seemed more an acknowledgement of Oliver's essay topic than a truce to our morning argument. How could I make her understand? Her education was something I valued, something I was passionate about and wanted to contribute to.

"In reality, homosexuals aren't the oppressed," Oliver concluded, "but the oppressors. Until we learn to voice our opinions, to love ourselves, how can we expect others to love us?"

I thought Oliver's argument lacked teeth, and had told him so, but my horde of impressionable freshmen applauded. Oliver had ignored my wishes for more dialogue and scene—rather than his long-winded proselytizing. He was a stubborn man. I looked at Maggie in the back of the room, hunched over her reporter's notebook, nodding to no one. What was she puzzling over? Could she still be angry about our morning argument?

I dismissed the class, and the usual zippering of book bags ensued. Maggie approached me, and I hugged her, suggesting a restaurant for lunch. I sensed her distance. When Oliver passed us, Maggie tapped him on the shoulder.

"I loved your essay," she said. "Could I read a copy of it?"

Oliver clapped his hands at chest level. "I would be honored, Maggie!" He introduced himself, holding out his left hand, hinged at the wrist, as if he were royalty. Maggie clasped it warmly.

"You must be proud of your father," Oliver said. "He's a *fabulous* tutor." They turned and looked at me. Maggie's eyes narrowed with dissent.

I fastened the brass buckle of my satchel, staring at my daughter. She was still angry with me. Oliver continued to rant about our special relationship, then asked Maggie how long she was visiting me. Their banter—the easy familiarity—frustrated me, but I tried to play along. After a few minutes I held Maggie's elbow and whispered, "Let's hurry, honey. I want to beat the lunch crowd on Newbury Street."

Maggie looked at Oliver. She seemed to sense my impatience and shook me off, linking arms with Oliver. "Why don't you join us? We're celebrating my birthday today. George shouldn't be my only guest."

The crowded restaurant Maggie had chosen was not on Newbury Street as I hoped, but rather in Kenmore Square, and was decorated with a car-wash-style banner, a depressing mural of a fiesta, and a fireplace containing a television monitor—which in turn played a videotape of a crackling fire. The specialties were slow-cooked BBQ brisket and lime-green margaritas. Our waiter, a young man in no particular hurry, approached our table and stared at me in a direct manner for several seconds.

"Remember me, George? Rudy? I wrote the essay about the karaoke tournament I won in junior high?"

"Of course," I lied. He stretched his arm in the air like a basketball player, awaiting my slap. I lowered it and shook his hand.

Rudy sat unexpectedly in my booth and wrote down our drink order: a vodka martini for me, a Diet Coke for Maggie, and for Oliver, the house margarita. As he walked away, I told Maggie and Oliver that his writing was remarkable only for his overuse of semicolons.

Maggie unrolled her napkin, chiding me. She leaned toward Oliver. "Do you really think my father's a good teacher?"

"I'm not overstating when I say that George is quite remarkable. He has always encouraged me to write the truth." With his yellow handkerchief in the air, he winked at me.

I returned his confidence with a frown, smoothing my napkin in my lap.

"Good," Maggie said. "Because he's trying to convince me to follow in his footsteps."

There was an awkward silence. Oliver dipped a tortilla chip in salsa. I wondered if he had the gall to reveal our relationship to her.

Maggie said, "Your essay made a good argument for nature, Oliver, but I'm not sure it's necessarily true."

"Let's not discuss this right now," I said.

She fastened her eyes on me.

"It's *my* party, isn't it?" She turned to Oliver. "Did you ever lie to anybody about yourself?"

I tapped Oliver's boot beneath the table, trying to silence him with a glance. "My dear," he said, "I told my parents the terrible truth about their son when I turned 16."

"Really? How did they take it?"

"My mother threw a tantrum. And then my father had a heart attack."

Maggie's mouth dropped, and she expressed her sympathies. She turned to me and asked the same question. I ignored her, staring at the electronic flame across the room. Oliver sipped his lime-green margarita. I was willing to wait out the silence, but Oliver could not. He politely excused himself to the bathroom.

"You don't have to be so uptight," Maggie said.

"How could you invite him? This was supposed to be our celebration."

"I'm sick of arguing with you all the time."

I reached out and held her soft fingers atop the table. Her nails were painted a glossy white. "What can I do to please you, Maggie?"

"Just lighten up." She pulled her hand away. "Why can't you be more like Oliver?"

I crumpled my napkin beneath the table. "Oliver Neal is not a role model."

"I like him. He's got a good sense of humor."

He's a dandy, I wanted to yell, but held my tongue. What kind of man would I be if I carried myself like him? Maggie craned her neck toward the spot where Oliver had disappeared behind a pair of saloon doors.

She turned to me, her mouth pulled back at the corners. "It's obvious you hate him."

For a brief instant I wanted to tell her the truth. I wanted her to know about Oliver's cunning, his manipulation of me, his book deal. I wanted her to know that Oliver consented to everything that night beside the Muddy River. Over her shoulder, I saw Oliver talking near the rest room with Rudy. He had twisted his arm to show Oliver an intricate tattoo that circled the upper half. Oliver squeezed his biceps and cooed.

Maggie stared out the large plate-glass window.

"If you're ever to be an educator, a truly exceptional one," I said, "you must understand that teachers and students don't mix. It's asking for trouble. I hope you can understand."

She gave a weary sigh. When Oliver slid back into the padded booth, he unfolded a receipt and showed it to her. It was not until a few days later, when I dropped my daughter at Logan Airport, that she shared the contents. Rudy had given Oliver his phone number and, below it, reduced the bill for Maggie's birthday dinner by thirty percent.

*

Later that autumn, Pamela made plans for a cruise to the Bahamas with her partner. Maggie and I decided to celebrate Thanksgiving in my home. Oliver had quickly put together a passable first draft, 200-odd pages, and left it in my faculty mailbox before the holiday break began. It had finally become exciting, working on our book, and I had convinced myself that the story was not the actual event, but a dramatization. Years of deconstructing Eliot and Pound had taught me to separate the writer from the text. Our meetings centered on Oliver's voice, diction, occasional lapses of tone. He had surprised me with his professionalism and determined approach.

Maggie sat in my kitchen on Thanksgiving morning and read a tattered copy of *Vogue*. I cracked three eggs on the rim of a stainless-steel bowl.

"There's an article in this issue by a gay kid...I mean, the child of a gay couple. The interviewer asked him if he had a choice, who would he pick? Straight or gay parents? Guess how he answered."

"God forbid." I placed her toast on a porcelain plate and slid it with a small jar of marmalade across the counter.

"Gay, of course. Isn't that awesome?"

"No one, of course, would *choose* gay parents."

Maggie frowned, buttering her toast. The eggs congealed in an old frying pan on the stove. Maybe her mother never should have told Maggie my identity. I think it may have been too much for any young girl.

"You're so cynical, George. My roommate says pessimism is bad for your skin." She took her toast and her magazine and sprawled on my Turkish carpet. I sighed. Maggie's new bravado: she reminded me of one of my students.

The telephone rang, and Maggie looked at me. I ignored both, breaking the egg yolk in the pan. When the answering machine picked up, Oliver spoke. "I was thinking we should work on the sex scene, George. Do you think it's too graphic? Maybe we should make my attacker immediately regret hitting me. Just a thought. Ciao."

I slid the fried eggs to another plate. Maggie raised her dark eyebrows at me. I feigned interest in the sports section of the *Globe*, and when I failed to acknowledge her, she rose, touching my forearm.

"Did you know Mom wanted me to go to Grandma's house for Thanksgiving?" She sat on a high stool across from me at the counter. "She thinks your issues will rub off on me. I said, 'What issues?' but she wouldn't say."

Maggie laid her hand flat on the newspaper headline that I was reading. "Why can't we just talk like regular people, George?"

I stared at her delicate fingers. Though I loved Maggie and would support her unconditionally, I was unwilling to share this part of my life.

How could I possibly broach it? How could I explain to her that Oliver Neal had once engaged me in anonymous sex and then asked me to strike him under the Boylston Street Bridge?

I was her father. Yet I didn't want to invoke this cliché.

"Maggie, please," I said, placing my hand on top of hers. "Allow me to keep parts of my life private." What I did with other men, whom I chose to be physically intimate with, was no concern of hers.

She slinked to the bathroom as if she'd been reprimanded (or, upon reflection, hurt). I didn't know how to comfort her. She would spend the rest of that weekend talking to her mother long-distance, prodding me with existential questions, drinking coffee. Always, *always*, trying to steer the conversation to the topic of sexuality. *My* sexuality, *my* unwillingness to talk about it. She was infuriating, sulking from living room to bathroom. My 19-year-old daughter, impressionable and idealistic in her white polished nails, still hopeful for change in this world.

I heard the click of the bathroom door. I gathered her dirty plate and rinsed the remains of her toast in the sink.

Arnold, the manager at Devon's, filled a highball glass with plain-label gin and tonic water, then ran a thin lime wedge along the rim. I had dropped Maggie at Logan Airport with a small crate of tangerines and twenty minutes to spare before her flight back to New Jersey.

"My bartender called in sick for the third time this week. Can you believe it, George?" He set the drink before me. Despite his complaint, Arnold was smiling. I imagined that pouring cocktails in the crowded bar was better than paying invoices in his dingy office, surrounded by cases of beer and a metal desk where late one night, after one too many cocktails, he had lowered my trousers. I had allowed him to pleasure me.

Arnold lifted my gin-and-tonic from the bar and set a small napkin below it. I stirred the petite red straw and then sucked the gin from the end. Devon's was crowded with bare-chested men in leather pants and matching leather caps. There were a few put-together college students who talked in small tribes at high tables.

"Why so glum?"

"Oh, Arnold," I said, "my daughter loathes me."

He leaned on his chin and poured himself a Coke from the soda nozzle. "Things can only get better."

Arnold struck me as a "good old" type—welcoming to everyone, discriminating against no one. I'd always found it surprising, the fraternity of a gay establishment. Community newspapers and support-group flyers near the door, disco music blaring from mounted speakers, men cruising other men but also laughing with one another and greeting each other with kisses on the mouth.

Arnold nodded in the direction of the jukebox. "That boy in the corner? He's got a sweet smile for you."

I turned. The stocky red-haired boy looked barely out of high school. A Red Sox cap was level with his eyebrows, and he possessed a shy, unassuming smile. Dimples fast at work. He was seated at a table with two equally youthful friends.

"Thank you, Arnold, but he looks like one of my students." I finished my drink and walked away from the bar to the billiards table. The red-haired boy's gaze followed me. Soon he stood and went to the bathroom. I followed him, standing at the stall to his right. "What's your name?" I asked.

He smiled. "Chad Kline."

We moved to the porcelain sinks, and I introduced myself. Chad rubbed his hands beneath the faucet and then combed his wet fingers through his short hair.

"You don't look of age, Chad."

"How old do you think I am?"

"About sixteen."

"It's the zits. I just moved back from California. Do you know how much L.A. revolves around sex?"

I laughed, asking him if he'd like to have a nightcap. On the short walk to my apartment, he told me his life story: he had attended a private school in Cambridge, then, upon graduation, moved to Los Angeles to pursue acting. His accomplishments over the past three years, however, consisted of a diet-soda commercial and a management position at a pornography shop in West Hollywood. I encouraged him to keep at it, as I would with any of my students. "It's difficult to wend one's way through the Inferno," I added.

Half an hour later, inside my disorderly living room, I handed him a bottle of beer and told him to remove his baseball cap, make himself at home. He flashed that quick smile I'd noticed at Devon's and said he'd remove whatever I wanted.

Truthfully, boys did nothing for me. It was body hair I loved, the goatee circling a man's lips, the muscular thighs, the soft scratch of hair beneath the arms. These things aroused me and reminded me I was with another man. If I wanted smooth skin, I would have made love to women. When I removed Chad's shirt, the zits he'd mentioned in the bar covered his shoulders and back like small red ants.

When he was unclothed, he crouched in front of me at my piano bench and removed my loafers. He reached for my waist, and I helped him to remove my black belt, my dark linen trousers, my boxers. He threw my trousers on top of the piano. I wanted to fold them neatly. Instead I ran my hand through his short hair, and, when he looked up, he asked what I wanted to do.

"Hit me," I said, somewhat uncertainly.

"I'm sorry?"

I kissed him and then handed him my belt. "With this." His red lips were parted, not sure how to proceed; I grinned, noting that he was aroused.

Except for laying hands on Oliver Neal nearly three decades earlier, I can say that I had never struck, or been struck, by another man. Chad rose to his feet and gathered his clothes from the settee where they lay. I remained on the piano bench.

As he dressed, I repeated my request.

Chad shook his head, incredulous. He buttoned his baggy jeans. "You're fucked up," he said, lifting my trousers off the piano and hurling them at me. He squared his Red Sox cap across his brow. "Crazy old queen." Before I could reply, he had unlocked the dead bolt and let himself out. ଚ

The White Tide
Steven Church

Many writers and artists have been stricken with a psychological sickness known as the "white death," an all-consuming obsession with Herman Melville and his novel, *Moby Dick*. Junot Diaz, Laurie Anderson, Jackson Pollack, Tony Kushner, David Foster Wallace, Nick Flynn, and David Shields all had a touch of the sickness; the "white death" seemed especially infectious amongst a group of writers in New York City in the late 90's and early 2000's. Justin Hocking was one of these writers, riding the wave of Melville's resurgence with his own unique style and characteristic flow in an exciting debut memoir from Graywolf Press, *The Great Floodgates of the Wonderworld*.

Perhaps this movement toward Melville was a response to the spare minimalist prose and claustrophobic domestic tableaus that seemed to characterize so much contemporary and post-modern fiction. Perhaps it was the anti-imperialist, environmentalist ethos of his epic novel. Perhaps it was, as Hocking quotes another writer, because, "[*Moby-Dick*] speaks so deeply to us today because this state of alienated meaninglessness is so prevalent in twentieth-century man." For whatever reasons, Melville's book enjoyed a resurgence in popularity amongst some writers, artists, and intellectuals, many of them restless transplants in their twenties who'd found themselves working soul-crushing cubicle jobs in New York publishing or, like Hocking, working a soul-crushing cubicle job in New York publishing, delivering Indian Food on evenings and weekends, writing a doomed novel, attending a twelve-step program for co-dependency, and taking every other opportunity to escape to the ocean, "the one place that felt like home, a lush wave garden free from all the thorns and thistles of the broken world," forever in search of the "blissed out" feeling that only surfing seemed to provide.

Melville's postmodern moves (authorial intrusion, shifting points of view, overtly symbolic characters, structural and formal idiosyncrasies) were exciting and relevant, even revolutionary to a whole new generation of writers. *Moby Dick* was "bending genre" and mixing fiction and nonfiction long before it was en vogue or taboo, and reading the book made everything new in literature, especially postmodernism, seem old. Perhaps more significantly, it filled writers with sea dreams of subjects so vast and deep and dark that they threatened to swallow them whole.

Recently I read about the tragic and unexpected death in Uganda of freelance journalist, Matthew Power, while on a writing assignment for *Esquire*. Power was a writer I admired very much, enjoying immensely some of his more Melvillian essays for *Harper's Magazine*, particularly his March 2008 piece, "Mississippi Drift: River Vagrants in the Age of Wal-Mart." Power also lived in New York during those years of the rising white tide; having apparently also caught a bit of the "white death" himself, he was known, in conversation, to quote whole lines from *Moby Dick*. Donovan Hohn, another writer and editor, and a friend of Power's, who would go on to write his own critically acclaimed Melville-inspired book, *Moby Duck*, remembered Power's love for Melville's masterpiece, and what might be called Power's penchant for chasing "white whales," or those deep, dark, and ineffable ideas. In Power's writing and in the writing of Hocking and Hohn and others afflicted with the "white death," we discover that those "ungraspable phantoms of life," can consume, nourish, and enlighten us even as they threaten our very existence.

Hocking, avid skateboarder and publishing industry "pit" drone, was paddling against the existential pushback of New York City, searching for something like peace in the wake of failed relationships and generalized anxiety, and ultimately finding inspiration in an old book and a newly developed passion for surfing; surfing is one thing that both holds his memoir together and sets it apart from other books that explore the "white death," making it a "surfing book" about the ocean and the environment, a memoir of real-life love and loss, as much as it is also an ekphrastic celebration of *Moby Dick*.

Composed of short, essayistic meditations that bounce between surfing vignettes, personal stories of work, love, and life in New York, and reflections on Melville's character and writing, the book still never spins out of control, but instead moves with grace—smooth, flowing, tight and focused—like one imagines Hocking skates the wooden bowl in Greenpoint and surfs the breaks at Rockaway. Mixed in with some wry humor and haunted images of Melville lingering around the edges of his consciousness, Hocking's book also takes the occasional experimental turn, making the book as delightfully unpredictable in form as it is in subject.

The Great Floodgates is a stunningly beautiful, finely tuned and often lyrical and heartbreaking meditation on identity, anxiety, love, surfing, *Moby Dick*, and the search for spiritual transcendence. Just when you think Hocking might be the obsessed and self-destructive Ahab or, worse yet, end up a Bartleby living out his days in a paralyzed corporate angst-ridden existence, he instead becomes our Ishmael, the narrator-hero first pulled under by the dark tides of life in New York City ascending finally from the sinking wreck of his past, rising to a new world no less complicated but filled with the promise of something close to enlightenment. ❧

Thin, Brilliant Lines
Patrick Myers

Somewhere, a photograph. I couldn't say where. A dresser drawer, a coat pocket, a landfill. It could be anywhere. There are two things I know about the photograph. First—it's of me. Physically I'm in the picture. And second—the photograph is black and white. On cheap gloss paper splashes the darkest of darks, the brightest of brights, with only slight traces of gray in between.

A wave of fog rolls in on a road in eastern Montana and everything's white. A confused, chaotic sort of white that jumps around at random and at will. Ahead a car drives with all its lights out except for one, the brake light, and the only time it's clear that the car is still on the road and in the fog is when the car slows down and there's a quick, cherry-red blip. The blip is bright enough, barely, to turn all the white red, a large red space to drive through for a moment until the road's all white again. This happens again and again. The road is white, then red, then white, and then red, and the fog stays heavy. In other places, coastal places, fogs are falling down warm and nice, cloaking streetlights, like in films. But there's no coast, no warmth here. The temperature outside is negative two, soon enough it will be negative three, and the sun has set. Driving east is like that; the sun is always set or setting. At least it's been that way for me.

Negative three degrees now and soon negative four. People focus on the numbers but dark and wind really make cold cold on the plains. And the plains are cold, a cold biting and relentless and unforgiving, though the fog is turning the plains into what they're not and they shift and pulse and breathe as seas do. I'm in the middle of the sea and drifting, not driving, weightless. The moon is full and coming up in the sky on top of the road. Before the fog came in, the sky was clear and dark, and before that a gradient gray.

A small sign with simple print marks the North Dakota/Montana state border. I cross over the border and, as if on cue, tank trucks carrying oil pour onto the road. They're behind, a long line of them, some even passing, and they're coming from the other way as well. They come by every minute or so, and they're big and fast, stirring up the snow on the side of the road, which happens violently enough to make the road feel serious. The car with only the one brake light is still ahead of me and its driver starts to feel the same thing, I know, because he begins to brake more frequently. Gas flares pop up on the side of the road—tall, bright flames burning off excess oil from the ground, some of them close and some of them a little farther off, and the fog is still thick, and when the trucks come down the road snow goes swirling up again and the car ahead brakes, and the one red light turns everything red again still, and the flames on the side of the road are red, too. This is how North Dakota introduces itself, with the world white and covered in flames, except for those short moments of total red, and when everything turns red now it's *really* red, and *everything* is red, even the whites of my eyes, and all of this together makes the drive seem surreal and frightening and exciting too, in a way.

Negative five degrees. Soon negative six.

Williston, North Dakota is a modern day oil boomtown—a term used to imply lawlessness, or wildness, a term seeming to prove true upon my one a.m. arrival. The formerly quiet, small agrarian town is lit up and moving. Oil tankers, torrents of them, fall down the roads, men fall drunk out of bars, and there's enough light from the traffic and the buildings to turn night essentially into day.

My hotel room walls are paper thin. Also there's noise. All sorts of noise—groups of men outside on the sidewalk, tankers falling down on the highway, and the sort of sound machines make when thousands of them run together. Plus the couple next door. They've been yelling since I got here. One voice is deep and aggressive, the other high and defensive. She keeps saying she'll be there for him, no matter what. He keeps saying, "you stupid bitch." The time is four in the morning. The deeper voice goes deeper, nearly to a growl, and one of them stomps across the room—deep, heavy stomps that shake the walls of my own room. The lights are so many and so bright outside that, even with the curtains drawn, the window of the room shines out as a bright yellow square and casts shadows across the bed. Lying down I remember a time driving, not far from here, when my tire hit a nail and went flat. Outside the air had been cold in the usual winter way, so dry it seemed to break and fall apart, and it was cold enough to push me back into the car every couple of minutes as I changed the tire, which took quite awhile, but when the job was done I didn't go back in, not right away. I leaned back into the car and slid down to the ground. The air was lung-aching, the wind furious, making high, angry whistling noises, but the night still felt quiet, clean, and calm. There was no moon, no stars, just a black, unbroken space with wind flying across it, gaining speed for miles all around, and the subtle vibrations from the running car were a reassurance on my back.

One of the couple yells and throws something, some sort of glass or something else fragile, I think, and I hear it break against the wall and fall to the ground in pieces. The woman starts screaming "oh no, oh no, oh no," and her voice is raw and scratched from the yelling. I get up to go knock on their door, to get the man at the desk, something, but stop when I hear their voices turn soft and gentle, their quiet sorry murmurs coming through the wall, and awhile after that the not so quiet sounds of sex. Outside the men are playing loud music from car speakers, and then more cars pull up, and the golden box on the wall gets brighter, and the shadows grow longer against the floor's worn, pallid carpeting.

At a diner bar, the next morning, two men sit close and I can hear their conversation. I can't not hear them. One of them owns a high and piercing pitch that dominates the room, a voice sounding strange coming out of his face, a face heavy and covered by a beard that curls out thick and black like animal hair. The other man, his friend, nods but says nothing. The loud one is saying "let's go down to South Dakota this weekend, that's where all the women are." He tells a story about how he met his third wife, and his friend keeps nodding, but the story is long and involves so many of his other past wives I get lost in the details. A waitress comes by, and every time she does, he gives her a friendly smile and manages to touch her in some way on the shoulder, waist, or wrist, and she puts a smile on and laughs at his jokes. But she looks tired. Her eyes lay dead on her face. All the women working here look tired. The sun rises, then turns, breaking into the room by the windows, and the small, suspended particles that morning light holds so well seem to be missing. Their absence makes the room feel empty. Food from the plate sits dull in my mouth and goes coarse down my throat. The man says, "I just can't stand going alone to that bed another night. I can't," and his friend keeps nodding.

Walking out the diner I see two birds ambling underneath an oil truck in the parking lot. They're Hoary Redpolls, small finches with cone shaped bills and pale plumage across their chest and wings. I'm surprised to see them. Hoarys live in the arctic and rarely come south for the winter, and when they do they won't go much farther south than here. They have a bright, near perfectly circular red dot on their forehead, and they look similar to and would be easy to mistake with their cousin, the Common Redpoll. But these two are Hoary. They're Hoary, not Common, because their feathers are paler than the Common's would be, feathers that blend in well enough with the snow on the ground that when squinting from across the lot, the red dot is all I see. The birds linger underneath the truck, close to the thick rows of tires. They are attractive, unique looking animals. It's unclear what they're doing, but I never find out because before I realize or can react, the truck starts to move, and one of the Redpolls opens its wings and flies away, but the other doesn't, not in time.

I learn more about the Hoary Redpoll then.

I learn that when the tire of a two ton oil tanker runs over a Hoary Redpoll, its body makes several quick, thin popping noises. I learn that after a Hoary Redpoll's been run over in this way, its body doesn't look flattened, or bloodied, or all twisted up like you might expect it would. The bird just lies there, its wings stretched out, like it's still trying to get out of the way, and its eyes stay open, and its body looks so intact that it seems as if it's going to get up and fly away at any second, except for the thin, barely noticeable lines of blood running out of its eyes and bill. Those lines fall over the back of its head and mix in with the patch of red on its forehead, and after awhile the blood falls to the ground and makes slight red drips on the snow.

I pick up the dead bird and place it in bushes away from the road so it won't get run over again. The other Redpoll flies over and lands on the bush next to the dead one. Then, after a moment, it flies away.

Now all there is is black. I feel black everywhere. The road to Williston is black, and the tires of my car are black, and the tires that killed the Redpoll are black, too, and so are the eyes of the waitresses in the diner. The man at the diner went home after his long day of work, and his world was hushed and black, and when I drove, black ran through the engine and underneath my feet and burned up, all of it, smelling black, into the sky. A sky that was grey and dark and might as well have been black. None of it the same black of the night on the road, after I changed my tire. It was down and dirty, it leaked and poured in and onto everything, onto me, even, it was apart of me, I was apart of it, and I needed to get away.

White Earth Valley.

It's night when I arrive in the valley and the sky is cloud-covered and I can only see the edge of the light of my headlamp, which flickers on/off because the battery hasn't been changed since I can't remember when. I walk down into the valley, to White Earth River, hiking along for an hour or so until I find a place that seems o.k. for camping. The ground is dark and hard next to the river, which is frozen, but somewhere still there's a slight trickle of running water, and there's wind too, but besides the trickle and the wind everything is quiet. And cold, of course, but not as cold as it could be. In the tent I wrap up, every inch of skin covered by rigid wool, or fleece, and I slide down into my sleeping bag and more or less pass out.

But the cold wakes me before the sun's up. The coldest part of the day is the moment right after the sun rises, I've been told, not before it, and though I know this and realize I should pack up and move towards the car, I decide not to move, to stay wrapped up and out of the wind. As I grow colder the pain comes in waves, mostly in my hands and face. Every breath I take rises up into the empty space above me before dispersing, and then another breath replaces it. Shuddering sets in after an hour. My eyes clench and my teeth shake. What I think about in that hour is a guess. Maybe nothing, besides the pain.

When the sun does rise I move to the edge of my tent to meet it, but my fingers are dead and stiff, so when I bring them up to the fly it feels like

I have to tell them what to do again and again in my head. After awhile I abandon my fingers and grab the zipper with my teeth to pull it down. The flap falls, and I see mist rising off the river, and the rising sun coming through the mist, and everything else I couldn't see the night before. The surrounding valley is subtle, covered in snow and dead prairie grass, and a little ways in the distance, at the valley's mouth, I can see a couple of old buildings that make up the town of White Earth, decrepit and in various stages of decay. And White Earth Valley really is white. A layer of frost covers everything—the shoes I left outside, the fly of the tent, all the dead and dried up shrubs and grasses; it's all white, and the sun is coming through the mist off the river, deepening the valley in a way that makes me forget the cold.

The only visible living thing in White Earth Valley is a dog. I drive out of the valley and she comes running up to the car from a trailer on the side of the road, runs alongside the car and throws herself onto the pavement. I slam on the brakes. My tires lock and slide on the ice. She stands in front of my car as it slides. She refuses to move. Refuses to wince, even. I see her pregnant stomach. I press down harder. My toes whiten from the pressing. The bumper comes within a couple of inches of her before the car comes to a stop. She looks directly at me and begins to howl—long, sorrowful howls, her belly swollen and sagging and swaying with her movements. In her eyes is loathing. She would have let herself die here, on this morning road. She is protecting her place, I suppose. This will be her children's place after it is hers, and after they are gone this place will be their children's place, and then their children's place—a place worth protecting despite the danger or impossibility of stopping what's coming her way. After several long moments she moves aside, though she's slow and reluctant to do so. I drive past, watching in one of the mirrors as she walks back into that same spot in the middle of the empty road, where she sits quietly and follows my leave.

I keep driving, can't seem to stop driving, and later that night my car breaks down, somewhere under the hood oil leaks and the engine runs dry. It's late at night, and cold, still. Negative six or around there. I've stopped dead in an intersection. A traffic light blinks above. In the car, cold pours down into every crevice, in and over the windows and through the sides of the doors, as water might to a sponge. All around the road is quiet, besides the odd driver pumping their brakes and swerving around. One of the these drivers pulls over next to me and opens the door to my car and shouts, "what did you *do* to this thing?" and laughs a manic, raspy laugh that bounces around and out of his throat. His face is round, bright, flushed from the cold.

The two of us push the car into a nearby lot. He's breathing loud, and despite the cold sweat falls down his face in weighted beads. He offers to drive me to the nearest hotel, and I accept, but he drives like he's blind, and the dash of his car is filled with old paper, dried crusted tissues, and other dark objects that run and fall down onto my lap as he makes his desperate turns.

"It's suicide," he says. "There's an accident almost every week, somebody dying over by Williston, Dickinson, all those towns, they run into the oil tankers on the road. They say it's an accident. I don't believe it. There's too many to be accidents. It's suicide. Just like in homestead days, when guys came and looked for work and couldn't stand living in the cold. They killed themselves, too."

Later that night I would learn more about this man. I'd learn that in town, where he lives, everybody's got heads bowed down out and out of the cold, but he keeps his up and takes it full on, with a face flushed and stretched across by a toothless grin. He goes to a bar called the Mint Bar and he drinks a pint, maybe two, and the side of the bar is painted green with big white letters that say *you're only a stranger once*. Up and down main street the people of the town have put up small stereos that sputter familiar songs in an unfamiliar, distorted way, but he's been here so long he doesn't take notice. He tells everyone he's a madman, an old Norwegian, and they can see it in his face, in his old blue eyes and wispy wild blonde hair.

Back in the car he says, "watch this," and swerves into the empty hotel parking lot, wrenching the wheel and hitting the gas, spinning the car into a donut. He rolls down the window and barks that same wild laugh around and out of his throat. The lights of the hotel lobby come on and a man and a woman walk out, looking concerned at first, then relieved when they recognize his face. The woman yells, "you stupid bastard!" Both smile and laugh. This is what they see: his bright-eyed, red face sticking out of the window, the car spinning in circles, his hand raised up toward the sky and the breath pouring out of his mouth, rising up to meet the smoke coming off the burning tires. Then the two misty bodies coming together, floating in the air, demurely, spreading out across the sky, threading in and out of each other above the spinning car with its self-proclaimed madman behind the wheel.

All of this in motion, all in flux.

A mechanic tells me the next day that the car is wrecked, that I'll have to leave it and come back for it in a couple of weeks. I can take a train if I need to get out of town.

In the station there's a stagnation to the air, a thick, malleable sort of stillness. The train is five hours late. Pale fluorescent light hits different objects in the room—benches, tables, old crumpled newspapers on the floor—and the shadows that fall off of them feel equally pale. Across the room, a mother sits with her son. The mother sleeps, sitting upright with her head slouched to the side, but the son is awake and wide-eyed. He's holding a disposable camera, and every once in a while he'll bring it up to his eye and take a picture. The snap of the shutter reverberates all over the room, followed by the thick, mechanical click of the dial. He hops off the bench, without waking his mother, and starts to walk around the room. His steps are slow and careful. He spends large amounts of time examining his subjects before capturing them. His subjects are a rotten banana peel, a rubber band, and an old discarded bag of chips. He makes his way all around the room, stands in front of me.

I say, "hello."

And without a word, the boy brings the camera up to his eye, snaps a quick picture, then turns around and walks back to the bench to sit next to his mother, still asleep. He doesn't look in my direction again, just fidgets with the camera and looks out the window. He takes one more picture. The light from the window is soft and composed, and when it hits his mother's hair, the hair glows. Their train comes an hour later, going the opposite direction of mine. The boy wakes his mother and together they leave.

My train comes two hours after theirs, seven hours late.

The cabin I'm assigned is empty. My plan is to fall asleep and stay that way until I reach Chicago, but when then the train pulls away the sun is setting, which makes sense, because whenever I'm headed east, the sun is always setting. But I look out the window and all I can see is red. And this is the red that does it. As to why this particular red, the red most far away, is the red that takes over, that finally pulls me up and out of my vapidity, I'm unsure.

Maybe it's the largeness of it, or the slight tint to the window, that makes the color feel so much more vibrant, so much more alive than it would have otherwise. Or, my best guess, it's that I have a chance to be still and take the place in. The color takes up the whole earth, and I can hardly breathe, and I don't want to blink because I'm afraid I'll miss a second of it. Red washes over in waves, and I can feel it, even inside the train—thin, brilliant lines running and pulling together the places and people. Actual red, like the Redpoll's forehead or of the flushed faced man, but also the cold pain of the night in the valley and the burning eyes of the pregnant dog on the road. Those moments are red, too. If I could, I would walk off the train and surround myself in the feeling, delve into the madness of it, take in its vehemence. But the train moves at full speed. Instead I sit and watch the red out of the window, watch the color fill up everything—the white and even the black, watch all of it become a large red space for me to live in and hold onto for as long as it will allow.

And a wind picks up, running alongside the train. A wind strong enough as to nearly be visible, a wind touching everything. Trees next to the track hunch their shoulders, their empty branches waver, and on the ground, in every direction, dead grass falls and bends, and the train itself even seems to lean over, a little, and the whole scene really, truly, just moves. ❧

Salamander

POETRY✦FICTION✦MEMOIRS

READING PERIOD:
SEPTEMBER 1-APRIL 30

SUBMIT AND SUBSCRIBE ONLINE AT
SALAMANDERMAG.ORG

OR SEND
BY MAIL TO:

SALAMANDER
SUFFOLK UNIVERSITY
DEPARTMENT OF ENGLISH
8 ASHBURTON PLACE
BOSTON, MA 02108

DIE LEIDEN DES JUNGEN WERTHERS (THE SORROWS OF YOUNG WERTHER) by Johann Wolfgang von Goethe

David Samuel Levinson

I first read *The Sorrows of Young Werther* a few days after I returned to New York from being abroad for a couple of years. I had been living in Berlin with a man, a German lit scholar, who used to give me German novels because, as he said, I had a gap in my literary education. (He was right, and I read everything he gave me.) I had no idea Goethe's slim volume had traveled back with me until I started unpacking and found it in a side pocket of my suitcase. I thought I had lost it and remembered the afternoon the scholar had presented me with his own frayed copy. He'd already gifted me *Elective Affinities*, and though he didn't like *Sorrows* as much, thought it should also be a part of my sentimental education. As I was already in the middle of reading *Elective Affinities*, I set *Sorrows* aside and then subsequently forgot about it, as I'd forgotten about so many things those first few months in Berlin.

Relocating from one city to another can be disorienting, but relocating to a foreign city in which one doesn't speak the language involves its own particular brand of disorientation. In general, those first few months in Berlin were a harried, turned-around time for me, as I tried my best to acclimate. I thought I was doing a fine job of it, until the scholar announced he was breaking it off with me.

"I wanted you to fall in love with Berlin," he said, "but you haven't. You're homesick all the time."

It was true. I was homesick, though not for New York. I was homesick for a home in Berlin, a home I thought he and I would create together. Instead, we lived separately—his choice—and though we saw each other all the time, it felt as if we were living in different cities. He had his friends, I had mine, and we never could seem to bridge the gulfs, socially, domestically, and otherwise. A real pity, because I'd never met anyone with whom I shared such a ravenous appreciation for and love of books, though not even this was enough to bind and keep us together.

I mention all of this because it seems a fitting introduction to *Sorrows*, a paradigmatic story of a great love affair gone awry and the messy, complicated treacheries of the human heart. While I wouldn't necessarily recommend reading the novel the way I did—directly on the heels of a breakup—I will say that, given its darkly gleaming subject matter and wholly unexpected, if shocking, conclusion, it is a remarkable novel in and of itself.

We begin then with a letter from Young Werther to his best friend, Wilhelm, detailing his life in the fictional village of Wahlheim. A stand-in for Goethe himself, Werther is drawn as a sensitive painter with a moody, artistic temperament. Something of a misanthrope, he detests all of the societal norms placed upon him and wiles away his time outdoors, finding the natural world far more accessible and easily apprehended than the people who populate it. That is, until he meets the ravaging Charlotte, who beguiles Werther, until his "whole soul was absorbed by her air, her voice, her manner." It's love at first sight for our naïve hero, who had been warned early on in the novel to guard his heart against Charlotte, who is engaged to the worthy, moneyed Albert.

Unfortunately for Werther, he is far too young and too besotted to heed the warning and soon enough his heart belongs to her: "I found penetration and character in everything she said: every expression seemed to brighten her features with new charms,—with new rays of genius,—which unfolded by degrees, as she felt herself understood."

So begins the true sorrows of young Werther, who spends the rest of this short, epistolary novel falling further and further into love, unrequited though it may be. By the end, unable to justify his existence without her, the exasperated, unhappy Werther borrows Albert's pistols and shoots himself in the head. It's a gruesome final scene, though in the context of this breathtaking, sentimental novel, which launched the twenty-four-year-old Goethe into literary stardom, it is surprisingly apt, even moving, for which of us has not thought about suicide in the wake of love gone wrong?

"I have carefully collected whatever I have been able to learn of the story of poor Werther," the preface tells us. "To his spirit and character you cannot refuse your admiration and love: to his fate you will not deny your tears. And thou, good soul, who sufferest the same distress as he endured once, draw comfort from his sorrows; and let this little book be thy friend, if, owing to fortune or through thine own fault, thou canst not find a dearer companion."

Sorrows came along at a time in my life when I, too, thought I wouldn't be able to go on, when I, too, couldn't believe in a world without my love. Yet in some odd way it is also a novel about having to go on, about surviving our passions, and releasing the objects of our affection back into the world, not as the people we created and idealized out of existence but as the simple people they were, full of flaws and foibles and sadness of their own. Though it was not written as a cautionary tale, *The Sorrows of Young Werther* remains one of those novels I continue to cherish because of the hope it lent me—I read it, devoured it, put it away, then joined the living once again, because, unlike Werther, what other choice did I have? ❧

Chiara

Jonathan Wilson

In February 1975, a week or so before my 25th birthday, I accompanied my girlfriend Chiara Elefterides on a trip from England to Russia: Londoners both, we had been living together for almost three years in the village of Wivenhoe near its estuary, far from the city and the disapproving glare of our respective parents. Chiara was a graduate student at the nearby University of Essex, while I, ambitious and delusional, believed that I was a poet. Our workman's cottage featured no bathroom, a decidedly unpoetic outside toilet, and walls so thin that the neighbors' voices came through no softer than our own. The wife could be harsh. "Pick, pick pick," we heard her yell at her husband as we sat down to eat, "You stick your finger so far up your nose that you're gonna pick your bloody guts out one of these days."

In order to cover the five pounds a month rent due for our luxurious accommodation, I worked as a general dogsbody at The Station Inn, the pub next door, where I piled crates of beer, worked the pumps, swept the floor. Chiara had higher things on her mind: Dostoyevsky and the Russian Orthodox Church. The blue candlewick counterpane on our bed was weighted down with her books, works by obscure (to me) Russian saints and philosophers, Tikhon of Zadonsk and Vladimir Solovyov among them. She fell asleep reading and woke, as I did, always at 4 A.M. when the express from Colchester jolted into the station over the street, like the train carrying Strelnikov in *Dr. Zhivago*, all lights, smoke, and screeches. That train did a lot for our sex life.

Chiara thought, like so many before her, that marriage was a prison, a view perhaps augmented by close study of her own parents who had divorced when she was twelve. After three years, even though she tormented me, or perhaps because she did, I was ready to settle down. I was part Vronsky and part Gustav von Aschenbach, in pursuit of Tadzio, the tears running in rivulets down my painted face. Chiara was a dark-eyed, dark haired beauty, with a tight body and a punkish look. Unlike most of her contemporaries, she had no interest in hippie stuff; it was all black leather and zips. Lots of men desired her and were unafraid to approach. Some, professors mainly, thought they had a right to bed her as a kind of *droit de seigneur*. A guy from the English department with a red goatee, a high powered anthropologist who had just returned from Brazil, for example, and, of course, all the Russianists, men and women. Chiara never failed to let me know whom she found attractive and whom less so. She wanted to give me a lesson in freedom and she had nothing but disdain for jealousy. "Are you crying?" she once asked me during a phone call from hell in which she had described in detail the recent advances of a senior member of the faculty twice her age. "I'd never fuck him," she said, and when I'd replied, "I hope not," she'd added, "I'm not attracted to him at all." A pause. "My god you *are* crying. Well, *that* I really can't stand." And down went the phone.

The invitation to Moscow came out of the blue. Chiara's official supervisor, Angela Strug, had been away for months in the Soviet Union doing nobody knew quite what. In those days the Iron Curtain was still clanked pretty heavily shut and communication in and out of it tended to be cryptic. In Angela's absence, Leo Burnett, a junior member of the faculty (big beard, corduroy trousers, glasses, much emphatic yearning and desire) who taught and wrote about those brilliant, tragic Russian poets, Akhmatova, Tsvetayeva and Mandelstam, had been seconded to take over duties with Chiara, but all he had managed so far was, like all the others, to make her an offer that she'd chosen to refuse. "Come," Angela had written to Chiara, "I have someone interesting for you to meet."

We booked with a group tour through Intourist, the Russian travel agency: it was almost impossible to move without an official guide in the Soviet Union unless you had special dispensation. We planned a few days in Leningrad to be followed by a train journey to Moscow, where Angela would meet us at our hotel, and we hoped, spirit us away from our minders.

I had imagined, somehow that the flight from London would take seventeen hours, all that Churchillian enigma wrapped in a pastry stuff had permeated my consciousness as distance: Australia, whose sports teams, singers and politics were a daily feature in British newspapers, seemed closer. Yet, a quick churn through cloudy winter skies and we were in Leningrad looking out from our hotel room toward the icy Neva and its moored memory of Revolution 1917, the battleship Aurora.

I had been looking forward to having sex in Russia (or anywhere, really) but Chiara had a stomachache and sent me down to the bar to see if I could procure the Soviet equivalent of Coca Cola. She thought that a carbonated drink would settle her queasiness. We had been warned not to drink the local water—the murky swamp on which Leningrad stood and back into which it was slowly sinking had somehow poisoned the wells—but Chiara's ailment seemed premature. She hadn't even brushed her teeth yet.

I had been anticipating a throwback atmosphere for the hotel, although just how far back I wasn't sure. Certainly the women at the bar (hookers most likely), peroxide blondes with beehive hairdos and exemplary mini-skirts, were predictably retro, but to my surprise the men, in expensive suits, shirts, ties and shoes, with well-groomed hair and bright, scrubbed faces, looked as if they had stepped out of a high end prime time American soap opera. The reason for this, it turned out, is that they *were* American. Before I even had time to buy the soda, I was bear hugged by a friendly giant, a tipsy Jack Nicklaus lookalike who offered to buy me a drink then let me know that he was part of a delegation of small town U.S. mayors that, puckishly, had decided to hold their annual conference in the Communist stronghold. "Comrade," he said, "any time you want to visit Manhattan Beach we'll be glad to have you." "I'd love to come to New York," I said. The beach was in California.

While the mayors were knocking back vodka, preparing to fuck the hookers and have their pictures secretly taken by the KGB, I returned to our room with a bottle of "nature identical" soda water. Chiara wasn't there. She had a history of disappearance: sometimes she'd take off for days, returning without explanation or apology but usually in high spirits. If I asked her where she'd been, she would say, "I was busy," and then kiss me so sweetly that I gave up on my resentment. Why did I stay? I was enchanted by her beauty, in awe of her persuasive rationalizations (she had a brilliant mind), unhinged by her megawatt smile, and so on. When she was with you, she donated her full attention (it was a gift), especially in bed, but when it was time to move on, she moved—if you reached out to stop or delay her all you grasped was airy nothing.

For three days, we wandered after our guide through grey air and snowflakes in the direction of gold domes, churches of spilt blood, palaces, and the landmark homes of great and approved Russian writers. On the day that we were to depart for Moscow, the morning hours were designated as "free time." You could not purchase a map of Leningrad, nor a guide to its transport system, but Chiara persuaded Sveta, our cheerful Intourist guide, to help her make a pilgrimage to Dostoyevsky's tomb in the Tivkin cemetery. We went alone. The grave, when we arrived, turned out to be a not too impressive bust of the writer fronting a plinth headed by a large cross. Dostoyevsky was fenced off by wrought iron, there were no flowers, this was not Jim Morrison at Père Lachaise, and the bare branches of the surrounding trees advanced our sense of gloomy isolation. Then a boy appeared in a long coat and floppy eared fur hat. He addressed us in English. He said his name was Dmitry and that he liked Pink Floyd. He asked if when we got back to England we would send him some LPs. Chiara was silent. I said we would do as he asked. He gave me his address and then he left. Chiara stood for a long time in front of the tomb. She was, I thought, quite capable of overwhelming stones and trees with desire and it wouldn't have surprised me at all if Dostoyevsky's likeness had asked her what she was doing that night.

We were late getting back to the hotel and Sveta, who in the space of twenty-four hours appeared to have plagiarized both Chiara's hairstyle and her manner of dress, was angry with us. As punishment she withheld the sandwiches that had been distributed to our fellow travelers to sustain them during the seven-hour train ride to Moscow. Once we were in our carriage (we hadn't been *that* late) a kind-hearted American couple tried to slip us some of their bread and cheese but Sveta spotted the transaction in progress and intervened. This was our gulag experience.

Angela in a fur coat, her long white hair untrammeled, was on the platform to meet us. Sveta did not want to give her prisoners up, but fortunately her jurisdiction ended in Moscow and before the new guide could come to replace her, we were down in the Metro, that marvelous chandeliered Soviet tribute to the worker's state, the Winter Palace for commuters. "We'll go to your hotel later," Angela said, "We have an invitation for dinner."

We traveled on the Zamoskvoretskaya line to Dinamo station whose white and gray marble tiled walls were interspersed with sport-themed bas-reliefs: a javelin thrower, a hurdler, a boxer. I was thrilled to be there. I knew that when we emerged onto Leningradsky Avenue I would see the great football stadium, home to Moscow Dynamo, where the world's greatest goalkeeper, Lev Yashin, had once stood between the sticks to parry and punch with his massive hands. I was goalkeeper myself and knew well the magnificent solitude of that position. Neither Chiara nor Angela had any interest in football; their concentration was elsewhere, on Nabokov's haughtiness, or Bunin's dark avenues, or the poet whose lover in waiting wanted her to describe how she kissed and how men kissed her.

We crossed tramlines under darkening skies, passed a line of men and women queuing to buy kvass, and arrived outside a high-rise apartment block. Our host for the evening, Angela had told us as we emerged from the Metro, would be Zhenia Levitin, an old friend of hers who worked for the Pushkin Museum of Fine Art. A specialist on Rembrandt, he had published a number of articles in journals, and introductions to books. Chiara pretended to be interested but I had a feeling that she couldn't have cared less. She was an idea person and old-style scholarship left her cold. As for me, my obsession was Chiara; it was pathetic, but that's how it was. All my poems were about her. She was happy with that, although once she had become enraged when I had written a few lines from her point of view, as if she had spoken them. "You know nothing about me," she'd yelled, "Do not write through me ever again." On the other hand if I told her I was working on something new, she inevitably asked, sunnily and without shame, "Is it about me?" She wanted to inspire, entice, seduce, and then, with her lover on his knees as men adore god at the altar, vanish.

We rose up several floors via a rickety old elevator and emerged into a narrow, dimly lit corridor. Zhenia greeted us at his door, a small man with a solemn look, his large, slightly bulging, intense eyes behind black-framed glasses. In his tiny kitchen he served us chicken and bread, then opened a bottle of wine. He went about his business of hospitality in a manner that was almost stern. I did not participate, of course, in the Russian conversation, but afterwards I learned that Zhenia had described how he had recently been refused an exit visa to visit Yugoslavia on the grounds that (a) he was a Jew, (b) he was not married, (c) he was not a member of the Communist party—though whether these were the reasons officially given (to the extent that anything in those days was distinctly "official" in the Soviet Union), or he just guessed that they were the operative reasons, Angela did not know. It was, I learned, a miserable fact of life for Zhenia that he could not go abroad. I don't know what Angela had told him about me, but at one point when the conversation ebbed he stared hard at me and then asked, in English, if I had ever visited Israel. "Yes," I replied, "I had," but before our conversation could progress, he stopped it short, nervous perhaps about the infamous listening devices in Soviet apartments.

Zhenia never smiled once throughout the evening, but he sang. At the end of our meal he began, slowly and firmly, a song that seemed to have many verses and which he sang to the end very solemnly.

That night, in bed at the Hotel Intourist, Chiara's beautiful brown eyes closed to the world, her gold-standard breasts peeking out from under the sheet, I whispered that I loved her and she sleepily responded, "thank you." On the first night we had slept together, she had told me with great certainty, "You will never get what you want from me." It was true, I never had, if what I wanted was to feel something like possession. Chiara was of the opinion that human beings were by and large unknowable to one another, and that her own intelligent mystery was more opaque than most. She was a puzzle. In all the time we had been together, she had never once bought me a gift; she believed that presents, although she enjoyed receiving them, were manipulations, demands for reciprocation. Once, in a moment of assertion, I had asked her to give me something for my birthday. "What do you want?" she said. "Anything." "O.K.," she replied. But then I instantly backtracked. "You won't do it, forget I asked." "How do you know?" "Because I know you." This last, like the poem I had written in her voice, sent her into a fury. I knew five words in Russian, and one was "Dasvedanya"—goodbye. I told Chiara that if she ever wrote a memoir, she should call it "You Can't Know Me—Dasvedanya." She laughed, but it was laughter in the dark.

In Moscow, we saw jaundiced Lenin in his mausoleum and visited the department store GUM, where Libby, one of the American women on our tour, described the bra counter with its unadorned, uniform display of white B-D cups as "like the Himalayas."

On our last evening, when the cold felt like fifteen pound lead weights on our heads and we regretted not having splurged on fur hats in one of the tourist Berioszka shops, Angela brought Chiara and me to dinner with Yevgeny Borisovich, the son of the great novelist Boris

Pasternak. This was the "interesting person" Chiara had been promised. Angela, as it turned out, had spent the last months in Moscow officially researching a book on Tolstoy but clandestinely translating Pasternak's memoir *Safe Conduct* into English. Yevgeny, as far was he was able, oversaw the foreign publication of his father's works. There were, it seemed, numerous obstacles to the English edition. "Pasternak," Chiara had declared, as we were leaving our hotel, "was a great poet and a terrible novelist." I didn't know enough to argue with her; for me *Dr. Zhivago* was only a movie in which, horribly, Omar Sharif had found and then lost the love of his life, Julie Christie, and everything had ended in tears and a hydro-electric station.

Yevgeny Pasternak, strikingly handsome, bore an uncanny resemblance to pictures that I had seen of his father. He was an engineer by trade, a branch line away from the occupations of his father and grandfather Leonid, whose portraits covered the walls of his apartment. Several guests arrived, and a samovar appeared on the table. The atmosphere was convivial, with smoking and laughter, but the conversation was exclusively in Russian and I was a silent observer. Chiara was the center of attention. Later I learned that she had offered some brilliant, incisive comments on Pasternak's descriptions of Mayakovsky's suicide in *Safe Conduct* (Mayakovsky, larger than life, much desired and expressively over-the-top, was her kind of guy). I was used to Chiara's magnetic appeal, but whenever I witnessed it in action, pride and envy burned in me as simultaneous low fires. I was also aware that Chiara didn't like it much if I became withdrawn or morose as the men around her preened and displayed their feathers—after all what was the point of a lover who wasn't going to be fun? Eventually, out of pity I suppose, one of the guests turned to me and asked in English who I preferred, Tolstoy or Dostoyevsky, and when I replied "Dostoyevsky," he said, "Are you Jewish?" as if my answer had somehow predetermined that probability. He went on to inform me that many Russian Orthodox priests in the city were in fact converted Jews, severely restricted in the practice of their first religion and searching for a spiritual outlet. "The priests are rabbis," he said. Later in the evening, the same guest whispered to me, "This country is shit."

Feigning sickness, Chiara exempted herself from the next two days of our tour. In place of sightseeing, she visited the Lenin library while my fellow Intourists and me were introduced via coach stops to the frozen pond behind Tolstoy's Moscow home where his children and grandchildren had skated, to St. Basil's candy striped domes, and to restaurants where we flashed our foreign passports and were ushered to the front of the queue past long lines of Muscovites waiting in the cold.

Late in the evening when she returned from the library, Chiara was as sweet as could be. Books were palliatives for her racing consciousness; they softened and soothed her. She was too tired to make love so we cuddled in bed and plotted our morning escape from Ludmilla, the powerful concierge built like a Bulgarian weightlifter, who ruled our floor of the hotel as her personal fiefdom. Chiara closed her eyes and I kissed them, then she turned on her side. The curtains were not fully closed and a thin light from streetlamps illuminated a constellation of tiny birthmarks on Chiara's back. I kissed from one to the other, as if by joining them up I could somehow chart and cement our cosmic destiny together.

I lost her. Six months later, Chiara decamped to New York, ostensibly to pursue her Slavic studies in one of the great universities on the Eastern seaboard but more, I think, because she sensed that England was too small and belated for her exuberant personality: her killer smile, her combustible moods, her pre-punk punkishness were all better suited to the challenge of a city of high-rise ambition and unorthodox benedictions.

In those days, before Facebook, before Switchboard, discreet disappearance was still an option and I would not have been able to find her even if I had wanted to. If she wrote her book, it never appeared. Nothing like Chiara ever happened to me again.

Seventeen years passed. I married and divorced, and worked as an English teacher in a London comprehensive school, not happy, not unhappy, simply one of the host of conative individuals trying to get through the day, and with the help of a joint or a drink, stalk the night for its gifts until sleep.

In the spring of 1992, during the Easter vacation from school, I was in Tel Aviv on a visit. A London friend from my childhood, Gabriel Gurevitch, who had moved to Israel as a young man, was celebrating his fortieth birthday with a huge bash for himself at a restaurant in the old port of Jaffa. Because he was a warm-hearted man, generous and hospitable, father of five, and a successful lawyer, Gaby's invitation seemed like a good opportunity to revisit a country that I had not seen for twenty-five years since, as a young volunteer. I had spent a summer fixing sprinkler heads in the irrigation workshop of a kibbutz close to the Lebanese border.

On the day before the party Gaby asked me if I wanted to accompany him to visit a client of his, a recent Russian immigrant who he had been helping with certain tricky tax matters. The man had arrived in Israel a few months earlier and was living with his wife in an apartment in Gilo on the outskirts of Jerusalem near Bethlehem. The client had been crippled by a stroke back in Moscow, and was confined to a wheelchair. He couldn't walk and had use of only one hand. He had been told that physical therapy could improve his condition but he was resisting treatment.

We drove to Gilo, a journey of almost an hour. We entered the front room, and there was Zhenia. His wife, whose name it turned out, was also

Zhenia (Evgenia) stood next to the wheelchair. She was considerably younger than her husband, tall with pale blue eyes, high, Slavic cheeks with a touch of pink, and straight straw blonde hair. Later I learned that in Moscow she had been first his student, then his lover. Zhenia stared at me with his bulging eyes. "Zhenia!" I said, "I can't believe it's you. We met in Moscow many years ago. You asked me about Israel." He looked at me for a long time, everyone in the room was silent, and then, with what seemed like an extraordinary effort to speak, he said, "You came with beautiful Greek girl." "Well," I replied, "Her father was Greek, her mother Italian..." It seemed an unnecessary correction.

The afternoon progressed, blonde Zhenia, visibly devoted to her husband, catered to his every need and then, when he grew tired, lifted him from the wheelchair in her strong arms and carried him to a day bed set up by a window in the small room. The living conditions seemed not much different to what he had known in Russia, a depressing lack of both space and furniture. Apparently their earnings came from the piecemeal selling of the few drawings from Zhenia's private collection that he had managed to bring out of Russia. The art works and their sale were what had led to the tax issues.

Zhenia was still at once strangely stern and delicate, fragile and serious as Chiara and I had known him in Moscow. Blonde Zhenia told us that Nadezhda Mandelstam—the widow of the great poet Osip Mandelstam—whom they'd visited from time to time when in Moscow—used to call him "the little sparrow." Because of the odd affinity I felt with Zhenia, as if I had known him far, far better than I did, I took it upon myself to try to persuade him to pursue a course of physical therapy. "Gaby tells me that if you did, you could really improve your health," I said. Again, he stared at me before responding, "If you continue to talk to me like that I will begin not to like you."

The sun, having reached its zenith, collapsed into the room through the shades as a tired warrior: dusty, impeached, as if it hadn't done enough. We were about to leave when Zhenia, who had fallen half-asleep on the day bed, roused himself. "She came twice," he said to me, "once with you and once a few days later with the other Englishman."

"The other Englishman?"

"Yes. But he gave himself a Russian name, 'Lev.'"

"Lev?"

"Yes?"

"Did he have a beard?"

Zhenia nodded, and then for the first time in the spare few hours that I had known him which bracketed all the years that had passed, he smiled.

Two years later I heard from Gaby that Zhenia had died following a massive second stroke. I wrote to Angela; long retired, she had moved to Wales to be near her daughter but still worked on her translations of Russian poetry. A fortnight passed before I received a reply. She had received notice of Zhenia's death from Moscow friends and been saddened by the news. She remembered taking the two Zhenias to a Spring Fair at Midsummer Common in Cambridge on their only visit to England in 1989. There she persuaded Zhenia to ride on the carousel. "I looked round from my horseback to see that he was safe, and there he was, bouncing up and down on one of the painted gallopers, looking as serious and focused as if in the midst of giving a lecture."

To be twenty-four and in love with a woman who everyone tries to fuck, and who snaps your heart like a breadstick, is a testing thing. To be forty-two and extract an ounce of truth from the depths of delusion is even harder. Men, if the ancients are to be believed, once went to war over beautiful women, but I was not about to track down Leo Burnett and declare an intention against him. You couldn't have Chiara other than as she was; she may never have brought me a present but she gave me the gift of hours, the attractions of her slender body under white sheets, her beautiful face on plumped pillows, kisses that made me feel as if all the churches in Moscow and Leningrad that had been turned into dull museums were about to ring their bells. ஓ

redivider is...

- » the longest palindrome in the English language!
- » one of the top literary journals in New England (*Boston Globe*)
- » a 57th Annual New England Book Show Literary Journal winner
- » featured in Best American Poetry, Best American Fantasy, Pushcart Prize (special mention)
- » publishing work by Marion Winik, Kate Magnolia Gasgow, Sherman Alexie, Richie Hofmann, Ronda Broatch, and Robert Olen Butler
- » accepting FICTION, NONFICTION, POETRY, and ART submissions year round

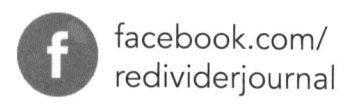

facebook.com/redividerjournal

@redividermag

redividerjournal.org

BECOMING ABIGAIL by Chris Abani
Laura K. Warrell

A young Nigerian woman sits on an embankment of the River Thames smoking cigarettes as she prepares for a fateful jump. Gazing across the water where she imagines "the ghosts of those who had also ended it here," the young woman recalls the men she has slept with for money and the way she wrote "me" on her breasts to reclaim her body afterward. She also tries to recall her mother's funeral though the memory remains unclear no matter how intently she attempts to piece it together.

So begins *Becoming Abigail*, a coming-of-age story about a strong-willed girl struggling to transcend unfathomable hardship. The titular character of Chris Abani's 2006 novella has been forced into prostitution by her family, a fact that counts for only one of the harrowing events in a lifetime of brutalities. *Becoming Abigail* is a devastating read, but one that ultimately reveals the dignity and courage inhabiting even the most ravaged of human spirits.

Abani, whose 2005 debut *Graceland* won the Hemingway/PEN Award among other honors, seems to enjoy playing with literary convention, in particular the structure of time. In *Becoming Abigail*, chapters titled "Now" find the character contemplating life as a London prostitute whose only happiness is an affair with a social worker. Chapters titled "Then" tell the story of how she arrived at this decisive moment by the Thames, including her mother's death, her visits with psychiatrists and witches to diagnose her rebellious behavior, and the sexual violence perpetrated by her cousin who eventually facilitates her move from Nigeria. The book goes back and forth between these "Now" and "Then" chapters, a movement that reflects how our internal lives rarely progress in a linear fashion but rather loop in cycles as the past and present continuously affect each other. Meanwhile, the extreme interiority of the narrative reflects Abigail's isolation, which works to give the book an intensity and intimacy rarely found in contemporary fiction.

But perhaps *Becoming Abigail* is so engaging because it reads much like an extended prose poem. Abani is also an award-winning poet, and he creates a world for Abigail where the moon is "tired" and sunlight is "lazy," where traffic does not simply go by but "winks past." Abigail's father is "a tall whip of blackness like an undecided but upright cobra" while the jazz music the old man listens to when he drinks too much "was something you find down a dark alley taken as a shortcut, and brushing rain from your hair in the dimness of the club found there, you hear the singer crying just for you." The lyricism of Abani's prose is as musical—and the imagery as vibrant—as anything one might find in a Toni Morrison novel, which makes Abani one of those rare authors whose skills as a poet and storyteller combine to make extraordinary fiction.

Abani once told *The Rumpus* that *Becoming Abigail* is "a love letter to my inability to see women for everything they are and offer." Indeed, the care with which he tells the story of this young woman "caught in the sheath of men's plans" feels like an act of love, though perhaps not in the traditional sense. Justice does not necessarily win out in Abigail's story, and her final act of self-recovery and empowerment may not rest well with all readers. *Becoming Abigail* reminds us that not every human story has a happy end, but in telling those stories we find their power and grace.

Index

The following is a listing in alphabetical order by author's last name of works published in *Post Road*. An asterisk indicates subject rather than contributor.

Abend, Lisa	THE DEPTFORD TRILOGY BY ROBERTSON DAVIES (recommendation)	PR23, 165
Abraham, Pearl	JOHN DOS PASSOS: USA TRILOGY (recommendation)	PR20, 49
Abrams, Eve	REDEMPTION WINDOW (nonfiction)	PR15, 143
Adnot, Becky	A NATURAL PROGRESSION OF THINGS (fiction)	PR17, 17
Aguero, Kathleen	WE DIDN'T COME HERE FOR THIS: A MEMOIR IN POETRY, BY WILLIAM B. PATRICK (recommendation)	PR15, 193
Albergotti, Dan	JACK GILBERT'S THE GREAT FIRES (recommendation)	PR18, 19
Albert, Elisa	STACEY RICHTER KICKS ASS (recommendation)	PR17, 123
Albert, Elizabeth	PAINTINGS (art)	PR18, 65
Albertsen, Dawsen Wright	CHRIS STOPS THE BOYS (fiction)	PR16, 14
Albo, Mike	KILL FEE LIT—AFTER READING GEORGE GISSING'S NEW GRUB STREET (recommendation)	PR13, 207
Alfier, Jeffrey	ASBURY PARK, JUST BEFORE WINTER (poetry)	PR20, 145
	WORDS FOR A NIGHT SINGER (poetry)	PR20, 147
Allen, Joy	SUNDAY LUNCH AND BLACK HOLE (fiction)	PR27, 163
Allison, Will	HITLESS WONDER: A LIFE IN MINOR LEAGUE ROCK AND ROLL BY JOE OESTREICH (recommendation)	PR25, 127
Almond, Steve	THE EMPEROR BY RYSZARD KAPUSCINSKI (recommendation)	PR6, 141
	ESSAY: AN INQUIRY INTO THE PSYCHOLOGICAL ROOTS OF AMERICA'S DEATH FETISH, OR, WHERE'D YOU HIDE THE BODY? (etcetera)	PR11, 197
Alvarez, Julia	RECOMMENDED READING (recommendation)	PR5, 129
Ames, Jonathan	A BOY'S GUIDE TO DRINKING AND DREAMING (recommendation)	PR2, 153
	DEEP IN QUEENS (theatre)	PR7, 123
	THE STORY OF MY SON (theatre)	PR7, 125
	TWENTY QUESTIONS (etcetera)	PR11, 216
Anderson, E. Kristin	WHEN WE LEFT MEDICINE BEHIND (poetry)	PR24, 167
	QUANTUM PHYSICS AND YOU (poetry)	PR24, 168
Ansay, A. Manette	MARILYNNE ROBINSON'S HOUSEKEEPING (recommendation)	PR13, 196
Anthenien, Catherine	BAZAAR (art)	PR1, 11
Antosca, Nick	YOUNG MEN AND FIRE, BY NORMAN MACLEAN (recommendation)	PR14, 191
Apostol, Gina	BUT FOR THE LOVERS, BY WILFREDO NOLLEDO (recommendation)	PR19, 16
Aptowicz, Cristin O'Keefe	WHAT I MEANT WHEN I SAID FAILURE (poetry)	PR26, 161
	THROUGH THE LOOKING GLASS (poetry)	PR26, 162
Armbrust, Hannah	WHEN ASKED TO EXPLAIN THE FALL OF MANKIND	

	(poetry)	PR20, 78
Armstrong, Mary	PAINTINGS (art)	PR7, 66
Armstrong, R.S.	MOST FERTILE SOIL (poetry)	PR17, 59
	PHRASES FROM OVERWHELMING DESIRE (poetry)	PR17, 60
Aronstein, A-J	#GENTLEMANLYPURSUITS IN PAUL KAHAN'S CHICAGO (criticism)	PR24, 23
Attenberg, Jami	A FEAST OF SNAKES, BY HARRY CREWS (recommendation)	PR15, 90
Ausherman, Stephen	CONQUEST, TOURISM, AND ETERNAL CANADIAN RAPTURE (nonfiction)	PR15, 93
Awad, Mona	THE GIRL I HATE (fiction)	PR27, 125
Ayala, Michael	PHOTOGRAPHS (art)	PR6, 66
Baggott, Julianna	MARY MORRISSEY, OLENA KALYTIAK DAVIS, AND MARISA DE LOS SANTOS (recommendation)	PR5, 132
Baker, Aaron	NOTEBOOK (poetry)	PR6, 27
	BONES (poetry)	PR6, 30
Bakerman, Nelson	WILDWOOD (art)	PR3, 96
Bang, Mary Jo	A SELECTION (recommendation)	PR4, 98
Barber, Jennifer	JUDENPLATZ (poetry)	PR26, 99
	CABIN (poetry)	PR26, 100
Barkan, Ross	FLUTTER FLAKE (fiction)	PR24, 33
Barnes, Rusty	O SADDAM! (fiction)	PR15, 129
Barot, Rick	SELF-PORTRAIT AS VIDEO INSTALLATION (poetry)	PR9, 128
	DECEMBER SONNET (poetry)	PR9, 130
Barrodale, Amie	CHENDRU (fiction)	PR26, 239
Barter, Christian	PEOPLE IN HISTORY (poetry)	PR13, 51
	THE DEVIL'S PARTY (poetry)	PR13, 52
	THE TURNS THEY HAVE TAKEN FROM BYE-BYE LAND (poetry)	PR23, 147
Bassiri, Kaveh	NOTEBOOK OF ANSWERS (theatre)	PR23, 131
Bauer, Douglas	THE GOODLIFE, BY KEITH SCRIBNER (recommendation)	PR1, 157
Bazzett, Michael	ANOTHER DAY (poetry)	PR27, 106
Beam, Alex	VARIOUS (recommendation)	PR6, 155
Beard, Jo Ann	SEVEN BOOKS IN SEVEN DAYS (recommendation)	PR24, 149
Beck, Lisa	HIDDEN PLACE (art)	PR23, cover
Beck, Sophie	CUT TO THE CHASE (nonfiction)	PR13, 209
Beeber, Steven Lee	"DIRTY WEDDING" (recommendation)	PR26, 138
Beeder, Amy	BOTANY NOTES (poetry)	PR9, 121
	NO CHILD WILL CHOOSE IT (poetry)	PR9, 122
Beilin, Caren	MEET ME AT THE HEDGE, MY LOVE (fiction)	PR21, 49
Bell, Currer (see also Brontë, Charlotte)	NOTE: BIOGRAPHICAL NOTICE OF ELLIS AND ACTON BELL (etcetera)	PR15, 99
Bell, Matt	KAMBY BOLONGO MEAN RIVER BY ROBERT LOPEZ (recommendation)	PR20, 99
Beller, Thomas	KAROO, BY STEVE TESICH (recommendation)	PR3, 65

Bellows, Nathaniel	NAN (fiction)	PR14, 89
	THE BOOKSHOP, BY PENELOPE FITZGERALD (recommendation)	PR15, 11
Bergin, Josephine	THE SINGLE GIRL GOES TO TOWN BY JEAN BAER (recommendation)	PR9, 178
Bergman, Megan Mayhew	OUT OF AFRICA BY ISAK DINESEN (recommendation)	PR25, 24
Bernard, April*	INTERVIEW (etcetera)	PR7, 169
Berne, Suzanne	SISTERS BY A RIVER BY BARBARA COMYNS (recommendation)	PR11, 169
Bernier, Nichole	CROSSING TO SAFETY BY WALLACE STEGNER (recommendation)	PR25, 52
Bibbins, Mark	HIATUS (poetry)	PR1, 87
	BY THE TIME (poetry)	PR1, 88
Bickford, Ian	INTRODUCTION TO ANGIE DRAKOPOULOS: PAINTINGS (art)	PR8, 41
Bierce, Ambrose	EXCERPT FROM THE DEVIL'S DICTIONARY (etcetera)	PR2, 119
Bird, Peter	IT'S LIKE BEING RAISED IN THE WILD, BUT WITH MORE STYLE (nonfiction)	PR2, 67
Birkerts, Sven	VARIOUS (recommendation)	PR1, 159
	REMINISCENCE: JOSEPH BRODSKY (etcetera)	PR8, 166
Bitetti, Kathleen	INTRODUCTION TO MICHELA GRIFFO: PAINTINGS AND DRAWINGS (art)	PR9, 66
Bjorklund, Patricia	SIMPLY NATURAL (fiction)	PR9, 30
Black, Alethea	"ARE YOU MAKING FUN OF ME?" (recommendation)	PR22, 137
Black, Sophie Cabot	THE STRAY (poetry)	PR6, 32
	PULLING INTO MORNING (poetry)	PR6, 33
Blackman, Andrew	FINDING MY WAY HOME (nonfiction)	PR17, 165
Blair, Sheila	WHY VEILING? (art)	PR17, 33
Bland, Chloe	BARGAIN DONUTS (fiction)	PR5, 108
Block, Stefan Merrill	LIGHTS, CAMERA, LESSON (recommendation)	PR23, 123
Bloom, Jonathan	WHY VEILING? (art)	PR17, 33
Bochan, Toby Leah	WHY (fiction)	PR4, 68
Bockman, Jeffrey M.	CITY STORMS (nonfiction)	PR7, 52
Boesky, Amy	INTRODUCTION: WRITING THE BODY: CREATIVE NONFICTION (nonfiction)	PR24, 81
Boggs, Belle	WINTER READING: JANE BROX'S BRILLIANT (recommendation)	PR21, 147
Bohince, Paula	THE GOSPEL ACCORDING TO LUCAS (poetry)	PR14, 177
	THE GOSPEL ACCORDING TO JOHN (poetry)	PR14, 178
Boice, James	SANCTUARY BY WILLIAM FAULKNER (recommendation)	PR23, 63
Bolin, Chris	ANNAPOLIS (poetry)	PR19, 77
	VIEW (poetry)	PR19, 78
Boobar, James	TOUR: THE DOSTOEVSKY WALK (etcetera)	PR11, 17
Booker, Brian	THE BOARDWALK (fiction)	PR12, 121

Post Road | 239

Borden, Sarah Gardner	THE PEACOCK SPRING BY RUMER GODDEN (recommendation)	PR24, 30
Borders, Lisa	WHAT'S IT ALL ABOUT? A NOVEL OF LIFE, LOVE, AND KEY LIME PIE, BY WILLIAM VAN WERT (recommendation)	PR9, 168
Bottum, Joseph	SARO'S LOVE SONG (poetry)	PR20, 69
Boudinot, Ryan	LOSING THE VIRGINITY OF TIME: THE LITERARY COORDINATES OF BRUNO SCHULZ AND ISAAC BABEL (etcetera)	PR8, 193
	READERS AND WRITERS (fiction)	PR24, 131
Bourgeois, Louis E.	A LONG TIME AGO IT RAINED (nonfiction)	PR12, 15
Boutell, Amy	YOUR TRANSLATOR, MY BRUNETTE (fiction)	PR23, 125
Boyd, Rebecca	WHO I WAS SUPPOSED TO BE: SHORT STORIES, BY SUSAN PERABO (recommendation)	PR2, 158
Bradway, Becky	BLOOD AND LUCK (nonfiction)	PR12, 211
Braffet, Kelly	DOROTHY L. SAYERS (recommendation)	PR25, 183
Braunstein, Sarah	"A LOUD, LONELY CRY FOR HAPPINESS": THE LATE GEORGE APLEY BY JOHN P. MARQUAND (recommendation)	PR22, 26
Braver, Adam	EXCITABLE WOMEN, DAMAGED MEN, BY ROBERT BOYERS (recommendation)	PR12, 119
	CONVERSATION: AMY HEMPEL (etcetera)	PR14, 83
	CONVERSATION: PHILLIP LOPATE (etcetera)	PR15, 21
	CONVERSATION: MARION ETTLINGER (etcetera)	PR16, 27
Braverman, Melanie	JANE HAMILTON (recommendation)	PR4, 101
Braziatis, Mark	IF LAUGHTER WERE BLOOD, THEY WOULD BE BROTHERS (fiction)	PR18, 163
Breckenridge, Zak	THINKING/CARTOONING (criticism)	PR28, 40
Breen, Susan	ROBERT CREELEY'S COLLABORATIONS (recommendation)	PR1, 170
Bremser, Wayne	MATTHEW BARNEY VERSUS DONKEY KONG (criticism)	PR10, 113
Brennan, Valerie	PEANUT GALLERY (art)	PR24, 65
Brimhall, Traci	A LOVE LETTER FOR LOVE, AN INDEX (MCSWEENEY'S POETRY SERIES) (recommendation)	PR24, 37
Brink, Elisabeth	I AM CHARLOTTE SIMMONS, BY TOM WOLFE (recommendation)	PR15, 104
Brink, Jolene	MATISSE IN NORWEGIAN MUSEUM ONCE NAZI LOOT, FAMILY WANTS RETURNED (poetry)	PR26, 177
	CATACHRESIS (poetry)	PR26, 178
Brontë, Charlotte (see also Bell, Currer)	NOTE: BIOGRAPHICAL NOTICE OF ELLIS AND ACTON BELL (etcetera)	PR15, 99
Brouwer, Joel	AND THE SHIP SAILS ON (poetry)	PR8, 24
	BECKETT'S ENDGAME (poetry)	PR8, 25
Brown, J. Camp	ARNOLD SCHULTZ TELLS THE HUG-EYED BOY (poetry)	PR27, 121
Brown, Jason Lee	MY OLDER BROTHER, JUNE BUG (poetry)	PR16, 165
	NAME I WILL NEVER FORGET (poetry)	PR16, 166

Brown, Jericho	TRACK 4: REFLECTIONS AS PERFORMED BY DIANA ROSS (poetry)	PR15, 9
	TRACK 1: LUSH LIFE (poetry)	PR15, 10
Brown, Peter	SINCE IT'S YOU (fiction)	PR7, 89
Browne, Jenny	TWIN CITIES, NO SIGN (poetry)	PR5, 27
	BEFORE (poetry)	PR5, 29
Browne, Nickole	ONTOGENY (poetry)	PR15, 159
	STRADDLING FENCES (poetry)	PR15, 161
Brownell, Mia	STILL LIFE WITH LOST MIGRATION (art)	PR26, cover
Brunner, Edward	EXTENDING HARRY CROSBY'S "BRIEF TRANSIT" (etcetera)	PR3, 179
Buchbinder, Jane	MURMURINGS (fiction)	PR28, 23
Buckley, John F. (with Martin Ott)	RALLYING IN RHODE ISLAND (poetry)	PR21, 26
	DUOLOGUE IN DELAWARE (poetry)	PR21, 27
Burt, Stephen	CATHEDRAL PARKWAY SUBWAY GATE (poetry)	PR4, 25
	OUR SUMMER JOBS (poetry)	PR4, 26
Butler, Blake	LIST OF 50 (11 OF 50): WORM LOOP (nonfiction)	PR19, 71
	LIST OF 50 (25 OF 50): DOPPELGANGER (nonfiction)	PR19, 74
Butler, Robert Olen	MIKHAIL BULGAKOV (recommendation)	PR16, 35
Calhoun, Kenneth	ULTRAVIOLET (fiction)	PR27, 107
Cameron, Nora	SLIDING DOOR (fiction)	PR23, 65
Campana, Joseph	SUITE FOR THE TWENTIETH CENTURY (FOR CAROLE LOMBARD) (poetry)	PR16, 37
	SUITE FOR THE TWENTIETH CENTURY (FOR MARILYN MONROE) (poetry)	PR16, 43
Cantor, Rachel	CHULIAK (fiction)	PR19, 125
Canty, Kevin	ROBERT WALSER (recommendation)	PR7, 140
	LONG STORIES (etcetera)	PR15, 151
Capossere, Bill	SWEET CORN (nonfiction)	PR18, 17
Capps, Ashley	READING AN EX-LOVER'S FIRST NOVEL (poetry)	PR12, 187
	HWY 51 (poetry)	PR12, 188
Carl-Klassen, Abigail	DONNA AND THE COUNTRY QUEENS (nonfiction)	PR27, 103
Carlson, Stacy	SIX MEMOS FOR THE NEXT MILLENNIUM, BY ITALO CALVINO (recommendation)	PR22, 43
Carr, Susan	BURNT MATTRESS, BIRTHDAY PHOTO (art)	PR28, 79
Carter, Joaquin	THE CONFRONTATION (art)	PR28, 66
Carter, Teri	THE STAGES OF CIVILITY (nonfiction)	PR25, 129
Castellani, Christopher	THE LIFE TO COME AND OTHER STORIES, BY E. M. FORSTER (recommendation)	PR8, 151
Casey, Brenna	A PENNY AND A NICKEL (nonfiction)	PR19, 79
Casey, Maud	SISTERS BY A RIVER, BY BARBARA COMYNS, THE GIRL FROM THE COAST, BY PRAMOEDYA ANANTA TOER (TRANSLATED BY WILLEM SAMUELS), AND "GUSEV" BY ANTON CHEKHOV (TRANSLATED BY RICHARD PEVEAR AND LARISSA VOLOKHONSKY) (recommendation)	PR14, 217

Cataldo, Jesse	DAVEY (fiction)	PR20, 101
Catone, Anna	WANTING A CHILD (poetry)	PR14, 207
	THE PARACHUTE (poetry)	PR14, 208
Cernuschi, Claude	INTRODUCTION TO PAINTINGS BY MARY ARMSTRONG (art)	PR7, 66
	INTRODUCTION TO PAINTINGS BY STONEY CONLEY (art)	PR7, 73
Chabria, Priya Sarukkai (with Ravi Shankar)	AANDAAL: THE AUTOBIOGRAPHY OF A GODDESS (poetry)	PR22, 121
Chace, Rebecca	BOOKS WITH PICTURES (recommendation)	PR20, 149
	THE PERIODIC TABLE BY PRIMO LEVI (recommendation)	PR26, 227
	THE REVOLUTION CONTINUES, WHY DO YOU WATER THE GRASS? (nonfiction)	PR27, 19
ChaoChun, Tan	THE LESHAN GIANT BUDDHA (poetry)	PR25, 55
	A SICKLE (poetry)	PR25, 56
Chapman, Maile	A LOVE TRANSACTION (fiction)	PR1, 33
Chariott, Katherine Lien	SELF-PORTRAIT, NUMBER 1 (nonfiction)	PR20, 97
Chasin, Alexandra	BY'M BYE (fiction)	PR18, 153
	AN ALTERED BOOK BY CARA BARER (recommendation)	PR28, 172
Cheever, John*	INDEX: CHARACTERS FROM THE STORIES OF JOHN CHEEVER (etcetera)	PR11, 149
Chelotti, Dan	EATING A DEVIL'S LUNCH WITH ALEKSANDAR RISTOVIĆ (recommendation)	PR26, 59
Chinquee, Kim	BODY LANGUAGE (fiction)	PR16, 183
	BALLOONS AND CLOWNS AND POPCORN (fiction)	PR16, 184
	MASH (fiction)	PR16, 185
Choi, Susan	JOHN DOLLAR AND EVELESS EDEN, BY MARIANNE WIGGINS (recommendation)	PR12, 13
Chopan, Jon	THE CUMULATIVE EFFECT (fiction)	PR19, 189
Church, Steven	APOLOGY TO HENRY AARON (nonfiction)	PR5, 111
	A LETTER TO THE BIONIC MAN (nonfiction)	PR5, 113
	THE WHITE TIDE (recommendation)	PR28, 213
Chute, Hillary	"I SAID I'M NOT YR OILWELL": CONSUMPTION, FEMINISMS, AND RADICAL COMMUNITY IN BIKINI KILL AND "RIOT GIRL" (criticism)	PR1, 185
	COOL FOR YOU, BY EILEEN MYLES (recommendation)	PR4, 103
Clabby, Paul	BAT (art)	PR26, 36
	SODS (art)	PR26, 37
Clarke, Brock	THE PRIME OF MISS JEAN BRODIE, BY MURIEL SPARK (recommendation)	PR13, 171
Clarke, Jaime	DESPERATELY SEEKING PACINO (etcetera)	PR1, 143
	FIVE ESSENTIAL MODERN SHORT STORIES (recommendation)	PR3, 72
	MORVERN CALLAR, BY ALAN WARNER (recommendation)	PR8, 161

Clements, Marcelle	MADAME BOVARY, BY GUSTAVE FLAUBERT (recommendation)	PR10, 73
Clinch, Jon	MORE REAL THAN REALITY: THE FROZEN ART OF ALISTAIR MACLEOD (recommendation)	PR16, 219
Cline, Emma	GOLDEN STATE (fiction)	PR20, 11
Cloutier, Martin	BRIGHT SHINY THINGS (fiction)	PR26, 51
Cockey, Tim	TIME'S WITNESS, BY MICHAEL MALONE (recommendation)	PR9, 174
Coffin, Jaed	THE SOUND OF WAVES, BY YUKIO MISHIMA (recommendation)	PR17, 83
Cohen, Leah Hager	A LONG AND HAPPY LIFE, BY REYNOLDS PRICE (recommendation)	PR11, 53
	THE DREARIEST ART, OR WHY I WRITE BOOK REVIEWS (nonfiction)	PR22, 81
Coig, Luis	PAINTINGS (art)	PR20, 33
Colburn, John	IN SALES (poetry)	PR10, 13
	PAST THE BITTER END (poetry)	PR10, 20
Cole, Lori	ON THE AESTHETIC AGENDA OF THE ANTIWAR MOVEMENT (criticism)	PR7, 57
Collins, Billy	ANIMAL BEHAVIOR (poetry)	PR26, 85
Collins, Michael	DROP IT (theatre)	PR9, 139
Collins, Wilkie	REPRINT: MY MISCELLANIES. A PETITION TO THE NOVEL-WRITERS (COMMUNICATED BY A ROMANTIC OLD GENTLEMAN) (etcetera)	PR14, 159
Coman, Carolyn	WHY I WRITE FOR CHILDREN (nonfiction)	PR22, 84
Comer, Carrie St. George	MORBIDEZZA (poetry)	PR17, 141
	LA LINGUA (poetry)	PR17, 145
	PAST THE BITTER END (poetry)	PR10, 20
Conley, Stoney	PAINTINGS (art)	PR7, 73
Connelly, Shannon	THE KIN-DER-KIDS, LITTLE ORPHAN ANNIE, AND MASTERS OF AMERICAN COMICS (criticism)	PR15, 49
Connor, Jackson	RARA AVIS: HOW TO TELL A TRUE BIRD STORY (nonfiction)	PR16, 249
Conway, Patrick	HOW IT'S DONE: A CRIMINAL DEFENSE INVESTIGATOR AT WORK (nonfiction)	PR27, 63
Cook, Kenneth	EASTER WEEKEND (fiction)	PR5, 95
Cooley, Martha	BLAISE CENDRARS (recommendation)	PR2, 160
Cooper, T	SEX AND [AUTO] GENOCIDE: THE SLUTS, BY DENNIS COOPER & SWIMMING TO CAMBODIA, BY SPALDING GRAY (recommendation)	PR13, 126
Copperman, Michael	THE POSSIBILITY OF OCEAN (nonfiction)	PR18, 197
Corbett, William	INTRODUCTION TO JOSH DORMAN DRAWINGS (art)	PR4, 82
	SHEEPSHEAD BAY, BY ED BARRETT (recommendation)	PR4, 124
Corcoran, Olisa	SHOUTING OBSCENITIES AT GEORGE BUSH THE YOUNGER (nonfiction)	PR3, 126
Cording, Robert	SHAME (poetry)	PR17, 61

Corral, Eduardo C.	ALL THE TREES OF THE FIELD SHALL CLAP THEIR HANDS (poetry)	PR13, 169
	OUR COMPLETION: OIL ON WOOD: TINO RODRIGUEZ: 1999 (poetry)	PR13, 170
Cotler, T. Zachary	HOUSE WITH A DARK SKY ROOF (poetry)	PR17, 63
Cowgill, Erin	NATIONS CUP (art)	PR12, 33
	MATCH 2 (art)	PR26, 39
	COLORADO PARIS 1 (art)	PR26, 41
	ROOM (CADIZ, SPAIN) (art)	PR26, 44
Cox, Elizabeth	STRONG OPINIONS BY VLADIMIR NABOKOV (recommendation)	PR11, 81
Craig, Hannah	AFTER READING ABOUT CANNIBALS (poetry)	PR18, 115
	WORLD, YOU NEED MORE CALCIUM (poetry)	PR18, 116
Crane, Hart*	GUGGENHEIM APPLICATION (etcetera)	PR14, 63
Crane, Kate	SEA MONSTERS (nonfiction)	PR7, 31
	A WOMAN IN BRINE (nonfiction)	PR24, 20
Cravens, Astrid	THE WATER AND THE WEAKENED LINK (art)	PR17, 97
	HURRICANE ESP (art)	PR28, 70
Crews, Harry*	ANTHOLOGY OF BLURBS (etcetera)	PR6, 186
Crucet, Jennine Capó	GETTING LOST IN THE CITY WITH EDWARD P. JONES (recommendation)	PR18, 149
Cummings, Don	THE WINNER (theatre)	PR25, 111
Curtis, Rebecca	THE SWEATER, THE PAIR OF SHOES, AND THE JACKET (fiction)	PR3, 13
Cutter, Weston	SAINT RUST (poetry)	PR21, 157
	SAINT SAY IT (OVER AND OVER AGAIN) (poetry)	PR21, 158
Czyzniejewski, Michael	VICTOR (fiction)	PR15, 163
D'Agata, John	A GENRE YOU HAVEN'T LOVED ENOUGH (recommendation)	PR15, 63
Dahlie, Michael	AN AUTOBIOGRAPHY, BY ANTHONY TROLLOPE (recommendation)	PR19, 200
Dalton, Quinn	VARIOUS (recommendation)	PR15, 197
Dalton, Trinie	CONFESSIONS (fiction)	PR25, 123
Dameron, Jim	TWO BIRDS (nonfiction)	PR8, 97
Danford, Natalie	SHINING EXAMPLES OF LITERARY BASTARDS (recommendation)	PR20, 117
Daniel, David	A CONFEDERACY (poetry)	PR7, 11
	MR. SWEATNER'S PARADE (poetry)	PR7, 12
Darby, Ann	A POETICS OF RISK (etcetera)	PR4, 131
Davidson, Karin C.	THE LAST I SAW MITSOU (fiction)	PR25, 69
Davies, Tristan	RECEIPT: TACO BELL (etcetera)	PR9, 191
Davis, Alan	THE MOVIEGOER, BY WALKER PERCY (recommendation)	PR13, 111
Davis, Carol V.	THE ORCHARD, BY BRIGIT PEGEEN KELLY (recommendation)	PR17, 133

244 | Post Road

Davis, Lisa Selin	"THE ORDINARY SON," BY RON CARLSON (recommendation)	PR12, 167
Davis, Olena Kalytiak	THE LAIS OF LOST LONG DAYS (poetry)	PR7, 20
	STRIPPED FROM THE WAIST UP, LOVE (poetry)	PR7, 21
Dawidoff, Nicholas	A RIVER RUNS THROUGH IT, BY NORMAN MACLEAN (recommendation)	PR4, 105
Day, Adam	LETTERS ON SPACE AND HANDS (poetry)	PR20, 51
	HAMAL (poetry)	PR20, 53
Day, Cathy	PIG BOY'S WICKED BIRD: A MEMOIR, BY DOUG CRANDELL (recommendation)	PR11, 107
deBlanc-Knowles, Jaime	HAYSTACKS (fiction)	PR26, 121
Decker, Stacia J. N.	WAITING ROOM (nonfiction)	PR6, 127
de Gramont, Nina	NOW IT'S CLEAN (fiction)	PR10, 161
Dempster, Brian Komei	GRAFFITI (poetry)	PR5, 37
	THE CHAIN (poetry)	PR5, 39
	JAP (poetry)	PR24, 39
	'NAM (poetry)	PR24, 43
Dick, Mina Pam	YOU ARE THE ROBERT WALSER! (recommendation)	PR26, 235
Dickson, Rebecca	THE FAITH OF OUR FATHERS (nonfiction)	PR12, 191
Dickstein, Morris	KEROUAC'S ON THE ROAD AT FIFTY (recommendation)	PR16, 163
DiClaudio, Dennis	SCENES FROM THE LIFE AND TIMES OF LITTLE BILLY LIVER (theatre)	PR8, 113
Didyk, Laura	FAREWELL (nonfiction)	PR16, 61
Dierbeck, Lisa	LYNNE TILLMAN'S NO LEASE ON LIFE (recommendation)	PR14, 209
Dietz, Maggie	MEDITERRANEAN (poetry)	PR23, 74
	GALILEE (poetry)	PR23, 75
Dinerstein, Joel	TO FACE THE MUSIC AND DANCE (nonfiction)	PR19, 87
Di Paoli, Matthew	WORSHIP (fiction)	PR21, 87
Dixon, Jonathan	PRESTON FALLS BY DAVID GATES (recommendation)	PR25, 202
Dolin, Sharon	FIRST WHY (poetry)	PR10, 79
	AND HOW (poetry)	PR10, 80
Donner, Rebecca	ASK THE DUST, BY JOHN FANTE (recommendation)	PR9, 172
Donovan, Matt	SARGENT ADRIFT AT THE TRENCHES (poetry)	PR19, 11
	THE OWL FOR AT LEAST A FEW STEPs (poetry)	PR19, 14
Dop, Gary	MAZATLAN (poetry)	PR24, 127
	LEARNING THE FASTBALL (poetry)	PR24, 128
Dorman, Josh	DRAWINGS (art)	PR4, 82
Dowd, Kevin	THE ICEMAN COMETH AGAIN (recommendation)	PR26, 146
Dowd, Will	THE CAVE AND ITS CAVEMAN: FIRST PROPHET (poetry)	PR17, 79
	SEVENTEEN HAIKU FOR THE END OF THE WORLD (poetry)	PR17, 81
	REASONS TO SEARCH FOR EARTH-LIKE PLANETS (poetry)	PR20, 83
	ASCENSION IN THE UFFIZI COURTYARD (poetry)	PR20, 84
	THE LITTLE THINGS (etcetera)	PR28, 31

Drain, Kim	FAMOUS CAKE (fiction)	PR13, 85
Drakopoulos, Angie	PAINTINGS (art)	PR8, 41
Dryansky, Amy	THE BED WAS MADE (poetry)	PR17, 64
Dubie, Whitney	A VISION OF INDIA (poetry)	PR20, 72
Duff-Strautmann, Valerie	MARK SLOUKA'S ESSAYS FROM THE NICK OF TIME (recommendation)	PR22, 98
Dumanis, Michael	MY MAYAKOVSKY (poetry)	PR13, 61
	CRIME SPREE (poetry)	PR13, 63
Dungy, Camille T.	POET, HEAL THYSELF (nonfiction)	PR22, 87
Dunlap, Murray	ALABAMA (fiction)	PR13, 10
Dunn, Meghan	SOAP SIRENS (poetry)	PR15, 91
	ADVICE FOR A SOAP SIREN (poetry)	PR15, 92
Durham, David Anthony	A SCOT'S QUAIR BY LEWIS GRASSIC GIBBON (recommendation)	PR11, 141
Eberlein, Xujun	A HUNDRED YEARS AT 15 (nonfiction)	PR13, 107
Eberly, Paul	HOT WATERS (fiction)	PR5, 84
Edgar, Natalie	SOUTH FERRY (art)	PR28, 65
Edwards, C. Ronald	THE COFFIN HANDLES WERE STALKS OF WHEAT (nonfiction)	PR22, 57
Egan, Jennifer	QUESTIONNAIRE (etcetera)	PR15, 219
Elam, Chris	INTRODUCTION TO DESTRUCTION AND CONSTRUCTION OF THE HUMAN FACE, BY TAKAHIRO KIMURA (art)	PR5, 194
Eldridge, Courtney	BECKY (fiction)	PR2, 35
Ellis, Sherry	INTERVIEW WITH ELIZABETH SEARLE (etcetera)	PR8, 199
Ellison, Lori	CREASES (art)	PR28, 68
Engel-Fuentes, Brian	GOD ON SIDE (poetry)	PR11, 49
	SO DIRTY A SMILE (poetry)	PR11, 51
Eno, Will	BOOKS FOR READERS AND OTHER DYING PEOPLE (recommendation)	PR2, 164
	TWO MONOLOGUES (theatre)	PR4, 39
	EXCERPT FROM GINT (AN ADAPTATION OF HENRIK IBSEN'S PEER GYNT) (theatre)	PR16, 169
Eprile, Tony	THE RADETZKY MARCH BY JOSEPH ROTH (JOACHIM NEUGROSCHEL, TRANS.) (recommendation)	PR18, 227
	THE REVENGE OF UMSLOPOGAAS (fiction)	PR24, 153
Erian, Alicia	AYITI BY ROXANE GAY (recommendation)	PR27, 101
Espaillat, Rhina P.	TWO CAMEOS (poetry)	PR23, 70
Ettlinger, Marion*	A CONVERSATION (etcetera)	PR16, 27
Evenson, Brian	WHITE SQUARE (fiction)	PR3, 20
Fallon, Peter	A WINTER WOUND (poetry)	PR26, 94
Faries, Chad	THIRD STREET. STAMBAUGH, MICHIGAN: LATE SPRING, 1972 (nonfiction)	PR7, 48
Farrell, Charles	THINGS I COULDN'T FIX (nonfiction)	PR19, 95
	HOW I WORK (KO 0) (nonfiction)	PR27, 49
Fath, Lauren	HAYSTACKS (nonfiction)	PR24, 169

Fazio, Joseph	A LOCAL MYTH (fiction)	PR25, 71
Febos, Melissa	MANUAL DE ZOOLOGÍA FANTÁSTICA (recommendation)	PR27, 135
Feinberg, Ezra	IS PSYCHOANALYSIS TOO SERIOUS? (criticism)	PR25, 27
Feitell, Merrill	"SONNY'S BLUES," BY JAMES BALDWIN (recommendation)	PR11, 143
Ferrell, Monica	AFTER A REST: PALIMPSEST (poetry)	PR9, 133
	ECHO DIGRESSION (poetry)	PR9, 135
Ferrer, Elizabeth	YOLANDA PETROCELLI (art)	PR22, 65
Field, Miranda	BIRTH MARK (poetry)	PR2, 85
	COCK ROBIN (poetry)	PR2, 86
Finkelstein, Norman	EXCERPT (poetry)	PR21, 11
	DECISION (poetry)	PR21, 12
Fitch, Janet	THE MEMORY ROOM, BY MARY RAKO (recommendation)	PR5, 133
Fitzgerald, Adam	THE ARGUMENT (poetry)	PR20, 88
	PROUD HAND (poetry)	PR20, 90
Fitzgerald, F. Scott*	CONTRACT FOR THE GREAT GATSBY (etcetera)	PR1, 152
Fix, Nicole	GENETIC DISORDERS (fiction)	PR18, 121
Fleming, Colin	CHIX AND QUARTERS (fiction)	PR27, 179
Flint, Austin	EEVA-LIISA MANNER (recommendation)	PR1, 161
Flook, Maria	INSIDE THE SKY: A MEDITATION ON FLIGHT, BY WILLIAM LANGEWIESCHE, AND STICK AND RUDDER: AN EXPLANATION ON THE ART OF FLYING, BY WOLFGANG LANGEWIESCHE (recommendation)	PR8, 142
	TWENTY QUESTIONS (etcetera)	PR12, 219
Flores-Williams, Jason	NORTH DALLAS FORTY, BY PETER GENT (recommendation)	PR9, 164
	THE DINNER PARTY (theatre)	PR12, 71
Fluger, Marty	DIRECTING GRAND GUIGNOL (theatre)	PR1, 61
	COMPOSING FOR GRAND GUIGNOL (theatre)	PR1, 78
Flynn, Nick	AMBER (poetry)	PR1, 90
	STATUARY (poetry)	PR1, 92
Foix, J.V.*	FOUR SHORT POEMS, trans. Susan Lantz (etcetera)	PR9, 205
Foos, Laurie	DONALD ANTRIM'S THE AFTERLIFE (recommendation)	PR14, 57
Ford, Katie	IT'S LATE HERE HOW LIGHT IS LATE ONCE YOU'VE FALLEN (poetry)	PR5, 30
	ELEGY TO THE LAST BREATH (poetry)	PR5, 31
Fortini, Franco	TRADUCENDO BRECHT (poetry)	PR4, 28
Fortini, Franco*	TRANSLATING BRECHT, trans. John P. Welle (poetry)	PR4, 29
Fountain, Carrie	JORNADA DEL MUERTO (poetry)	PR19, 163
	LATE SUMMER (poetry)	PR19, 164
Fox, Sarah	SHADOW OF THE VALLEY (poetry)	PR5, 32
	HOW TO GET THE LOVE YOU WANT (poetry)	PR5, 35
Foy, D.	DIRT (nonfiction)	PR21, 159
Franco, James	FILM SONNET (poetry)	PR27, 17
	FILM SONNET (poetry)	PR27, 18
Frank, Elizabeth Bales	RONDO (nonfiction)	PR21, 155

Frank, Rebecca	LOCAL CARNIVAL (poetry)	PR18, 207
Morgan	THE BLESSING OF THE ANIMALS (poetry)	PR18, 209
Franklin, Emily	LITERARY FEASTS (recommendation)	PR17, 31
Franklin, Tom	TRUE GRIT, BY CHARLES PORTIS (recommendation)	PR7, 145
Freeman, Ru	HALF & HALF: WRITERS ON GROWING UP BIRACIAL+BICULTURAL (recommendation)	PR18, 177
Fried, Daisy	TONY HOAGLAND'S HARD RAIN (recommendation)	PR18, 49
Fried, Seth	THE WORK OF STANLEY ELKIN (recommendation)	PR24, 175
Frumkin, Rebekah	MONSTER (fiction)	PR16, 201
Funkhouser, Margaret	ESTIMATED DRIFT (poetry)	PR6, 34
	ITS OWNERS BECAME A DIM (poetry)	PR6, 35
Furr, Derek Lance	YELLOW PAJAMAS (nonfiction)	PR8, 93
Gaitskill, Mary	PETER PAN (recommendation)	PR14, 29
Galaviz-Budziszewski, Alexai	AN EXCERPT FROM JUST SAY GOODBYE (nonfiction)	PR19, 116
Galvin, Brendan	ON THE SEA OF THE HEBRIDES (poetry)	PR17, 75
	A LATE, AROMATIC MOMENT (poetry)	PR17, 77
	A SEA PIECE (poetry)	PR17, 78
Garcia, J. Malcolm	RELIEF: AFGHANISTAN, 2001 (nonfiction)	PR9, 99
Garden, Joe	WHAT IT IS BY LYNDA BARRY (recommendation)	PR27, 27
George, Diana	PATERNITY WITHIN THE LIMITS OF REASON (fiction)	PR4, 67
Gerard, Christian Anton	DEFENSE OF POETRY 1 (poetry)	PR27, 29
	DEFENSE OF POETRY 2 (poetry)	PR27, 31
Gerstler, Amy	HEADLESS, BY BENJAMIN WEISSMAN (recommendation)	PR8, 144
Giannelli, Adam	DARK DAISY (poetry)	PR24, 63
	THE LINGERING (poetry)	PR24, 64
Gibson, Dobby	VERTICAL HOLD (poetry)	PR12, 201
	THE WORLD AS SEEN THROUGH A GLASS OF ICE WATER (poetry)	PR12, 202
Gifford, Barry	THE CINÉ (fiction)	PR5, 79
	THE ROSE OF TIBET, BY LIONEL DAVIDSON (recommendation)	PR6, 144
	HOLIDAY FROM WOMEN (fiction)	PR10, 75
Gilberg, Gail Hosking	PLAN OF A STORY THAT COULD HAVE BEEN WRITTEN IF ONLY I HAD KNOWN IT WAS HAPPENING (nonfiction)	PR1, 119
Gilsdorf, Ethan	HOW TO LIVE SAFELY IN A SCIENCE FICTIONAL UNIVERSE BY CHARLES YU (recommendation)	PR24, 139
Ginsberg, Debra	GREEN DARKNESS BY ANYA SETON (recommendation)	PR26, 25
Girdish, Jen	THE IMPOSSIBLE RETURN (nonfiction)	PR19, 135
Gitterman, Debra	BAGGAGE CLAIM (poetry)	PR15, 107
	THOSE WERE DESERT YEARS (poetry)	PR15, 108
Glassberg, Roy Ira	OVERTURE: A RIFF ON THE SIN OF DESPAIR (theatre)	PR19, 165
Glassgold, Peter	E.R.B. AND THE RED PLANET (recommendation)	PR26, 193
Glick, Jeremy Martin	COLLATERAL DAMAGES: CONTEXTS FOR THINKING OF THE LIBERATION OF JAMIL ABUL AL-AMIN (H. RAP BROWN) (criticism)	PR4, 12
Goldberg, Kim	BIRTHDAY (nonfiction)	PR16, 49

Goldberg, Len	JOURNAL: BLACK ROCK CITY JOURNAL (etcetera)	PR16, 133
Goldberg, Myla	BRUNO SCHULTZ AND BOHUMIL HRABAL (recommendation)	PR3, 66
Goldberg, Tod	REPORT: VEGAS VALLEY BOOK FESTIVAL (etcetera)	PR12, 183
	THE LAWS OF EVENING, BY MARY YUKARI WATERS (recommendation)	PR16, 179
Goldstein, Ellen	LANTERN FESTIVAL (nonfiction)	PR26, 185
Goldstein, Naama	"THE BOUND MAN," FROM ILSE AICHINGER'S THE BOUND MAN (recommendation)	PR12, 181
Goldstein, Yael	SPIN, BY ROBERT CHARLES WILSON (recommendation)	PR16, 95
Gonzalez, Elizabeth	THE RECLAMATION SPECIALIST (fiction)	PR18, 39
Gornick, Lisa	PITY (fiction)	PR28, 83
Grandbois, Peter	ALL OR NOTHING AT THE FABERGÉ (fiction)	PR11, 93
Graver, Elizabeth	A GOOD HOUSE, BY BONNIE BURNARD; AND BLINDNESS, BY JOSÉ SARAMAGO (recommendation)	PR5, 134
	INTRODUCTION, GUEST FOLIO	PR25, 67
Graves, Michael	BALLOONS (fiction)	PR24, 121
Griesemer, John	ERNEST HEBERT (recommendation)	PR5, 127
Griffith, Michael	THE DANGEROUS HUSBAND, BY JANE SHAPIRO (recommendation)	PR10, 29
Griffo, Michela	PAINTINGS AND DRAWINGS (art)	PR9, 66
Grimm, Mary	WAR AND PEACE AS HYPERTEXT (recommendation)	PR12, 81
Grinnell, Max	TREASURE ISLAND: AN APPRECIATION (recommendation)	PR20, 61
Gritsman, Andrey	OVERHEARD: WAKE UP NEW YORK CITY, SEPTEMBER 2001 (etcetera)	PR10, 21
Grodstein, Rebecca	EVAN S. CONNELL'S MRS. BRIDGE (recommendation)	PR18, 29
Gross, Gwendolen	STONES FOR IBARRA, BY HARRIET DOERR; AND OF KINKAJOUS, CAPYBARAS, HORNED BEETLES, SELEDANGS, AND THE ODDEST AND MOST WONDERFUL MAMMALS, INSECTS, BIRDS, AND PLANTS OF OUR WORLD, BY JEANNE K. HANSON AND DEANE MORRISON (recommendation)	PR8, 155
Grubin, Eve	THE NINETEENTH-CENTURY NOVEL (poetry)	PR7, 13
	THE NINETEENTH-CENTURY NOVEL II (poetry)	PR7, 14
Hadari, Atar	THE PASSOVER WEDDINGS (poetry)	PR23, 83
	TIE A YELLOW RIBBON (theatre)	PR26, 229
Hagy, Alyson	A GOOD MAN IS HARD TO FIND, BY FLANNERY O'CONNOR (recommendation)	PR13, 93
Haigh, Jennifer	PIZZA MAN (fiction)	PR14, 113
Haines, Lise	WHY DID I EVER, BY MARY ROBISON (recommendation)	PR6, 157
Haley, Melissa	SHE, UNDER THE UMBRELLA, WENT (nonfiction)	PR11, 171
Halovanic, Maria	FEMMÁGE (poetry)	PR15, 137
	AFTERIMAGE FROM A TRAIN (poetry)	PR15, 138
Hambleton, Richard	RICHARD HAMBLETON: THE AMERICAN POP EXPRESSIONIST (art)	PR27, 33

Hamburger, Aaron	THE WONDERFUL WIZARD OF OZ, BY L. FRANK BAUM (recommendation)	PR17, 15
Hamilton, Saskia	ROOM (poetry)	PR4, 27
	EXTEND (poetry)	PR4, 30
Hanning, Jenny	PROPERTY (poetry)	PR18, 179
	BICKFORD AVENUE (poetry)	PR18, 180
Hansmann, V.	GOODNIGHT, MOON (nonfiction)	PR28, 149
Harding, John Wesley (see also Stace, Wesley)	LISTERINE: THE LIFE AND OPINIONS OF LAURENCE STERNE (etcetera)	PR5, 174
	THE LOST STRADIVARIUS, MOONFLEET, AND THE NEBULY COAT: THE ABNORMAL RESPONSES OF JOHN MEADE FALKNER (recommendation)	PR11, 89
	JOURNAL: (UNEXPURGATED) TOUR JOURNAL (etcetera)	PR16, 221
Hardy, Edward	APOLOGY NUMBER 21, OR WHAT YOU SHOULD KNOW ABOUT THE LIBRARY (fiction)	PR25, 72
Harnetiaux, Trish	THE DORSAL STRIATUM (theatre)	PR13, 129
Harris, Kathrin	THE DOLPHIN LADY OF SIESTA KEY (nonfiction)	PR27, 171
Harrison, David L.	Q&A REFLECTIONS (recommendation)	PR26, 29
Harrison, Donald MacLeod	THE GOLDEN BRAIN (fiction)	PR21, 91
Hart, JoeAnn	CROSS CREEK, BY MARJORIE KINNAN RAWLINGS (recommendation)	PR12, 189
Hart, Matt	IN MEMORY OF SOMEBODY ELSE'S FEELINGS (poetry)	PR19, 143
	UPON SEEING AGAIN THE THRIVING (poetry)	PR19, 147
Hartley, Heather	PARTNER MY PARTNER (poetry)	PR14, 59
	THE KHARMA CLUb (poetry)	PR14, 61
Harvey, Matthea	THE DIFFERENCE BETWEEN THE NEED FOR CONSISTENCY & THE STATE OF EXPECTATION (poetry)	PR4, 31
	DEFINITION OF WEATHER (poetry)	PR4, 32
Harwood, Seth	FISHER CAT (fiction)	PR12, 169
Hausler, Pete	FROM HELL, BY ALAN MOORE, ILLUSTRATED BY EDDIE CAMPBELL (recommendation)	PR1, 172
	WIND, SAND AND STARS, BY ANTOINE DE SAINT-EXUPÉRY (recommendation)	PR8, 137
	THE WINE WENT DOWN IN THE BOTTLE: THE PASSIVE BEAUTY OF JOHN STEINBECK'S TORTILLA FLAT (recommendation)	PR25, 86
	THE DEATH OF MR. BALTISBERGER BY BOHUMIL HRABAL (recommendation)	PR27, 13
Hawley, Michael	ALLAPATTAH (fiction)	PR28, 97
Hazlewood, Carl E.	ABOUT ANGELS (art)	PR25, 33
Healey, Emma	LOAN SUITE (fiction)	PR26, 15
Healey, Steve	GOD (poetry)	PR17, 121
	RANDOM VIOLENCE (poetry)	PR17, 122
Healy, Lorraine	WHAT WE'VE FORGOTTEN (poetry)	PR16, 25
Hearst, Michael	THREE SHORT STORIES (nonfiction)	PR15, 157
Heine, Karl	GREEN PANES—BROKEN SKY (art)	PR28, 67
Hemery, Michael	PAUL'S BOOTS (nonfiction)	PR17, 117

Hempel, Amy	PEARSON MARX (recommendation)	PR1, 16
Hempel, Amy*	A CONVERSATION (etcetera)	PR14, 83
Hergenrader, Trent	THE MOUTH OF THE VOLGA (nonfiction)	PR21, 21
Herman, Molly	SILVERPOINT SERIES (art)	PR24, 70
Hernandez, Sonne	FLOATER (art)	PR26, 33
	BLIND-SIDED (art)	PR26, 35
	SHOWTIME ON DEMAND (art)	PR26, 38
Hero, Claire	MARGINALIA (poetry)	PR5, 41
	DIVINATION (poetry)	PR5, 42
Hershon, Joanna	MRS. BRIDGE, BY EVAN S. CONNELL (recommendation)	PR6, 145
Heti, Sheila	KURT VONNEGUT (recommendation)	PR14, 175
Hett, Jim	JIM HETT: THEY'RE ALL THE SAME EXCEPT THEY'RE ALL DIFFERENT (art)	PR23, 33
Higgs, Christopher	HOLD YOUR HORSES THE ELEPHANTS ARE COMING (nonfiction)	PR16, 155
Hill, Daniel	PAINTINGS (art)	PR8, 34
Hill, Owen	PIKE BY BENJAMIN WHITMER (recommendation)	PR23, 23
Himmer, Steve	THE ISLANDS OF GEORGE MACKAY BROWN (recommendation)	PR25, 196
Hoagland, Edward	THE CIRCUS OF DR. LAO, BY CHARLES G. FINNEY (recommendation)	PR5, 135
Hobson, Brandon	RED OWL (fiction)	PR25, 137
Hoch, James	GLEANERS (poetry)	PR6, 36
	SCARIFICATION (poetry)	PR6, 37
Hodgman, Jan	SMALL WORLD (nonfiction)	PR4, 46
Hoffman, Alice	TRANSFORMATIONS (fiction)	PR16, 267
Hoffman, Richard	AFTER LONG SILENCE, BY HELEN FREMONT (recommendation)	PR10, 56
	NOTHING TO LOOK AT HERE (fiction)	PR13, 197
Holder, Jakob	SUMATRA MANDHELING (theatre)	PR18, 109
Holdsworth, Kevin	MOVING WATER (nonfiction)	PR3, 121
Holland, Noy	A SPORT AND A PASTIME, BY JAMES SALTER (recommendation)	PR16, 127
Hollander, David	WHATEVER HAPPENED TO HARLAN? A REPORT FROM THE FIELD (nonfiction)	PR16, 51
Holliday, Frank	DAVID SPIHER: A NEW YORK PAINTER (art)	PR13, 65
Hollmeyer, Jenn	WE SHARED A DUPLEX (fiction)	PR23, 18
Holman, Virginia	AN AMERICAN MEMORY AND I AM ZOE HANDKE, BY ERIC LARSEN (recommendation)	PR8, 135
Holmes, Martha Stoddard	BODY WITHOUT ORGANS (nonfiction)	PR24, 111
Hood, Ann	FIRST NOVELS (recommendation)	PR11, 47
	CROONING WITH DINO (fiction)	PR14, 145
	MAN'S BEST FRIEND (fiction)	PR22, 45
Hoover, Michelle	JOHN EDGAR WIDEMAN: THE LAST GREAT RADICAL (recommendation)	PR21, 29

Horrocks, Caitlin	TRAVELS IN MOOMINVALLEY (recommendation)	PR23, 91
Hosking, Gail	THE ABCS OF PARTING (nonfiction)	PR24, 55
Hotchner, A. E.	P. G. WODEHOUSE (recommendation)	PR6, 146
Houle, Adam	THE COUNTY FAIR BUILDING FOR ANIMAL HUSBANDRY (poetry)	PR24, 21
	WE ARE FEWER THAN BEFORE (poetry)	PR24, 22
Hryniewiez-Yarbrough, Ewa (trans.)	DE SE IPSO, BY JANUSZ SZUBER (poetry)	PR9, 131
	NEW LABORS, BY JANUSZ SZUBER (poetry)	PR9, 132
Huber, K. M.	VISIT WITH A FORGOTTEN PEOPLE (nonfiction)	PR10, 107
Huey, Amorak	HARMONICA (poetry)	PR22, 41
	HARMONICA II (poetry)	PR22, 42
Hughes, Mary-Beth	BEL CANTO BY ANN PATCHETT (recommendation)	PR4, 106
Hummel, Maria	NEW YORK SELVES: AN ELEGY (poetry)	PR11, 193
	GOD MACHINE ON ADVERSITY (poetry)	PR11, 196
Hunt, Jerry	FOUR VIDEO TRANSLATIONS (theatre)	PR10, 33
Iagnemma, Karl	ITALIAN DAYS, BY BARBARA GRIZZUTI HARRISON (recommendation)	PR7, 134
Ihara, Nathan	HITTING HARMONY (nonfiction)	PR8, 100
Inciarte, Rachael	THE WOMAN WHO CAME FROM THE GARDEN (fiction)	PR26, 179
Innis, Julie	LITTLE MARVELS (fiction)	PR22, 153
Ireland, Perrin	THE DOG OF THE MARRIAGE, BY AMY HEMPEL (recommendation)	PR16, 195
Ison, Tara	MENDEL'S DWARF BY SIMON MAWER (recommendation)	PR2, 166
Iyer, Lars	A LITERARY MANIFESTO AFTER THE END OF LITERATURE AND MANIFESTOS, OR NUDE IN YOUR HOT TUB WITH A GOOD VIEW OF THE ABYSS (criticism)	PR22, 139
Izzi, Matt	THE SUMMER HANNAH WORE A HAT (fiction)	PR26, 158
Jackson, Major	INDIAN SONG (poetry)	PR2, 87
	URBAN RENEWAL ix. (poetry)	PR2, 88
James, Henry	ON TURGENEV (etcetera)	PR7, 183
Janovitz, Bill	THE ROAD BY CORMAC MCCARTHY (recommendation)	PR18, 15
Jenkinson, Len	THE MUSEUM OF SPEED (fiction)	PR3, 26
Jiaxin, Wang	GLENN GOULD trans. by Diana Shi & George O'Connell (poetry)	PR28, 169
	MEETING RAIN, WUTAI MOUNTAIN trans. by Diana Shi & George O'Connell	PR28, 171
Jie, Zhong (trans.)	THE LESHAN GIANT BUDDHA BY TAN CHAOCHUN (poetry)	PR25, 55
	A SICKLE BY TAN CHAOCHUN (poetry)	PR25, 56
Johnson, Samuel	LAST WILL AND TESTAMENT (etcetera)	PR4, 149
Johnston, Mat	WHAT WE DO (fiction)	PR7, 100
Jones, Alden	SECRET LIFE, BY MICHAEL RYAN (recommendation)	PR4, 108
	POLITE SOCIETY, BY MELANIE SUMNER (recommendation)	PR9, 170
	THE BURMESE DREAMS SERIES (nonfiction)	PR19, 23
Jones, Allen Morris	WILLIAM FAULKNER'S "THE BEAR" (recommendation)	PR16, 101

252 | *Post Road*

Jones, Ben	THE ANCESTOR'S TALE, BY RICHARD DAWKINS (recommendation)	PR11, 200
Jones, Jeff	RIVEN (fiction)	PR18, 55
Juster, A.M.	A PLEA TO MY VEGAN GREAT-GRANDCHILDREN (poetry)	PR20, 63
	MY BILLY COLLINS MOMENT (poetry)	PR20, 64
Kadetsky, Elizabeth	THE MEMORY PAVILION (nonfiction)	PR22, 29
Kadish, Rachel	LAWRENCE WESCHLER'S VERMEER IN BOSNIA (recommendation)	PR12, 65
Kalfus, Ken	CONFESSIONS OF ZENO, BY ITALO SVEVO (recommendation)	PR2, 168
Kalotay, Daphne	WOMEN IN THEIR BEDS: NEW AND SELECTED STORIES, BY GINA BERRIAULT, AND THE TEA CEREMONY: THE UNCOLLECTED WRITINGS OF GINA BERRIAULT (recommendation)	PR11, 31
Kaluza, Kobun	EXCERPT FROM INERT DEMENTIA (theatre)	PR14, 193
Kamentsky, Gina	SAGA #2 (art)	PR28, cover
Kaminski, Megan	THE POLITICS OF PLAY (nonfiction)	PR20, 139
Kane, Jessica Francis	NIGHT CLASS (fiction)	PR24, 44
Kantar, Annie	FOR YOU, A POEM (poetry)	PR2, 89
	I SEE MY GRANDMOTHER AGAIN (poetry)	PR2, 90
Karapetkova, Holly	DEATH AND THE FOUR-YEAR-OLD (poetry)	PR25, 199
	LAST MEETING (poetry)	PR25, 200
	CHRISTMAS (poetry)	PR25, 201
Karlin, Katherine	THE LEARNING TREE BY GORDON PARKS (recommendation)	PR28, 152
Kasischke, Laura	FOR THE YOUNG WOMAN I SAW HIT BY A CAR WHILE RIDING HER BIKE (poetry)	PR26, 86
	ATMOSPHERE (poetry)	PR26, 89
Kearney, Meg	PENGUINS (poetry)	PR26, 97
Kearney, Simone	A KIND OF DUCTILITY (poetry)	PR20, 75
	MORNING (poetry)	PR20, 76
Keast, Rob	35.4 SENTENCES ABOUT THE PICTURED ROCKS NATIONAL LAKESHORE (nonfiction)	PR19, 107
Keck, Sean	THE ACCIDENTAL STAGE (poetry)	PR23, 89
Keener, Jessica	MOVING WATERS, STORIES BY RACELLE ROSETT (recommendation)	PR26, 261
Kennedy, X. J.	THE FICTION OF J. F. POWERS (recommendation)	PR10, 123
Khan, J S	MINE DONT NEVER (fiction)	PR28, 135
Kilpatrick, Connor	THE LATE GREATS (fiction)	PR17, 89
Kim, Eson	TOUCH (nonfiction)	PR21, 57
Kimball, Michael	EXCERPTS FROM THE SUICIDE LETTERS OF JONATHAN BENDER (B. 1967, D. 2000) (fiction)	PR12, 155
	THE POSSIBILITIES OF FICTION (recommendation)	PR21, 164
	BIG RAY, OR SOME THINGS CONCERNING MY CHILDHOOD, WITH AN EMPHASIS ON MY FATHER (fiction)	PR23, 177
Kimura, Takahiro	DESTRUCTION AND CONSTRUCTION OF THE HUMAN FACE (art)	PR5, 194

Post Road | 253

King, Dave	IN A STRANGE ROOM BY DAMON GALGUT (recommendation)	PR23, 144
Kinstler, Dana	ANGELA CARTER'S THE BLOODY CHAMBER (recommendation)	PR17, 113
Klass, Perri	BIRDS OF AMERICA, BY MARY MCCARTHY (recommendation)	PR12, 203
Klein, Michael	PROVINCETOWN, 1990 (poetry)	PR19, 55
	WHAT I'M GOING TO DO IS (poetry)	PR19, 56
Klíma, Ivan	IRENA OBERMANNOVA (recommendation)	PR2, 169
Klink, Joanna	SHOOTING STAR (poetry)	PR2, 100
	RIVER IN DUSK (poetry)	PR2, 101
Knapp, Elizabeth	INDELIBLE (poetry)	PR11, 13
	UNINVITED GUEST (poetry)	PR11, 15
Knight, Karla	BLIND VIEW (art)	PR26, 34
	SIMPLE SPONGE (art)	PR26, 40
Knight, Michael	TEACHING J. D. SALINGER (recommendation)	PR17, 149
Konsterlie, Peter	DEEP VISION (art)	PR26, 45
	INDELIBLE NOISE (art)	PR26, 48
Koven, Suzanne	AN INHERITED CONDITION (nonfiction)	PR25, 59
Kozma, Andrew	INVADER (poetry)	PR14, 103
	WHAT IS (poetry)	PR14, 104
Kreines, Amy	WARNINGS (etcetera)	PR8, 165
Krimko, Stuart	THE SETTING EVENING (poetry)	PR20, 80
	SELF PORTRAITS (poetry)	PR20, 82
Krisak, Len	WINTER EXERCISES (poetry)	PR23, 76
Kronovet, Jennifer	A HISTORY OF KANSAS (poetry)	PR3, 37
	SCENIC OVERLOOK (poetry)	PR3, 38
Kuo, Alex	THE LUNCH (fiction)	PR15, 85
Kuzmanovich, Zoran, et al.	LOLITA A–Z (etcetera)	PR7, 151
LaFarge, Paul	YEARS ARE BEARING US TO HEAVEN: DONALD BARTHELME'S THE SLIGHTLY IRREGULAR FIRE ENGINE, OR THE HITHERING THITHERING DJINN (recommendation)	PR24, 129
Lahsaiezadeh, Caitlin	CHIRON, ON ACHILLES (poetry)	PR26, 104
	FIRST TATTOO (poetry)	PR26, 105
Lang, Andrew	EXCERPT: FROM ADVENTURES IN BOOKS (etcetera)	PR14, 127
Lanigan, Kerry	DA CAPO (fiction)	PR25, 15
Lantz, Susan (trans.)	FOUR SHORT POEMS, BY J. V. FOIX (etcetera)	PR9, 205
Larsen, Annabelle	URBAN GUERRILLAS (nonfiction)	PR26, 211
LaSalle, Peter	E.A.P. (etcetera)	PR9, 183
Lauenstein, Maria	BODY AND SOUL (nonfiction)	PR10, 173
Laughlin, Scott	THE STRANGE QUESTION OF ALBERTO DE LACERDA (recommendation)	PR25, 161
Lavender-Smith, Evan	BENNETT'S CHEAP CATHARSIS (fiction)	PR15, 109
Laverty, Rory	MY LIFE OF CRIME (nonfiction)	PR9, 89
Lawry, Vivian	THE EATER (fiction)	PR25, 101

Le, Jenna	SALISBURY (poetry)	PR19, 185
	THE HARVARD SQUARE STREET MUSICIANS (poetry)	PR19, 186
Leahy, Anna	GOOGLE MOON (poetry)	PR23, 69
Leavitt, Caroline	ONE GOOD BOOK LEADS TO ANOTHER (recommendation)	PR21, 137
Leavitt, David	A FAR CRY FROM KENSINGTON, BY MURIEL SPARK (recommendation)	PR16, 265
LeCraw, H. H.	AUGUST (fiction)	PR8, 53
LeCraw, Holly	NAKED WITH INNOCENCE (recommendation)	PR23, 104
Lee, Don	MYSTERY RIDE, BY ROBERT BOSWELL (recommendation)	PR10, 81
Lee, Marie Myung-Ok	JENNIFER EGAN IS BETTER THAN JONATHAN FRANZEN (recommendation)	PR22, 9
Lehman, David	AARON FOGEL (recommendation)	PR2, 172
Lemieux, Brenna W.	OLDER SISTER (poetry)	PR24, 143
	EARL GREY (poetry)	PR24, 144
Lemon, Alex	BELOW THE NEARER SKY (poetry)	PR10, 157
	SILT (poetry)	PR10, 158
	THE NICE (poetry)	PR18, 11
	GHOST IN THE LATRINE (poetry)	PR18, 13
Lennon, Brian	SOME STORIES ARE PARABLES, BUT (fiction)	PR8, 51
Leone, Marianne	MA PICKS A PRIEST (nonfiction)	PR28, 59
Lerner, Ben	FROM THE LICHTENBERG FIGURES (poetry)	PR3, 39
LeRoy, J. T.	THE STORIES OF BREECE D'J PANCAKE, BY BREECE D'J PANCAKE (recommendation)	PR10, 211
Lethem, Jonathan*	INTERVIEW (etcetera)	PR5, 153
Levinson, David Samuel	PEOPLE ARE JUST DYING TO MEET YOU (fiction)	PR26, 197
	DIE LEIDEN DES JUNGEN WERTHERS (THE SORROWS OF YOUNG WERTHER), BY JOHANN WOLFGANG VON GOETHE (recommendation)	PR28, 223
Lewis, Jim	EASY (recommendation)	PR23, 67
Lewis, Sinclair	LECTURE: THE AMERICAN FEAR OF LITERATURE (etcetera)	PR15, 119
Lichtenstein, Alice	DEAD FRIENDS (fiction)	PR18, 155
Lifson, Hannah	TINY MONUMENTS: A LOOK AT SNAPSHOT PHOTOGRAPHY (criticism)	PR16, 83
Ligon, Samuel	ANIMAL HATER (fiction)	PR6, 83
Lima, José Lezama*	RHAPSODY FOR THE MULE, trans. G. J. Racz (etcetera)	PR4, 127
Lindquist, Mark	MOTHER NIGHT, BY KURT VONNEGUT (recommendation)	PR10, 171
Lisicky, Paul	BEACH TOWN (fiction)	PR25, 149
	LIBERTY (fiction)	PR25, 151
Liu, Elliott	THE END OF HISTORY (poetry)	PR14, 109
	THE RISE OF THE MIDDLE CLASS (poetry)	PR14, 111
Livesey, Margot	BLOOD, BY PATRICIA TRAXLER (recommendation)	PR4, 110
Livingston, Reb	INTERVIEW WITH APRIL BERNARD (etcetera)	PR7, 169

Lobko, William	SELF-PORTRAIT IN MY BROTHER'S BULLET (poetry)	PR18, 223
Michael	CHIPOTLE (poetry)	PR18, 224
Lock, Norman	BEYOND RECOGNITION: A MONOLOGUE IN 12 SECTIONS (theatre)	PR5, 49
Lombardi, D. Dominick	THE GRAFFOO (art)	PR19, 33
	URCHIN #7 (art)	PR26, 43
	URCHIN #6 (art)	PR26, 46
Lombardi, Joyce	YAMBA (nonfiction)	PR1, 111
Long, Priscilla	O IS FOR OLD (nonfiction)	PR24, 84
lonsinger, dawn	THE ICE FIELDS (poetry)	PR18, 99
	AGAINST PLUGGING AWAY (poetry)	PR18, 101
Lopate, Phillip*	A CONVERSATION (etcetera)	PR15, 21
Lopes, Frankie	ROOM FOR MY KNEES (nonfiction)	PR26, 141
Lopez, Robert	SCAR (fiction)	PR5, 82
Lorberer, Eric	SONNET (poetry)	PR4, 33
	OUR WILL (poetry)	PR4, 34
Lowenthal, Michael	ANTARCTICA, BY CLAIRE KEEGAN (recommendation)	PR7, 138
	MARGE (fiction)	PR14, 167
	BRAZILIAN ADVENTURE, BY PETER FLEMING (recommendation)	PR25, 49
Lucenko, Kristina	JANE BOWLES (recommendation)	PR1, 176
Luna, Cari	I LOVE DICK BY CHRIS KRAUS (recommendation)	PR28, 95
Lutz, Gary	EMINENCE (fiction)	PR1, 25
Lutz, Kevin	DOWN IN THE VALLEY (nonfiction)	PR13, 145
Lvovich, Natasha	BALAKOVO (nonfiction)	PR18, 103
Lynch, Allesandra	UNTITLED (poetry)	PR17, 65
Lynn, Allison	DIGRESSIONS ON SOME POEMS BY FRANK O'HARA, BY JOE LESUEUR (recommendation)	PR16, 81
Maazel, Fiona	MY LIFE AND HARD TIMES, BY JAMES THURBER (recommendation)	PR4, 112
Madden, Patrick	DIVERS WEIGHTS AND DIVERS MEASURES (nonfiction)	PR6, 133
Maher, Ronnie E.	PHOTOGRAPHS (art)	PR15, 65
Mahoney, Lesley	ROOTED (fiction)	PR25, 74
Makhno, Vasyl	THE ELEPHANT'S HEAD (art)	PR19, 153
Malech, Dora	FACE FOR RADIO (poetry)	PR13, 181
	QUICK STUDY (poetry)	PR13, 182
Malone, Cynthia Northcutt	WRITERS AND CRITICS AT THE DINNER TABLE: TRISTRAM SHANDY AS CONVERSATIONAL MODEL (criticism)	PR23, 13
Malzhan, Tim	INTRODUCTION TO MICHAEL AYALA: PHOTOGRAPHS (art)	PR6, 66
Mamet, David	TWENTY QUESTIONS (etcetera)	PR13, 221
Manning, David	THE MAN WHO WASN'T THERE (nonfiction)	PR1, 123
Mao, Sally Wen	FLIGHT PERILS (poetry)	PR23, 49
	SONNETS FOR KUDRYAVKA (poetry)	PR23, 52

Marchant, Fred	NON SUM DIGNUS (poetry)	PR12, 67
	ARD NA MARA (poetry)	PR12, 68
	ALMOST PARADISE: NEW AND SELECTED POEMS AND TRANSLATIONS, BY SAM HAMILL (recommendation)	PR13, 81
	SIXTEEN (poetry)	PR26, 106
	BODY, BODY (poetry)	PR26, 108
Markus, Peter	WHAT OUR FATHER IS HERE TO TELL US (fiction)	PR6, 89
Marsh, Erin Lynn	PORTRAIT OF CRIPPLED POET AS WOMAN (poetry)	PR22, 23
	ART LESSON (poetry)	PR22, 25
Marshall, Megan	THREE LIVES (recommendation)	PR28, 131
Martin, Knox	WOMAN: BLACK AND WHITE PAINTINGS (art)	PR21, 33
Martin, Lee	MY WORD: MEMOIR'S NECESSARY BETRAYAL (nonfiction)	PR3, 113
	THE END OF THE STRAIGHT AND NARROW BY DAVID MCGLYNN (recommendation)	PR18, 151
	CONFIRMATION (fiction)	PR18, 161
	THROUGH THE CLOSED DOOR (fiction)	PR25, 76
Martin, Manjula	ON THE DATING PROSPECTS OF FEMINIST DAUGHTERS, OR DEAR MAUREEN (criticism)	PR12, 49
Martone, Michael	CHILI 4-WAY (fiction)	PR21, 149
Marvin, Cate	WHY SLEEP (poetry)	PR3, 41
	OCEAN IS A WORD IN THIS POEM (poetry)	PR3, 43
Mastroianni, Mark	PAINTINGS (art)	PR10, 50
Matar, Rania	PHOTOGRAPHS (art)	PR17, 35
Matthews, Sebastian	IN MY DREAM I'VE BECOME A GREAT TRUMPETER (poetry)	PR6, 39
	THE FISH HAWK AT SANDERLING (poetry)	PR6, 41
Mattison, Alice	OTHER PEOPLE'S HOUSES AND HER FIRST AMERICAN BY LORE SEGAL (recommendation)	PR11, 37
Maulucci, A. S.	DANTE AND BEATRICE, 2010 (theatre)	PR20, 151
	FUGUE FOR A MAN AND A WOMAN (theatre)	PR20, 158
McCallum, Shara	"ARE WE NOT OF INTEREST TO EACH OTHER?": THE SUBLIME IN ELIZABETH ALEXANDER'S AMERICAN SUBLIME (recommendation)	PR13, 143
McCann, Richard	A SORROW BEYOND DREAMS, BY PETER HANDKE, TRANSLATED BY RALPH MANNHEIM (recommendation)	PR6, 139
McCarty, Anne	THE BOOK OF DISQUIET, BY FERNANDO PESSOA (recommendation)	PR3, 80
McClanaghan, Jen	PERSONAL AD WITH LOBSTERS (poetry)	PR17, 66
McCorkle, Jill	A MIRACLE OF CATFISH, BY LARRY BROWN (recommendation)	PR15, 43
McDonough, Jill	JULY 19, 1692: SUSANNA MARTIN (poetry)	PR12, 117
	SEPTEMBER 18, 1755: MARK AND PHILLIS (poetry)	PR12, 119
McGinnis, Ralph	THE OMISSION OF COMICS (criticism)	PR11, 55
McGlynn, David	RERUNS NEVER LIE (fiction)	PR11, 130
McIlvain, Ryan	U AND I AND I (recommendation)	PR27, 161
McLeod, Charles	MICROCLIMATES (fiction)	PR19, 17

Post Road | 257

McLeod, Eric Tyrone	SELLING OUT: CONSUMER CULTURE AND COMMODIFICATION OF THE MALE BODY (criticism)	PR6, 11
McMahon, Kate	SWAPPED (fiction)	PR28, 175
McMurry, Evan	DRUNK IN ENGLISH (fiction)	PR17, 153
McNair, Wesley	DELIGHTS & SHADOWS, BY TED KOOSER, SEARCH PARTY, BY WILLIAM MATTHEWS; AND JACK AND OTHER NEW POEMS BY MAXINE KUMIN (recommendation)	PR11, 191
McNally, John	THE PROMISE OF FAILURE, OR WHY YOU SHOULD DROP EVERYTHING YOU'RE DOING AND READ RICHARD YATES'S REVOLUTIONARY ROAD RIGHT NOW! (recommendation)	PR16, 113
Medina, Pablo	LETTER FOR MY FATHER (etcetera)	PR2, 131
Medwed, Mameve	VARIOUS (recommendation)	PR15, 81
Melleri, Arto *	SEA WINDS, trans. Niina Pollari (poetry)	PR17, 69
Mellis, Miranda F.	FROM RUNE TO RUIN: AN ALPHABET (EXCERPTS) (fiction)	PR13, 113
Melnyczuk, Askold	NO WEDDING, NO CAKE: MOSELEY AND MUTIS (recommendation)	PR4, 114
Melvin, Jacob	MISSING (nonfiction)	PR25, 153
Menger-Anderson, Kirsten	THE DOCTORS (fiction)	PR16, 117
Mentzer, Robert	LATE (fiction)	PR9, 61
Mercer, Jeremy	ESSAY: OBSERVING VICTOR HUGO (etcetera)	PR14, 211
Merrill, Christopher	AGAINST UNCERTAINTY (poetry) AGAINST IMPERIALISM (poetry)	PR26, 92 PR26, 93
Merriman, Ben	THE SLUTS: A PLAY (theatre)	PR26, 131
Messer, Chris	ROTTEN FRUIT (fiction)	PR27, 11
Messer, Sarah	RABID DOG (poetry) LOOKING AT SATAN (poetry)	PR3, 44 PR3, 46
Michaels, Leonard	REPRINT: WHAT'S A STORY? (etcetera)	PR12, 59
Miller, Ben	V.F. GROCERY (fiction)	PR2, 54
Miller, Michael	RUDOLPH WURLITZER'S INFINITE WEST (criticism)	PR18, 33
Miller, Risa	PARTS AND PIECES: SVEN BIRKERTS, A. MANETTE ANSAY, STEVE STERN, CHRISTOPHER TILGHMAN, ELINOR LIPMAN, AND AMY HEMPEL (recommendation)	PR8, 140
Millet, Lydia	THE COMPLETE TALES OF MERRY GOLD, BY KATE BERNHEIMER (recommendation)	PR15, 155
Mink, Lucy	STRANGELY FAMILIAR PLACES (art)	PR24, 76
Mirvis, Tova	JANE SMILEY'S A THOUSAND ACRES (recommendation)	PR25, 156
Monahan, Jean	ANIMALS IN TRANSLATION, BY TEMPLE GRANDIN AND CATHERINE JOHNSON (recommendation)	PR11, 11
Monson, Ander	A HUGE, OLD RADIO (fiction) EXCISION (poetry) LIMB REPLANTATION, FAILED (poetry)	PR4, 64 PR8, 28 PR8, 30
Montemarano, Nicholas	LAST LAST LAST (fiction)	PR4, 73

Moody, Rick	ON MICHAEL DE MONTAIGNE (recommendation)	PR1, 163
	FLAP (fiction)	PR8, 66
	I LOVE DICK, BY CHRIS KRAUS (recommendation)	PR10, 9
	TOUR DIARY: THE DIVINERS, NORTH AMERICA, 2005 (etcetera)	PR12, 91
Moody, Rick (ed.)	LETTERS HOME FROM THE PACIFIC, 1944–46, FRANCIS ARTHUR FLYNN (etcetera)	PR3, 138
Moolten, David	THE MOIROLOGIST (poetry)	PR27, 175
	GEOMETRY (poetry)	PR27, 176
Moon, Michael	THE MEMOIR BANK (recommendation)	PR5, 139
Moore, Alexios	FIELD STUDIES (nonfiction)	PR18, 81
Moore, Alison	OKLAHOMA ON MY MIND (recommendation)	PR4, 116
Moos, Kate	IN A CERTAIN PLACE, AT A CERTAIN TIME (poetry)	PR3, 47
	THE PRINCE (poetry)	PR3, 48
Moran, Caitlin Keefe	NO GOOD WAY (nonfiction)	PR24, 92
	THE SLEEPING KINGDOM (fiction)	PR28, 179
Moran, John	THE EMPIRICAL SOCIETY (theatre)	PR6, 49
Morris, Eric	WILL OF THE STUNT DOUBLE (poetry)	PR20, 113
	ONCE A BOY (poetry)	PR20, 114
Morris, Mary	LUCY GAYHEART, BY WILLA CATHER (recommendation)	PR8, 147
	POSSUM (fiction)	PR15, 13
Morrissey, Donna	MIDDLEMARCH, BY GEORGE ELIOT (recommendation)	PR7, 129
Moser, Barry	SACRED AND VULGAR: THE INFLUENCES OF FLANNERY O'CONNOR ON THE ILLUSTRATIONS FOR PENNYROYAL CAXTON BIBLE (recommendation)	PR6, 148
Moulton, Katie	DEDICATIONS (fiction)	PR25, 78
Moyer, Linda Lancione	WALKING BACKWARDS IN TAKAMATSU (nonfiction)	PR11, 209
Mulholland, Meaghan	NOVITIATE (fiction)	PR25, 80
Mullins, David Philip	THE VALUE OF VOICE (recommendation)	PR26, 175
Murphy, Sarah	BREATHLESS, MY VENOM SPENT, I LAY DOWN MY WEAPONS (poetry)	PR16, 215
	HOROSCOPE (poetry)	PR16, 217
Murphy, Tom	INDEX TO THE GREAT GATSBY (etcetera)	PR8, 172
Murray, Sabina	THREE AUSTRALIAN NOVELISTS (recommendation)	PR7, 146
Myers, Patrick	THIN, BRILLIANT LINES (nonfiction)	PR28, 215
Myles, Eileen	HELL (etcetera)	PR10, 83
Nadelson, Scott	THE NEXT SCOTT NADELSON (nonfiction)	PR18, 131
Nadler, Stuart	"REUNION," CHEEVER AND FORD (recommendation)	PR26, 247
Nadzam, Bonnie	TREES IN THE CITY (fiction)	PR25, 159
Nankin, Sarah	UNTITLED AS OF YET (fiction)	PR7, 114
Nanos, Janelle	HOMELAND SECURITY (nonfiction)	PR19, 111
Nathan, Micah	THE STORIES OF JOHN CHEEVER (recommendation)	PR21, 14
Nettleton, Taro	STREETSTYLE: SKATEBOARDING, SPATIAL APPROPRIATION, AND DISSENT (criticism)	PR8, 123

Nicholl, Greg	A ROCKET TO VENUS (poetry)	PR24, 11
	WALK THROUGH (poetry)	PR24, 13
Nichols, Kelcey	AUSTIN (fiction)	PR1, 40
Nicorvo, Jay Baron	I HAVE HEARD YOU CALLING IN THE NIGHT BY THOMAS HEALY (recommendation)	PR25, 95
Niffenegger, Audrey	TRASH SEX MAGIC BY JENNIFER STEVENSON (recommendation)	PR10, 193
Nilsson, Kathy	THE SACRIFICE (poetry)	PR1, 96
	BLACK LEMONS (poetry)	PR1, 98
Nin, Anaïs*	MARRIAGE CERTIFICATE (etcetera)	PR14, 63
Nissen, Thisbe	SOME THINGS ABOUT KEVIN BROCKMEIER (recommendation)	PR8, 149
Nolan, Delaney	SEEDS LIKE TEETH (fiction)	PR23, 27
Nordbrandt, Henrik	CASA BLANCA (poetry)	PR10, 197
	ANKERPLADS (poetry)	PR10, 199
Nordbrandt, Henrik*	CASA BLANCA, trans. Patrick Phillips (poetry)	PR10, 196
	ANCHORAGE, trans. Patrick Phillips (poetry)	PR10, 198
Norman, Brian	AGEE'S ASTONISHMENT (criticism)	PR26, 147
Novakovich, Josip	BERLIN, JULY 18–AUGUST 11, 2002 (etcetera)	PR6, 172
Nutter, Jude	THE WINGS OF BUTTERFLIES (poetry)	PR8, 19
	THE EYES OF FISH (poetry)	PR8, 22
Nye, Naomi Shihab	THE ORANGE, THE FIG, THE WHISPER OF GRAPES (etcetera)	PR2, 137
Oates, Joyce Carol*	NOVELS OF JOYCE CAROL OATES (etcetera)	PR10, 127
Ockert, Jason	SAILOR MAN (fiction)	PR22, 101
O'Connell, George (trans.)	GLENN GOULD by Wang Jiaxin (poetry)	PR28, 169
	MEETING RAIN, WUTAI MOUNTAIN by Wang Jiaxin (poetry)	PR28, 171
O'Connor, John	THE PASS (nonfiction)	PR28, 159
O'Connor, Larry	THE MIDDLE-AGED MAN AND THE SEA (nonfiction)	PR7, 39
O'Donnell, Angela Alaimo	THE GUINNESS AT TIGH MHOLLY (poetry)	PR20, 74
Offutt, Chris	VEGETABLE ON THE HOOF (fiction)	PR3, 14
O'Keefe, Michael	CONVERSATION: MARK STRAND (etcetera)	PR13, 119
O'Nan, Stewart	THE TRUE DETECTIVE, BY THEODORE WEESNER (recommendation)	PR5, 141
Oria, Shelly	MIRANDA JULY'S IT CHOOSES YOU (recommendation)	PR28, 81
Orlen, Steve	THE ALPHABET IN THE PARK: SELECTED POEMS OF ADELIA PRADO, TRANSLATED FROM THE PORTUGUESE BY ELLEN WATSON (recommendation)	PR3, 67
Orner, Peter	OPEN DOORS, BY LEONARDO SCIASCIA (recommendation)	PR7, 142
Ott, Martin	RALLYING IN RHODE ISLAND (poetry)	PR21, 26
(with John F. Buckley)	DUOLOGUE IN DELAWARE (poetry)	PR21, 27
Pack, Robert	BUBBIE (poetry)	PR20, 66
	POWER (poetry)	PR20, 68
Page, Judith	PORTRAITS IN PLASMA (art)	PR16, 65

Paine, Tom	LITTLE BOYS COME FROM THE STARS, BY EMMANUEL DONGALA (recommendation)	PR2, 174
Papernick, Jonathan	THE PRICE OF ADMISSION (fiction)	PR26, 165
Papillon, Buki	ONLY SOFTLY (fiction)	PR25, 81
Park, Ed	THE FREUD NOTEBOOK 2006–2008 (criticism)	PR17, 85
Parke, Melanie	MORNING TABLE (art)	PR28, 78
Parnell, Catherine	WISTERIA (fiction)	PR23, 113
Parras, John	BIOGRAPHY OF THE ARTIST (fiction)	PR25, 82
Parrish, Tim	HEAD, BY WILLIAM TESTER (recommendation)	PR5, 137
Parvin, Roy	MICHAEL BYERS AND THE COAST OF GOOD INTENTIONS (recommendation)	PR7, 143
Patrick, Oona Hyla	THE SHACK OF ART AND HEALING (nonfiction)	PR4, 52
	THE THREE MARIAS: WHATEVER HAPPENED TO PORTUGAL'S PUSSY RIOT? (recommendation)	PR25, 119
Pearlman, Edith	DREAM CHILDREN (fiction)	PR7, 83
Pei, Lowry	EUDORA WELTY'S THE GOLDEN APPLES (recommendation)	PR13, 15
Perabo, Susan	HARRY POTTER AND THE HALF-BLOOD PRINCE, BY J. K. ROWLING (recommendation)	PR12, 31
Perkes, Logan	THE ILLUSION OF SYMMETRY (nonfiction)	PR15, 31
Perrotta, Tom	AUNT JULIA AND THE SCRIPTWRITER, BY MARIO VARGAS LLOSA (recommendation)	PR5, 143
	THE SMILE ON HAPPY CHANG'S FACE (fiction)	PR8, 75
	TWENTY QUESTIONS (etcetera)	PR10, 219
	NINE INCHES (fiction)	PR18, 211
Petro, Melissa	WORKING NIGHTS IN THE ARTIFICIAL DAY, WORKING DAYS IN THE ARTIFICIAL NIGHT (nonfiction)	PR14, 133
Petrocelli, Yolanda	YOLANDA PETROCELLI (art)	PR22, 65
Phillips, Patrick	THOSE GEORGIA SUNDAYS (poetry)	PR10, 25
	LITANY (poetry)	PR10, 26
Phillips, Patrick (trans.)	CASA BLANCA, by Henrik Nordbrandt (poetry)	PR10, 196
	ANCHORAGE, by Henrik Nordbrandt (poetry)	PR10, 198
Pinsky, Robert	JAMES MCMICHAEL (recommendation)	PR3, 71
	POEM WITH REFRAIN BY LINDA NATHAN (poetry)	PR26, 112
Pippin, Stephanie	GOOD SCIENCE (poetry)	PR8, 16
	HEART (poetry)	PR8, 18
Pollack, Neal	HEED THE THUNDER, BY JIM THOMPSON (recommendation)	PR8, 146
Pollard, Heidi	SWAT (art)	PR28, 69
Pollari, Niina	ISOTOPE (poetry)	PR17, 68
Pollari, Niina (trans.)	SEA WINDS, by Arto Melleri (poetry)	PR17, 69
Pomfret, Scott D.	WHAT GOD SEES (fiction)	PR6, 104
Pope, Dan	A SPORT AND A PASTIME, BY JAMES SALTER (recommendation)	PR10, 217
	DRIVE-IN (fiction)	PR11, 115
	AN INHERITANCE (fiction)	PR20, 167

Post Road | 261

Popielaski, John	INVASION (poetry)	PR19, 201
	DISCONNECTION (poetry)	PR19, 203
Potter, Dünny Josafat	VALERIE BRENNAN: PEANUT GALLERY (art)	PR24, 65
Powell, Caleb	MISS ANG HAS A VERY COMFORTABLE LIFE (fiction)	PR19, 181
Powell, Elizabeth	I SPY (poetry)	PR12, 9
	12. DISTRICT COURTHOUSE, DIVORCE COURT, WHITE PLAINS, NEW YORK (poetry)	PR21, 81
	1. APOCALYPTIC WIFE (poetry)	PR21, 82
Power, Allison	PRELUSION (poetry)	PR20, 91
	THE FUTURISTS (poetry)	PR20, 92
Prabhaker, Sumanth	ALAMO NIGHTS (fiction)	PR20, 119
Prater, Tzarina T.	"OLD MAN YOUR KUNG FU IS USELESS": AFRICAN AMERICAN SPECTATORSHIP AND HONG KONG ACTION CINEMA (criticism)	PR2, 185
Pratt, Gretchen Steele	TO MY FATHER ON THE ANNIVERSARY OF HIS DEATH (poetry)	PR18, 31
	AUTUMN POETICA (poetry)	PR18, 32
Presente, Henry	THE SAVAGE GIRL, BY ALEX SHAKAR (recommendation)	PR7, 131
Price, D. Gatling	STILL WRECK (fiction)	PR10, 185
	CHARCOAL FOR LOCUST (fiction)	PR23, 141
Proulx, E. Annie	A POSTCARD (recommendation)	PR1, 156
Pruett, Lynn	PLANT LIFE BY PAMELA DUNCAN (recommendation)	PR7, 136
Pynchon, Thomas*	ANTHOLOGY: THE BLURBS OF THOMAS PYNCHON (etcetera)	PR14, 11
Quinn, Casey	GRANDPAP'S BURIALS (fiction)	PR28, 53
Rabb, Margo	HAPPY ALL THE TIME: LOVING LAURIE COLWIN (recommendation)	PR16, 153
Racz, G. J. (trans.)	RHAPSODY FOR THE MULE, BY JOSÉ LEZAMA LIMA (etcetera)	PR4, 127
Raffel, Dawn	FURTHER ADVENTURES IN THE RESTLESS UNIVERSE (etcetera)	PR2, 143
Raines, Laurah Norton	SLOW FREEZE (nonfiction)	PR16, 197
Rakoff, Joanna Smith	OLIVE HIGGINS PROUTY'S NOW, VOYAGER (recommendation)	PR20, 17
Ramey, Emma	SERVANT (poetry)	PR8, 26
	SERVANT (poetry)	PR8, 27
Rawson, Joanna	LOGBOOK (poetry)	PR9, 123
	ELM & CANCER (poetry)	PR9, 127
Raza, Asad	FOR THE LOVE OF NEW YORK (criticism)	PR21, 15
Rector, Liam	DANGEROUS MUSE: THE LIFE OF LADY CAROLINE BLACKWOOD, BY NANCY SCHOENBERGER (recommendation)	PR3, 76
Reddy, Nancy	THE SECRET NANCY (poetry)	PR28, 29
Redel, Victoria	WILLIAM BRONK (recommendation)	PR2, 175
Reeves, Jennifer	YOUNG YELLOW (art)	PR22, cover

Reifler, Nelly	SUGAR (fiction)	PR5, 103
	OCTOBER SNOW, BY SAMUEL REIFLER (recommendation)	PR16, 187
	ELIZABETH ALBERT: PAINTINGS (art)	PR18, 65
Reifler, Samuel	THE DAY THEY WERE SHOOTING DOGS (fiction)	PR16, 145
	YOU CAN'T TELL A BOOK BY ITS TITLE (recommendation)	PR25, 108
Reiken, Frederick	WINTON, MUNRO, BERGER (recommendation)	PR3, 77
Reinbold, Craig	A TREMENDOUS (EXPERIENCE OF) FISH (nonfiction)	PR24, 145
Resetarits, C.R.	PASSAGES (fiction)	PR25, 84
Retzkin, Hannah	OPHELIA (nonfiction)	PR20, 55
Reymond, Jan	PASSAGE DE LA TOUR (art)	PR25, cover
Reyn, Irina	EAT, MEMORY (criticism)	PR14, 47
Rhoads, Edie	THIS IS THE MOON (poetry)	PR17, 11
	RISHIKESH (poetry)	PR17, 13
Rice, Jeremy	LITTLE ORANGE BOTTLES (nonfiction)	PR16, 103
Richard, Frances	ADJACENT (poetry)	PR2, 92
	GLANCING AT (poetry)	PR2, 94
Richmond, Andrew	ACTIVIST (fiction)	PR7, 116
	PHOTOGRAPHS (art)	PR11, 65
Rivkin, Joshua	HOW I FELL IN LOVE WITH JOE MCCARTHY (poetry)	PR17, 70
	TIKKUN (poetry)	PR17, 72
Robbins, Michael	FREDERICK SEIDEL'S BAD TASTE (criticism)	PR27, 137
Roberts, Matt	THE DOGCATCHER HATES POLITICS (nonfiction)	PR10, 49
Robillard, G. Xavier	MY NAME IS RED (recommendation)	PR18, 63
Robin, C.C.	UPROOTED (fiction)	PR28, 13
Robinson, Christopher	HOGWASH (poetry)	PR28, 129
	FULLBOAT (poetry)	PR28, 130
Robinson, Lewis	TRUMAN CAPOTE, RICHARD FORD, AND JOHN IRVING (recommendation)	PR8, 153
Rock, Peter	GOLD FIREBIRD (fiction)	PR12, 19
	ON HARUKI MURAKAMI'S A WILD SHEEP CHASE, OR HOW I GOT "SHEEPED" (recommendation)	PR13, 219
Rogers, Christie	AT SEA (nonfiction)	PR24, 97
Rohan, Ethel	THAT TIME HE FELT THE WORLD TURN (fiction)	PR24, 15
	THE SPLITTING IMAGE (fiction)	PR24, 17
	ALL THE RAGE BY A.L. KENNEDY (recommendation)	PR28, 63
Roleke, Margaret	CURRENT ABSTRACTION (art)	PR14, 65
Roley, Brian Ascalon	READING ISHIGURO IN CAMDEN TOWN (recommendation)	PR19, 29
Rooney, Kathleen	QUICKIES! AND THE DOLLAR $TORE (recommendation)	PR18, 107
Roper, Jane	EAST OF EDEN BY JOHN STEINBECK (recommendation)	PR23, 129
Rosenfeld, Lucinda	THE DAY OF THE LOCUST BY NATHANAEL WEST (recommendation)	PR25, 31
Rosenfeld, Natania	A YEAR ON THE PRAIRIE (nonfiction)	PR11, 33

Rosovsky, Michael	POACHERS, BY TOM FRANKLIN (recommendation)	PR1, 178
	ON BOXING, BY JOYCE CAROL OATES (recommendation)	PR9, 176
Roth, David	THE OTHER WOMAN (fiction)	PR10, 201
Rothman, Wesley	OUR TOWN (poetry)	PR28, 155
	SINNERMAN (poetry)	PR28, 157
Ruff, John	WHAT THEY TALKED ABOUT AND WHAT THEY SAID (poetry)	PR4, 35
	DE CHIRICO SHAVING (poetry)	PR4, 36
	DREAMING OF ROME (poetry)	PR16, 129
	WHILE READING PICO DELLA MIRANDOLA'S ORATION ON HUMAN DIGNITY (poetry)	PR16, 132
Ruffin, Joshua	EXACT SCIENCE (poetry)	PR23, 93
	HOLLOW (poetry)	PR23, 94
	SCALE (poetry)	PR23, 96
Ryan, Anney E. J.	ROCKS (fiction)	PR17, 125
Ryan, David	MY LAST SIGH: THE AUTOBIOGRAPHY OF LUIS BUÑUEL (recommendation)	PR1, 180
	STORIES IN THE WORST WAY, BY GARY LUTZ (recommendation)	PR8, 159
	JERRY HUNT: FOUR VIDEO TRANSLATIONS (theatre)	PR10, 33
Rysz, Ronnie	SECURED CREDITOR (art)	PR21, cover
Salinger, J. D.*	SALINGER V. RANDOM HOUSE, INC., 811 F.2D 90 (2nd Cir. 1987) (etcetera)	PR9, 193
Salopek, Paul	MISSIVES: FOUR WAYS OF TRYING TO HOLD ONTO IT (etcetera)	PR11, 83
Salvatore, Joe	UNHEMLECH (fiction)	PR10, 99
Sandler, Lauren	HIP HOP HIGH: MAINSTREAM BLACK CULTURE IN THE WHITE SUBURBS (criticism)	PR5, 13
Sardy, Marin	DISINTEGRATION, LOOPS (nonfiction)	PR26, 65
Saterstrom, Selah	DIVINATORY EXPERIMENT, A SELECTION FROM INSTALLATION #9: REVENGE OF THE NERDS: IDEAL SUGGESTION (LOVE) (fiction)	PR25, 89
Saunders, George	QUESTIONNAIRE (etcetera)	PR14, 219
Savelyev, Simon	THE DISAPPEARING WIFE (fiction)	PR28, 190
Savitch-Lew, Abby	BOOMBOX AND NEON FLOWERS (fiction)	PR18, 21
Scalise, Mike	WRITING HIM OFF (nonfiction)	PR15, 201
Scanlon, Elizabeth	CLOSING TIME (poetry)	PR5, 43
	QUARRY (poetry)	PR5, 44
Scapellato, Joseph	FATHER'S DAY (fiction)	PR20, 57
Schaffzin, Eliezra	ONCE IN CUBA (nonfiction)	PR22, 93
Schappell, Elissa	THE SELECTED LETTERS OF DAWN POWELL, 1913–1965, AS EDITED BY TIM PAGE (recommendation)	PR12, 160
Scheibe, Amy	NOX, BY ANNE CARSON (recommendation)	PR20, 181
Scheid, Liz	WHAT THEY DON'T TELL YOU ABOUT BREAST-FEEDING (poetry)	PR16, 259
	WHAT I'M NOT TELLING YOU (poetry)	PR16, 260
Schilpp, Margot	THE BONE PEOPLE, BY KERI HULME (recommendation)	PR4, 118

Schireson, Peter	CAULIFLOWER SOUP (poetry)	PR23, 25
	STORM DAMAGE (poetry)	PR23, 26
Schleifer, David	THE BEST WAY TO GET GOOD TASTE (criticism)	PR19, 49
Schlossberg, Linda	"GORILLA, MY LOVE" (recommendation)	PR26, 163
Schmidt, Heidi Jon	FUTILITY, BY WILLIAM GERHARDIE (recommendation)	PR9, 161
Schmidtberger, Paul	A CLASS ACT (nonfiction)	PR27, 81
Schmoll, Ken Rus	RESPONSIBILITY, JUSTICE, AND HONESTY: REHEARSING EDWARD BOND'S SAVED (theatre)	PR3, 51
Schrank, Ben	ALL SOULS DAY, BY CEES NOOTEBOOM (AND OTHER BOOKS THAT YEARN) (recommendation)	PR6, 151
Schubach, Alanna	RAW MATERIAL (fiction)	PR20, 131
Schuller, Kyla	THE AMERICANS WHO MATTER: MICHAEL MOORE'S WHITE LIBERAL RACISM IN BOWLING FOR COLUMBINE (criticism)	PR9, 11
Schulman, Audrey	PIPPI AND MR. HYDE (recommendation)	PR25, 13
Schutt, Christine	THE ARTIST AND HIS SISTER GERTI (fiction)	PR6, 91
Schutz, Lacy	INTRODUCTION TO DANIEL HILL: PAINTINGS (art)	PR8, 34
	THE WATER AND THE WEAKENED LINK (poetry)	PR17, 97
Schutzman, Steven	THE BANK (theatre)	PR11, 119
Schwabe, Liesl	BLUE WINDOW (nonfiction)	PR8, 108
Schwartz, Julia	1.9.31.24 (art)	PR28, 71
Schwartz, Lynne Sharon	A TREATISE ON SHELLING BEANS, BY WIESLAW MYSLIWSKI, TRANSLATED BY BILL JOHNSTON (recommendation)	PR28, 20
Schwartz, Matthew	THE ISLAND ITSELF, BY ROGER FANNING (recommendation)	PR18, 203
Scott, James	HOW WE LOOKED (fiction)	PR21, 65
	THE SISTERS BROTHERS BY PATRICK DEWITT (recommendation)	PR25, 147
Searle, Elizabeth	BLACK TICKETS, THEN AND NOW (recommendation)	PR4, 120
	LIBRETTO: TONYA AND NANCY: THE OPERA (etcetera)	PR12, 139
Searle, Elizabeth*	INTERVIEW (etcetera)	PR8, 199
Seigel, Andrea	BEHIND THE ATTIC WALL, BY SYLVIA CASSEDY (recommendation)	PR12, 217
Semanki, David	CINÉMA VÉRITÉ (poetry)	PR11, 145
	DOUBLE FEATURE (poetry)	PR11, 147
Seward, Scott	WHY BALTIMORE HOUSE MUSIC IS THE NEW DYLAN (criticism)	PR3, 85
Sexton, Adam Reid	THE CENTAUR BY JOHN UPDIKE (recommendation)	PR27, 167
Shankar, Ravi	CAPE SAGRES TO LISBON AND BACK AGAIN (poetry)	PR19, 31
	SURFACE TENSION (poetry)	PR19, 32
(with Priya Sarukkai Chabria)	AANDAAL: THE AUTOBIOGRAPHY OF A GODDESS (poetry)	PR22, 121
Shapiro, Janice	SLOW DAYS, FAST COMPANY: THE WORLD, THE FLESH, AND L.A. BY EVE BABITZ (recommendation)	PR21, 63
Shapiro, Norm	HENRY HITCHINGS' THE SECRET LIFE OF WORDS: HOW ENGLISH BECAME ENGLISH (recommendation)	PR18, 117

Shattuck, Jessica	THE STORIES OF JOHN CHEEVER (recommendation)	PR11, 139
Sheehy, Hugh	ON AKUTAGAWA'S KAPPA (recommendation)	PR26, 183
Sheffield, Derek	SONG OF ARGOS (poetry)	PR26, 96
Shelby, Ashley	A RIVER IN CHARLESTON (nonfiction)	PR5, 115
Shepard, Jim	THE INVENTION OF TRUTH, BY MARTA MORAZZONI (recommendation)	PR2, 177
Sherman, Rachel	HOMESTAY (fiction)	PR2, 57
Shi, Diana (trans.)	GLENN GOULD by Wang Jiaxin (poetry)	PR28, 169
	MEETING RAIN, WUTAI MOUNTAIN by Wang Jiaxin (poetry)	PR28, 171
Shields, David	LIFE AND ART (etcetera)	PR2, 147
Shippy, Peter Jay	CELLIST (poetry)	PR7, 24
	DOGS RESEMBLING THEIR OWNER (poetry)	PR7, 25
Shirley, Skye	DAUGHTERS OF A BOARDINGHOUSE KEEPER (poetry)	PR23, 77
Sholl, Betsy	STILL LIFE WITH LIGHT BULB (poetry)	PR26, 109
	POCO A POCO (poetry)	PR26, 110
Shonk, Katherine	"THE RETURN," BY ANDREI PLATONOV, FROM THE RETURN AND OTHER STORIES (recommendation)	PR9, 165
Shteir, Rachel	ANATOLE BROYARD'S KAFKA WAS THE RAGE (recommendation)	PR26, 117
Shutan, Suzan	FLOCK (DETAIL) (art)	PR28, 80
Siasoco, Ricco Villanueva	DANDY (fiction)	PR28, 200
Siegel, Gail	FALLING OBJECTS: CHICAGO (etcetera)	PR10, 191
Siegel, Robert Anthony	THE MAGIC BOX (fiction)	PR11, 178
	BLOOD MERIDIAN, OR THE EVENING REDNESS IN THE WEST, BY CORMAC MCCARTHY (recommendation)	PR15, 139
Siegel, Zoë	IMAGES OF SCULPTURES AND DRAWINGS (art)	PR2, 19
Simmons, Alessandra	THE BRIDGES ARE ON THE GROUND (poetry)	PR22, 159
	CHORD & HEM (poetry)	PR22, 160
Simon, Jeremy	HOW TO REACH ME: A MANUAL (nonfiction)	PR2, 70
Simonds, Sandra Isabel	RARE CHILDREN (nonfiction)	PR17, 49
Sinor, Shara	GHOST OF TEN (nonfiction)	PR13, 56
Skloot, Floyd	ELLIPTICAL JOURNEY (nonfiction)	PR24, 102
Slater, Tracy	JOURNAL: ERASING GENDER: A WOMAN'S JOURNEY THROUGH MEN'S LOCKUP (etcetera)	PR13, 23
Slavin, Julia	MAILE CHAPMAN (recommendation)	PR1, 167
	DREAM TRAILERS (fiction)	PR13, 173
Smith, Cary	LUCY MINK: STRANGELY FAMILIAR PLACES (art)	PR24, 76
	POINTED SPLAT #2 (art)	PR28, 73
Smith, Charles	DAN SHEA (recommendation)	PR1, 168
Smith, Curtis	HOW TO REMEMBER THE DEAD (nonfiction)	PR23, 19
Smith, Suzanne Farrell	THE PEARL (nonfiction)	PR25, 185
Smith, Tracy K.	A HUNGER SO HONED (poetry)	PR7, 15
	SELF-PORTRAIT AS THE LETTER Y (poetry)	PR7, 17

Smithee, Alan	THE STRANGE, ENTERTAINING, AND SOMETIMES BEHIND-THE-SCENES STORY OF CLEO BIRDWELL AND DON DELILLO (etcetera)	PR2, 105
Snediker, Michael	O. HENRY (recommendation)	PR3, 70
Snyder, Laurel	THE SIMPLE MACHINES (poetry)	PR6, 43
	HAPPILY EVER AFTER (poetry)	PR6, 44
Solar-Tuttle, Rachel	WORDS—LEAN, LYRICAL, AUTHENTIC—BRING CHILDREN FROM SHADOWS (recommendation)	PR8, 157
Solms, Liz	IN JAMAICA (nonfiction)	PR26, 22
Sorrentino, Christopher	LIGHT WHILE THERE IS LIGHT, BY KEITH WALDROP (recommendation)	PR14, 105
Soth, Alec	UNTITLED 04, BOGOTÁ (art)	PR19, cover
Soto, Renee	AT THE DRIVE-IN VOLCANO, BY AIMEE NEZHUKUMATATHIL (recommendation)	PR17, 168
Sousa, Brian	JUST KIDS BY PATTI SMITH (recommendation)	PR28, 56
Sowder, Michael	DINNER AND A MOVIE, GREEN CANYON, UTAH (poetry)	PR23, 86
Spackman, Elizabeth Senja	UNHEIMLICH (NOT AT HOME) (poetry)	PR19, 121
	AFTER THE SEX, SIMILE OR SOMETHING LIKE IT (poetry)	PR19, 122
Spalding, Lavinia	TEACHING KOREA (etcetera)	PR4, 134
Spark, Debra	SIZE MATTERS (recommendation)	PR15, 213
Spece, Joseph	YES, BUT TENDERNESS BECOMES ME BEST—A SORT OF DYINGNESS— (poetry)	PR17, 73
Spiher, David	PAINTINGS (art)	PR13, 65
Spiotta, Dana	TRANCE, BY CHRISTOPHER SORRENTINO (recommendation)	PR14, 43
Sprague, Devon	TRASH AND BASTARD OUT OF CAROLINA, BY DOROTHY ALLISON (recommendation)	PR22, 151
Stace, Wesley (see also Harding, John Wesley)	LISTERINE: THE LIFE AND OPINIONS OF LAURENCE STERNE (etcetera)	PR5, 174
	THE LOST STRADIVARIUS, MOONFLEET, AND THE NEBULY COAT: THE ABNORMAL RESPONSES OF JOHN MEADE FALKNER (recommendation)	PR11, 89
	JOURNAL: (UNEXPURGATED) TOUR JOURNAL (etcetera)	PR16, 221
Standley, Vincent	TRAVELOGUE (fiction)	PR8, 71
Starke, Jonathan	I PROBABLY LET SOME OF IT SLIP ONCE (nonfiction)	PR20, 179
Stattmann, Jon	TRIAL BY TRASH (nonfiction)	PR11, 39
Staudinger, Christopher	WINTER HOUSE (nonfiction)	PR27, 74
Steinbach, Meredith	SILVER JINGLE BOBS, THE IMPORTANCE OF (fiction)	PR21, 109
Stender, Oriane	ENDLESS COLUMN (art)	PR28, 77
Stenson, Peter	WE SMOKED IN SILENCE (nonfiction)	PR21, 139
Stern, Amanda	DE PROFUNDIS BY OSCAR WILDE (recommendation)	PR23, 194
Steward, D. E.	DESEMBRE (fiction)	PR6, 118
Stine, Alison	THREE MONTHS, NO KIDDING (poetry)	PR7, 26
	SALT (poetry)	PR7, 27

Stone, Bianca	PAVOR NOCTURNUS WITH RELATIVITY (poetry)	PR20, 85
	SOMEONE WILL HAVE TO TELL YOU (poetry)	PR20, 87
Strand, Mark*	A CONVERSATION (etcetera)	PR6, 118
Strayed, Cheryl	WHEN THE FARMER CLUTCHES THE RAKE: WRITING THE REAL (nonfiction)	PR22, 90
Strempek Shea, Suzanne	READING THE FUTURE: TWELVE WRITERS FROM IRELAND IN CONVERSATION WITH MIKE MURPHY, EDITED BY CLIODHNA NI ANLUAIN (recommendation)	PR13, 37
Stumpf, Jason	PROOF (poetry)	PR11, 105
	THE LESSON OF THE BIRDS (poetry)	PR11, 106
Sukrungruang, Ira	SPOTLIGHTING (nonfiction)	PR12, 83
Sullivan, Felicia C.	THE BUSINESS OF LEAVING (fiction)	PR6, 94
Sullivan, Mary	THE HOLY BIBLE: KING JAMES VERSION (recommendation)	PR5, 145
Suzuki, Naoe	SPLENDOR OF AMAZING BOYS, GIRLS AND ANIMALS (art)	PR18, cover
Swofford, Anthony	GERHARD RICHTER'S MOTOR BOAT (FIRST VERSION) [MOTORBOOT (ERSTE ASSUNG)] (poetry)	PR13, 17
	NINE RHYTHMS IN NINE DAYS: A-FRAME NEAR SISTERS, OREGON (poetry)	PR13, 18
Szporluk, Larissa	BARCAROLE (poetry)	PR1, 100
	SENSILLA (poetry)	PR1, 102
Szuber, Janusz*	DE SE IPSO, TRANS. EWA HRYNIEWICZ-YARBROUGH (poetry)	PR9, 131
	NEW LABORS, TRANS. EWA HRYNIEWICZ-YARBROUGH (poetry)	PR9, 132
Talusan, Grace	THE START (nonfiction)	PR24, 114
Tarkington, Ed	SOUTHERN CULTURE ON THE SKIDS (nonfiction)	PR9, 108
Taylor, Al	PORTRAIT, DRAWING, SCULPTURE (art)	PR2, 29
Taylor, Mark C.	L'ENTRETIEN INFINI (THE INFINITE CONVERSATION), BY MAURICE BLANCHOT (recommendation)	PR2, 178
Taylor, Ravenna	RHYME SCHEME V (art)	PR28, 74
Teicher, Craig Morgan	THE GROANING COWS (poetry)	PR15, 45
	THE STORY OF THE STONE (poetry)	PR15, 47
Terwilliger, Cam	THE SHUT-DOWN CLASS (fiction)	PR19, 57
Thayer, Cynthia	EVA MOVES THE FURNITURE, BY MARGOT LIVESEY (recommendation)	PR14, 157
Thompson, Tom	LITTLE HEAP (poetry)	PR17, 74
Tinkler, Alan	A COUPLE OF POLAROIDS (fiction)	PR9, 23
Tintocalis, Stacy M.	HONEYMOON IN BEIRUT (fiction)	PR18, 183
Tobin, Daniel	IN ESCHER'S ROOMS (poetry)	PR23, 78
	QUISSETT (poetry)	PR23, 80
	AND NOW NOTHING WILL BE RESTRAINED FROM THEM (poetry)	PR23, 81
Tolides, Tryfon	THE VISITOR (poetry)	PR20, 93
	WATCHING THE LIGHT (poetry)	PR20, 94
	FOR WHO KNOWS HOW LONG (poetry)	PR20, 96
Tonge, Jennifer	SO MANY WAYS I'VE TRIED TO HOLD YOU (poetry)	PR23, 109
	MASHALLAH (poetry)	PR23, 110

Topol, Jachym*	ANGEL STATION, trans. Alex Zucker (etcetera)	PR1, 131
Tozier, Christopher	SUMMER EVENING, HOPPER 1947 (poetry)	PR20, 129
	HOUSE OF THE FOG HORN, NO. 3, HOPPER 1929 (poetry)	PR20, 130
Treadway, Jessica	RICHARD YATES'S THE EASTER PARADE (recommendation)	PR13, 205
Triant, Randi	HORRIBLE ENDINGS: MY BROTHER AND THE COMPLETE WORKS OF SAKI (etcetera)	PR10, 213
Trivett, Vincent	ONE HUNDRED DEMONS AND SELF-REPRESENTATION (criticism)	PR13, 41
Tsai, Addie	PROLOGUE, A LETTER: THE TWIN & HER LOVER, LACAN & THE OTHER (nonfiction)	PR23, 191
Tschirgi, Katrin	GOING TO CALDWELL (poetry)	PR26, 91
Tsukakoshi, Alissa	THE BARE MINIMUM OF HIM (nonfiction)	PR23, 97
Twain, Mark	FENIMORE COOPER'S LITERARY OFFENSES (etcetera)	PR6, 161
Tweddell, Steven	SUNSET JUDAS (fiction)	PR24, 45
Twitchell, Lane	SELF CENTERED ASUNDER (art)	PR28, 75
Unruh, Melanie	THE PLACE CALLED MOTHER (nonfiction)	PR23, 54
Uren, Robert	OMNIPLANET (fiction)	PR26, 77
Uzgiris, Rimas	RECOMMENDING KING DRIFTWOOD (recommendation)	PR23, 189
Vandenberg, Katrina	CRETACEOUS MOTH TRAPPED IN AMBER (LAMENT IN TWO VOICES) (poetry)	PR16, 97
	PALINODE FOR BEING THIRTY-FOUR (poetry)	PR16, 99
Van Aelst, Kevin	PARADIGM SHIFT (art)	PR27, cover
van den Berg, Laura	VICTOR LAVALLE'S BIG MACHINE (recommendation)	PR20, 127
van Loenen, Rocco	TECHNICAL DRAWING I (theatre)	PR1, 59
	TECHNICAL DRAWING II (theatre)	PR1, 77
Vasicek, René Georg	CONFESSIONS OF A PILSNER DRINKER (nonfiction)	PR14, 179
Venugopal, Shubha	LALITA AND THE BANYAN TREE (fiction)	PR14, 19
Veslany, Kathleen	THE APERTURE BETWEEN TWO POINTS (nonfiction)	PR2, 76
Vida, Vendela	OLT, BY KENNETH GANGEMI (recommendation)	PR10, 189
Vines, Adam	CHARTER (poetry)	PR23, 71
	FLOUNDERING (poetry)	PR23, 72
Voigt, Jeremy	FREAKISHLY BEAUTIFUL HEAD (poetry)	PR26, 190
	OUT OF SORTS (poetry)	PR26, 192
Voisine, Don	DUB STRIDE (art)	PR28, 72
Volkman, Karen	UNTITLED (poetry)	PR1, 104
	UNTITLED (poetry)	PR1, 105
Volpe, Eugenio	THEATER OF THE CRUEL (fiction)	PR9, 44
Voras-Hills, Angela	IN WHICH I HOARD THE AIR ESCAPING (poetry)	PR26, 27
	WAIT IN THE BATHTUB AND IT WILL CARRY YOU (poetry)	PR26, 28
Wade, Barry K.	WINTER SKY (fiction)	PR21, 127
Wagoner, David	THE OTHER MAN (poetry)	PR26, 113
	SPENDING THE NIGHT (poetry)	PR26, 114
	THE CATEGORICAL IMPERATIVE POEM (poetry)	PR26, 115
Waite, Urban	THE LOST WORLD (recommendation)	PR25, 57

Waldman, Ayelet	AN ICE CREAM WAR, BY WILLIAM BOYD (recommendation)	PR14, 17
Waldrep, G. C.	LULLABYE FOR MY SISTER (poetry)	PR12, 163
	FEAST OF ALL WOUNDS (poetry)	PR12, 164
	DIE FLEDERMAUS (poetry)	PR16, 191
	SISYPHUS IN PARADISE (poetry)	PR16, 192
Walker, Nicole	DROUGHT-TOLERANT TAMARISK (TAMARIX) APHYLLA (nonfiction)	PR17, 133
Wallace, Eric J.	THE CHILD SHAMAN (fiction)	PR25, 167
Wallaert, Josh	UPCOUNTRY (fiction)	PR26, 251
Walsh, William	RECOMMENDING "FIRST LOVE" BY SAMUEL BECKETT (recommendation)	PR21, 55
Ward, Nicholas	THE BACKYARD (nonfiction)	PR28, 115
Warloe, Constance	INTRODUCTION TO FROM DAUGHTERS & SONS TO FATHERS: WHAT I'VE NEVER SAID (etcetera)	PR2, 129
Warrell, Laura K.	BECOMING ABIGAIL, BY CHRIS ABANI (recommendation)	PR28, 235
Washington, Thomas	HAVE YOU READ MY MANUSCRIPT? (nonfiction)	PR9, 83
Wasow, Oliver	HAY (art)	PR24, cover
Waters, Lindsay	REBUILDING AESTHETICS FROM THE GROUND UP (criticism)	PR20, 21
Watson, Brad	WILLARD AND HIS BOWLING TROPHIES, A PERVERSE MYSTERY, BY RICHARD BRAUTIGAN (recommendation)	PR10, 159
Watterson, Zachary	OPEN LATE HOURS (nonfiction)	PR23, 167
Weinberger, Eliot	AT THE SIGN OF THE HAND (etcetera)	PR9, 188
Welle, John P. (trans.)	TRANSLATING BRECHT, by Franco fortini (poetry)	PR4, 30
Weller, Anthony	THE WORKS OF ROBERT DEAN FRISBIE (recommendation)	PR12, 151
Weller, Sam	THE ILLUSTRATED MAN, BY RAY BRADBURY (recommendation)	PR15, 147
Whitcomb, Katharine	EARLY MEDIEVAL (poetry)	PR11, 202
	DREAM ON HIS BIRTHDAY (poetry)	PR11, 206
White, Derek	COATI MUNDI (fiction)	PR11, 207
Wickenden, Andrew	STORY (fiction)	PR27, 151
Williams, Dawn	DIRECTING GRAND GUIGNOL (theatre)	PR1, 61
Williams, Diane	WELL-TO-DO PERSON (fiction)	PR6, 103
	MY FIRST REAL HOME (fiction)	PR16, 247
Williams, E. Genevieve	SOLSTICE 6 (art)	PR26, 42
	SOLSTICE 7 (art)	PR26, 47
Williams, Greg	BLUE ANGEL, BY FRANCINE PROSE (recommendation)	PR12, 199
Williams, Tyrone	HOW ON EARTH (poetry)	PR25, 99
	WAH WAH (poetry)	PR25, 100
Wilson, Jason	WHAT IS THE COLOR OF HOPE IN HAITI? (etcetera)	PR3, 168
Wilson, Jonathan	CHIARA (fiction)	PR28, 225
Winn, Tracy	CYNTHIA MORRISON PHOEL'S COLD SNAP (recommendation)	PR21, 153
Winthrop, Elizabeth Hartley	DIRT MUSIC, BY TIM WINTON (recommendation)	PR14, 81

Wisniewski, Mark	CALCULUS (poetry)	PR14, 37
	LAND (poetry)	PR14, 40
Wolff, Rebecca	MAMMA DIDN'T RAISE NO FOOLS (poetry)	PR2, 96
	A GOOD IDEA, BUT NOT WELL-EXECUTED (poetry)	PR2, 98
Wolos, Gregory J.	THE WILD PANDAS OF CHINCOTEAGUE (fiction)	PR27, 89
Wood, Ann	THE ROAD TO LOS ANGELES, BY JOHN FANTE (recommendation)	PR14, 215
Wood, Monica	WE NEED TO TALK ABOUT KEVIN, BY LIONEL SHRIVER AND GEORGE ELIOT'S LATER NOVELS (recommendation)	PR13, 179
Woodward, Kristine	KNOX MARTIN – WOMAN: BLACK AND WHITE PAINTINGS (art)	PR21, 33
	RICHARD HAMBLETON: THE AMERICAN POP EXPRESSIONIST (art)	PR27, 33
Wormser, Baron	FICTIONAL ESSAY: JOHN BERRYMAN, B. 1914 (etcetera)	PR13, 95
	SOUTHERN CALIFORNIA ODE (1969) (poetry)	PR26, 101
	CLIMATE (poetry)	PR26, 103
Wright, Carolyne	BETTY CARTER AT THE BLUE ROOM (poetry)	PR27, 157
	DIXIE WHITE HOUSE PHOTO (poetry)	PR27, 159
Wright, Charles	W. G. SEBALD (recommendation)	PR2, 179
Wunderlich, Mark	DEVICE FOR BURNING BEES AND SUGAR (poetry)	PR8, 13
	IT'S YOUR TURN TO DO THE MILKING, FATHER SAID (poetry)	PR8, 15
Wuori, G. K.	THE HOME FOR WAYWARD CLOCKS BY KATHIE GEORGIO (recommendation)	PR27, 177
Xi, Xu	THE LONG MARCH (recommendation)	PR13, 53
Yang, Jeffrey	GOOGLE (poetry)	PR15, 195
	KELP (poetry)	PR15, 196
Yang, June Unjoo	GENTILITY (fiction)	PR4, 63
Yarbrough, Steve	LARRY MCMURTRY'S THE LAST PICTURE SHOW (recommendation)	PR10, 155
Yoder, Charles	AL TAYLOR (recommendation)	PR2, 180
	TREE RINGS (art)	PR28, 76
Yoon, Paul	ON THE HISTORY OF A BACKGAMMON BOARD (fiction)	PR12, 206
Yoshikawa, Mako	REVISITING OLD FLAMES OF LITERATURE (recommendation)	PR6, 153
Young, C. Dale	THE EFFECTS OF SUNSET (poetry)	PR1, 106
	REQUIEM (poetry)	PR1, 107
Zabalbeascoa, Julian	THE ZULO (fiction)	PR22, 13
Zafris, Nancy	WRITING LESSONS IN PEGGY RATHMANN'S GOOD NIGHT, GORILLA (recommendation)	PR26, 74
Zailckas, Koren	IN YOUTH IS PLEASURE, BY DENTON WELCH (recommendation)	PR21, 83
Zaiman, Elana	PSALM FOR RAFI (nonfiction)	PR11, 111
Zinn, Peter	A LITTLE TRIAGE (nonfiction)	PR19, 187
Zucker, Alex (trans.)	ANGEL STATION, By Jachym Topol (etcetera)	PR1, 131